Phonetics

Phonetics

The Science of Speech

Martin J. Ball
School of Psychology and Communication,
University of Ulster at Jordanstown

and

Joan Rahilly
School of English, The Queen's University of Belfast

A member of the Hodder Headline Group
LONDON
Co-published in the USA by
Oxford University Press, Inc., New York

First published in Great Britain in 1999 by
Arnold, a member of the Hodder Headline Group,
338 Euston Road, London NW1 3BH

http://www.arnoldpublishers.com

Co-published in the United States of America by
Oxford University Press Inc.,
198 Madison Avenue, New York, NY10016

British Library Cataloguing in Publication Data
A catalogue record for this book is available from the British Library

Library of Congress Cataloging-in-Publication Data
A catalog record for this book is available from the Library of Congress

ISBN 0 340 70009 2 (hb)
ISBN 0 340 70010 6 (pb)

1 2 3 4 5 6 7 8 9 10

Production Editor: Liz Gooster
Production Controller: Priya Gohil
Cover Design: Terry Griffiths

Typeset in 11/13pt Sabon by J&L Composition Ltd, Filey, North Yorkshire
Printed and bound in Great Britain by MPG Books Ltd, Bodmin, Cornwall

What do you think about this book? Or any other Arnold title?
Please send your comments to feedback.arnold@hodder.co.uk

Contents

Acknowledgements

We were fortunate to be able to discuss various aspects of this book with colleagues, and would like to thank them in particular as well as those whose general advice has been put to good use in preparing the text. We would also like to express our gratitude to those who helped in providing illustrations. Thanks, then, to Evelyn Abberton, Martin Barry, John Esling, Adrian Fourcin, Vince Gracco, Fiona Gibbon, Bill Hardcastle, Barry Heselwood, Sara Howard, Ray Kent, John Laver, John Local, Nicole Müller, Maureen Stone, Paul Tench, Tony Traill, Nigel Vincent, and David Zajac. Unfortunately, we are unable to lay remaining shortcomings in the book at their door.

We would also like to thank current and former staff at Arnold – especially Naomi Meredith and Christina Wipf-Perry – for commissioning the book, and for their help in seeing it through to publication.

Introduction

This book is about phonetics, but what does this term signify? As our sub-title suggests, we define phonetics as 'the scientific study of speech'; but to understand this we need to think about both what we mean by speech, but also what we mean by scientific.

By 'speech', we mean all the sounds used to represent the words and other units of language. Furthermore, we don't just mean the English language, but all the languages of the world. There are some sounds we can make easily enough (such as the various raspberry-type noises) that do not occur in any known language (though it's always possible we may one day discover a language that does use some of these!). So these sounds do not normally come under consideration by phoneticians. There are also sounds that can only be produced by people with an abnormal craniofacial development (such as a cleft palate). These sounds are of interest to the *clinical phonetician* (see Ball, 1993), but are normally not dealt with by the general phonetician.

By 'scientific' we mean that the phonetician is concerned with an objective description of how speech works, measuring speech characteristics as accurately as possible, and providing an account using agreed and understood terminology. The phonetician is not concerned with subjective accounts of speech, of the type 'this sound/accent/speaker is uglier/nicer/ more refined than that'. We are not in the business of saying any one form of speech is in any way better than any other. Of course, such attitudes are common among laypeople, with prejudices usually based not on the intrinsic qualities of the sounds themselves but on people's views of the area/social class/personal attributes of the speakers of the variety in question. This phenomenon is certainly of interest to sociolinguists (the term 'sociophonetics' has been proposed for such studies), but is usually felt to be outside the domain of mainstream phonetics.

We must always remember that, just as language is a symbol system whereby a word stands for an item or concept (i.e. it is not the same as the item itself), so speech is also a symbol system. The spoken word represents the word just as the word represents the item. We can show this by noting a variety of ways in which a word can be represented. We can speak it of course, but we could also write it down, sign it using sign language, send it by morse code or semaphore (although some of these alternatives are, of course, derived from speech or writing). Speech can be thought of as the primary symbol system of language, but it is not the only one.

We have just mentioned the link between speech and language. At this point, then, we need to consider that the study of speech abilities in general differs from the study of the speech of a specific language, or of speech patterns in groups of languages. 'Phonetics' is the study of speech in general: the whole range of possible human speech sounds, how they are produced, their acoustic characteristics, how they are heard and perceived. When we study the sound system of a specific language, we are interested not in these features, but in how sounds pattern together to make units, the number and type of consonants and vowels the language has, the permitted ordering of sounds in words, the meaning associated with specific intonation patterns, and so on. This area of study is termed 'phonology'.

We do not discuss phonology in any detail in this book as this is a text on phonetics. Nevertheless, we do need to grasp one important phonological concept, as it affects our decision-making regarding how detailed our descriptions of certain sounds should be. This is the notion of 'contrastivity'. The point of contrastivity is that two phonetically different sounds may occur in two different languages, but only in one will they contrast, and so distinguish one word from another. We can illustrate this with an example: in English the 'l' at the beginning of the word 'leaf' (a clear-l) is different from the 'l' at the end of the word 'feel' (a dark-l) in most accents (try saying these carefully to hear the difference). This difference in English is not contrastive, however, because it is a positional variant: the clear-l always occurs at the beginning of syllables, and the dark-l at the end, so we can never find a pair of words contrasted only by the use of one or other of these types of 'l'. In Irish, on the other hand, both clear-l and dark-l can occur at the beginning of syllables, and at the end of syllables, for example, 'poll' (dark-l, meaning 'hole' nominative) and 'poill' (clear-l, meaning 'hole' genitive). In other words, the choice of the clear-l as opposed to the dark-l (or vice versa) actually results in a different word.

As we noted above, when we study phonetics we are interested in the sounds of speech: both individual segments and aspects (such as intonation) that spread over stretches of segments. We are interested in how we use the various vocal organs to produce these sounds; we are interested in the physics of speech, that is the acoustic characteristics of the speech sound wave; we are interested in the hearing process and how speech is decoded by the listener; and we are interested in developments in instrumentation to help us with these tasks. In this book we attempt to cover all these areas: differences in the amount of coverage reflect general tendencies in phonetic research over the years, and the fact that certain areas may be more immediately useful than others to general students of phonetics.

This brings us to a final thought: why should we study phonetics? Apart from a general interest in all the abilities of the human species, phonetics is, in fact, the very practical end of language study. A knowledge of how speech works is needed for a wide variety of occupations; for example, drama students need to know some phonetics to deal with voice projection and accent learning; singing students also need to know about voice production. Those wishing to teach a foreign language (or indeed learn one) will find phonetics invaluable in their attempts to introduce target pronunciation, whereas people wishing to teach English as a foreign language need to know English phonology but also general phonetics if they want to teach aspects of English pronunciation as well as grammar. Students of linguistics and communication will find that phonetics not only complements their study of linguistic communication, but will allow them to understand many aspects of sociolinguistic variation that we touched on earlier. Finally, those interested in communication disorders and speech and language therapy need a detailed knowledge of speech production and perception in order not only to understand specific impairments, but to know how to treat them.

1 The anatomy and physiology of speech

Introduction	The laryngeal system
The vocal tract	The supralaryngeal system
The respiratory system	Monitoring speech

Introduction

For a spoken message to be passed from a speaker to a hearer, a complex set of physical operations must be undertaken. This chain of events (sometimes called the **speech-chain**) starts with chemical activity in the brain of the speaker who devises or constructs the message. This neurological stage ends with the sending of instructions down the neural pathways to a variety of muscles located throughout the set of vocal organs (the **vocal tract**): the result is a range of muscle contractions and physical movement of structures such as the rib-cage, the larynx, the tongue and so on. In turn, these movements give rise to an aerodynamic phase of the speech chain, whereby air flows through the vocal tract. This airflow interacts with continued movement of structures such as the vocal folds, tongue, lips and soft palate to produce the different features of speech.

This modified airflow through the vocal tract impinges on the air surrounding the speaker, influencing it in particular ways. Thus we have an acoustic stage in the speech-chain, for which we can describe the particular properties of the sound waves leaving the speaker and heading to the hearer. These properties include how large the waves are (amplitude), how often they re-occur (frequency), and how long individual acoustic aspects last (duration).

Eventually, the sound waves reach the ear of the hearer, and again we have a series of physical operations that allow the hearer to convert sound waves (basically the movement of air molecules) into a message understood in the brain. The ear contains a number of sections (the outer, middle and inner ear) whose function is to convert sound waves into physical movement, and then physical movement into electrochemical activity along the neurological pathways from the inner ear to the relevant parts of the brain. It is here that the final neurological stage is undertaken, whereby the message is decoded by the different speech and language components of the brain.

From this brief overview of the speech-chain, it becomes clear that we can think of a speech event as consisting of broadly three parts: the production of the message; the transmission of the message; and the reception of the message. The neurological aspects of production and reception are often considered as falling outside phonetics proper and we will therefore only touch on these at appropriate places through the book. Phoncticians have traditionally termed the three main stages of the speech event **articulatory phonetics**, **acoustic phonetics** and **auditory phonetics**, and we will follow these three stages in the presentation of phonetics in this book.

Articulatory phonetics (the term derives from the fact that vocal organs often articulate or move against each other in the production of speech) encompasses a very wide range of physical activity needed to produce the very large number of sound types possible in human language. We will therefore be spending several chapters of this book looking at articulatory phonetics. In order to do this efficiently, we will need to know some anatomy and physiology, i.e. those aspects relevant to speech production.

The vocal tract

The main functions of the vocal tract for speech are setting a column of air into motion, and then modifying this moving airstream in a number of ways to produce the sounds of speech. We can therefore view the vocal tract as an aerodynamic system, with the individual vocal organs contributing to this system. To initiate a moving column of air we need one of two types of device: a bellows or a piston. Luckily for us, the vocal tract has a very efficient bellows-like organ (the lungs) and also a piston-like structure (the larynx), and both of these can be used to initiate an airstream for speech. The larynx can also act in a valve-like manner, allowing free flow of air from the lungs, or metering it in small bursts producing what we term 'voice'.

Furthermore, we have a series of cavities above the larynx that can act as resonating chambers. The pharynx, and oral and nasal cavities can all be used to modify the moving airstream and so produce differences in speech sounds. We can modify the shape of the pharynx and oral cavity, in the case of the latter through movements of the tongue, lips and jaws, and so all of these must be considered as part of the anatomy and physiology of speech. The soft palate can act as a valve: allowing or stopping air from flowing through the nasal cavity. The soft palate, together with the back of the

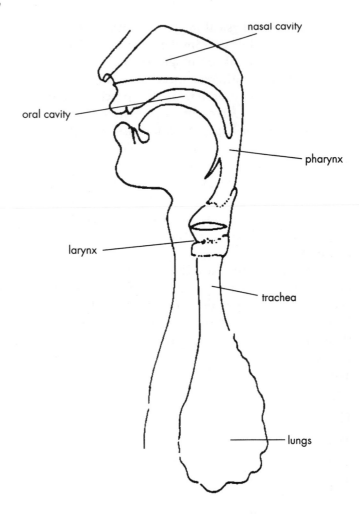

Figure 1.1 The vocal tract

tongue can also act in a piston-like manner, and so be yet another source of an airstream for speech.

As we can see in Figure 1.1, the vocal tract extends from the two lungs, via the trachea, the larynx and the pharynx, to the oral and the nasal cavities. We will examine these structures in turn, commencing with the lungs.

The respiratory system

The **lungs** are a pair of organs with an elastic or spongy nature. However, whereas we can characterize them as equivalent to a pair of bellows in their function of drawing air into the body and then expelling it again, they are unlike bellows in their make-up, as they do not consist of two balloon-like structures. It is more accurate to think of them as branching structures, consisting of many air-filled **alveoli** (around 300 million tiny air sacs) which

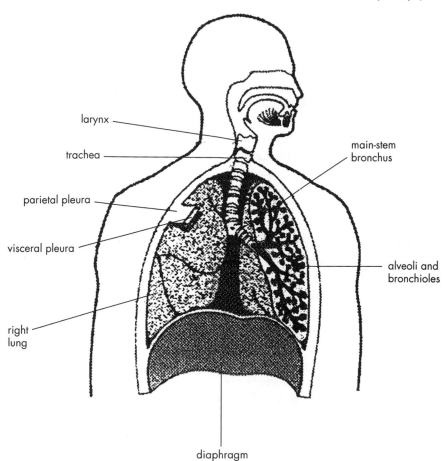

larynx

trachea

parietal pleura

visceral pleura

right
lung

main-stem
bronchus

alveoli and
bronchioles

diaphragm

Figure 1.2
The lungs

open into **alveolar** ducts, then into larger tubes (**bronchioles**), all of which
come together in the two **bronchi**. These unite at the base of the **trachea** (or
windpipe). This arrangement can be seen in Figure 1.2.

The lungs are contained within the **pleura**, which consists of one sac (the
visceral pleura) within another (the **parietal pleura**), the whole making up
an airtight entity within the thoracic cavity. The outer boundary of this
arrangement consists of the ribs while the lower one consists of the
diaphragm. The diaphragm is a large, dome-shaped muscle that separates
the thoracic from the abdominal cavities. Apart from the diaphragm, the
other important muscles concerned with lung activity are the **intercostals**.
The ribs are interconnected by two sets of intercostal muscles: the **external
intercostals**, which among other things help to expand the thoracic cavity
which creates a negative pressure within it, thus causing air to flow into the
lungs to help equalize pressure; and the **internal intercostals** which, among
other things, aids in the contraction of the ribs, thus creating positive

pressure leading to the expulsion of air from the lungs. Other muscles are also involved in breathing (for example the pectoralis minor muscles which connect ribs to the shoulder blade, and other abdominal and thoracic muscles), but we do not have the space here to go into all the muscular interactions needed for breathing and speech.

Stated simply, then, the breathing cycle of inspiration and expiration involves firstly the expansion of the rib cage and lowering of the diaphragm (causing negative air pressure as noted above), resulting in air flowing into the lungs (or **inspiration**). This is followed by a combination of gravity and muscular activity to expel air from the lungs. After filling with air, the lungs collapse under their own weight, causing air to start to flow outwards again (**expiration**). This is combined with raising of the diaphragm and activity by the internal intercostal muscles to create positive pressure and outward airflow. The lungs never empty completely (*see* Chapter 2 for discussion of amounts of air contained in the lungs at different points in the breathing cycle), but the speed with which they empty can be controlled. This is especially useful for speech, as we normally speak on an outward flowing airstream. By using the external intercostals as a kind of brake during expiration, we can slow this part of the cycle down to allow speech to take place over 2–10 seconds or, exceptionally, up to 25 seconds.

As noted above, the **trachea** commences at the union of the two bronchi of the lungs. It is a semi-flexible tube which is about 11 cm long and consists of a series of rings of cartilage, open at the back, connected by membranes; the top ring of the trachea is also the base of the larynx.

The laryngeal system

The **larynx** also consists of cartilage (in fact, nine separate cartilages), with connective membraneous tissue and sets of intrinsic and extrinsic laryngeal muscles (*see* Figure 1.3). For the purposes of speech production, we are mainly interested in the **cricoid** and **thyroid** cartilages, and the pair of **arytenoid** cartilages. The **epiglottis** can also have a speech function, but this is described in Chapter 3.

The cricoid cartilage is the base of the larynx and, as noted above, also functions as the top ring of the trachea. Unlike the other tracheal rings, the cricoid cartilage is a complete ring which has sometimes been compared to a signet ring in that the rear portion is flattened out into a large plate. Located above the cricoid cartilage is the thyroid cartilage. This is joined to the cricoid at the cricothyroid joint and the relevant ligaments allow the thyroid cartilage to move in a rocking or gliding motion against the cricoid cartilage.

The thyroid cartilage has been likened to a snow-plough, with the front

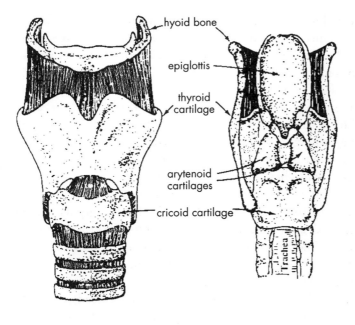

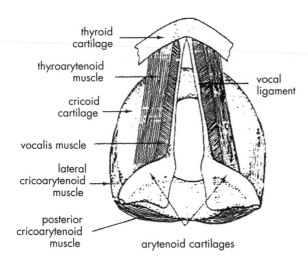

Figure 1.3 Front, rear and top view of the larynx

part of the plough being what we call the Adam's apple (or 'laryngeal prominence'). This prominence is more marked in men than in women, partly because the angle of the two thyroid lamina (or blades of the snow plough) is sharper in men than in women (90° as opposed to 120°).

Situated on the signet part of the cricoid ring are the two arytenoid cartilages, which resemble a pair of small pyramids (note that they are a mirror-image pair). They are attached to the cricoid via the cricoarytenoid joint, which allows both forward and backward movement, and side-to-side movement, this ability is important for speech as it allows us to adjust the tension of the vocal folds. The arytenoids have a series of small projections, which allow for muscular attachments (the 'muscular processes'), the cricoarytenoid joint just discussed, and (at the 'vocal processes') the attachments for the **vocal folds**.

The **vocal folds** run from the arytenoids forward to the interior of the front of the thyroid cartilage (*see* Figures 1.3 and 1.4). Each of the folds themselves (the older term 'vocal cords' is generally no longer used by phoneticians) can be thought of as consisting of a muscle (the **vocalis muscle**) covered by various layers, including the **vocal ligament** (there are different ways of classifying these layers that need not detain us here). The inner edges of the vocal folds, that come into contact when vocal fold vibration takes place (to produce 'voice'), are called the margins. These margins are usually divided into the upper and lower (or superior and inferior) margins: in vocal fold vibration the inferior margins make contact first, and separate first. Backward–forward movement of the arytenoids allows us to adjust the tension of the vocal folds (the more tense the vocal folds are, the higher pitch we perceive when voice is produced), whereas side-to-side movement allows us to bring the vocal folds together and move them apart.

Above the vocal folds (sometimes termed the 'true vocal folds') are the false vocal folds, or **ventricular bands** (*see* Figure 1.4). These resemble two shelves of tissue situated above the true vocal folds, and whilst they may be used by themselves or together with the true vocal folds in voice production for special effect, their use normally implies the speaker is suffering from a voice disorder.

The space between the vocal folds is termed the **glottis**. Although it may

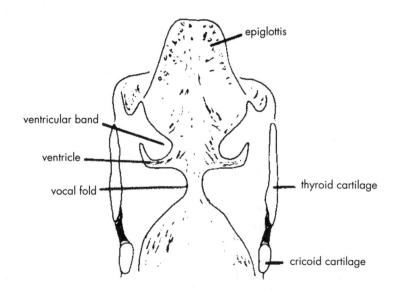

Figure 1.4 Cross-section of the vocal folds and the ventricular bands

seem strange to have a term for a space, rather than a structure, the glottis is important for speech, as the shape of the space between the folds determines many aspects of voice quality (*see* Chapter 2). The glottis can be open and closed (and various degrees in between), although there is always some resistance to airflow from the lungs, as the maximal glottal opening still covers just under half of the cross-sectional area of the trachea. This resistance to airflow actually causes acceleration to it, and can cause a certain amount of turbulence: the sound [h] is in fact turbulent airflow through a basically open glottis. Further aspects of glottal shape related to phonation and articulation are dealt with in future chapters.

Finally, we can also note that the larynx itself can be moved slightly upwards or downwards through the use of the laryngeal muscles. This aids in airflow initiation (*see* Chapter 2) by acting as a piston, but also aspects of voice quality derive from a raised or a lowered larynx (*see* Chapter 6). Superior to the larynx is the pharynx, which in turn leads to the oral and nasal cavities: it is these supralaryngeal (or supraglottal) structures that we will examine next.

The supralaryngeal system

The **pharynx** reaches up from the top of the larynx to the rear of the oral and the nasal cavities. The inferior part can be termed the 'oropharynx', with the superior called the 'nasopharynx'. The term 'laryngopharynx' has sometimes been used to denote that portion immediately above the larynx. As noted above, all the cavities described in this section are used as resonating chambers in speech production, which increase loudness and alter sound quality. The pharynx is less versatile in this regard than the oral cavity, as there are not many ways to alter the size or shape of the chamber. Nevertheless, certain changes can be made: the larynx may be raised, thus reducing the overall volume of the pharynx; the tongue root and epiglottis can be retracted into the oropharynx, again reducing its volume but also adding an obstruction to the airflow; and finally, the faucal pillars at either side of the back wall of the pharynx may be drawn towards each other thus contracting the back wall. This last modification generally results in an alteration to voice quality.

The **nasal cavity** is accessed through the **velopharyngeal port**, and this opening is effected through the lowering of the **velum** (or 'soft palate'): *see* Figure 1.5(a). In normal breathing, the velum is lowered all the time, so that air can flow freely through the nose down to the lungs and back out again. However, in speech the majority of sounds are purely oral (that is to say the outward flowing air on which speech is made does not enter the nasal cavity), so the velum must be raised. Nevertheless, a minority of speech sounds in most languages may involve the nasal cavity (for example, [m] and [n] in

(a)

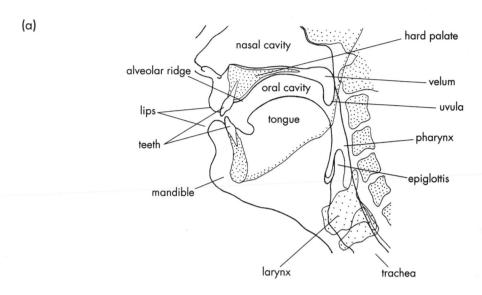

(b)

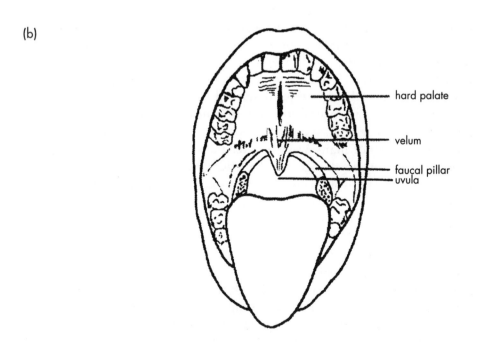

Figure 1.5 Oral cavity:
(a) side view; (b) front view

English), and for these sounds the velum is lowered and the air flows through the nasal cavity (it may also flow through the oral cavity at the same time; this is discussed further in Chapters 3 and 5). The nasal cavity cannot be modified in size or shape, and the air flow exits through the **nares** or nostrils.

The **oral cavity** is the most versatile of the three supralaryngeal cavities, and the important oral structures for speech are shown in Figure 1.5(a). At the front of the oral cavity, the lower jaw (or **mandible**) may be raised or lowered thus closing or opening the mouth. Linked to this, the upper and lower **lips** may be brought together or held apart. Also, the lips can adopt a rounded position (different degrees of rounding are possible), spread apart, or be in a neutral shape (*see* Figure 5.4 for illustrations of lip shapes). The **tongue** is the most flexible of the structures within the supralaryngeal system. Its **tip** and **blade** can articulate against the upper **teeth**, or the **alveolar ridge**; its **front** section can articulate against the **hard palate**; its **back** against the **velum** and the **uvula**; while its **root** can be retracted into the **pharynx** (*see* Figure 3.4 for a diagram of tongue divisions). The tip and blade are so flexible that they can be bent upwards and backwards such that the underside of tip and blade articulate against the roof of the mouth. Articulations at these places within the oral cavity can also be of different types (e.g. the tongue firmly touching the alveolar ridge, or leaving a small gap between the tip and the ridge), and these types are described in Chapter 3. All these articulations are used in the languages of the world to make individual sounds, and are described in detail in Chapter 3.

The modifications to the shape and volume of the oral cavity just described result in a large number of different sound qualities, which go to make up the vowels and consonants of language. We turn to look at this array of speech sounds in the next few chapters, but before that we also need to consider how the anatomy and physiology of speech allow us to monitor our speech as well as produce it.

Monitoring speech

In previous sections of this chapter we have been interested in the anatomy and physiology of speech production, but here we turn our attention to aspects of the monitoring of speech once it has been produced. (The hearing process and speech perception are dealt with in Chapters 10 and 11.) It is clear from listening to the speech of hearing-impaired people who learned to speak before suffering their hearing loss (termed 'post-lingual hearing loss') that monitoring of speech through hearing plays an important role. This **auditory feedback** is clearly used to monitor our accuracy in the production of prosodic aspects of speech such as intonation, loudness, tempo and voice quality (e.g. harsh, breathy or modal [= normal]), as these are among the most obvious disruptions in the speech of post-lingually hearing-impaired individuals; especially when their hearing loss occurred some time previously.

Phonetic disruptions also occur at the level of individual speech sounds with these speakers. So, we find inaccuracies in the vowel system, and precision in the production of many consonants also deteriorates over time. It seems clear, therefore, that auditory feedback is most important for the continued accurate production of speech. We can even test this with non-hearing-impaired speakers by temporarily blocking auditory feedback (usually through the use of padded headphones to block most sound from the ears). If you attempt this experiment, remember to record your own speech on a tape-recorder, or ask a colleague to let you know how you speak with the headphones on. Certain prosodic features are the first to be affected: loudness and tempo especially. It would appear then that these are under immediate control of auditory feedback, whereas the stored neuro-muscular patterns required for intonation, individual sound production and so on, take longer to degrade without this feedback.

However, it has long been known that auditory feedback is not the only monitoring mechanism in speech. For one thing, auditory feedback takes a comparatively long time (in speech production terms; *see* Figure 1.6 for a model of speech production and feedback): the time it takes from the movement of the speaker's articulators until the resultant sound is heard and any necessary alterations can be made is between 160 and 250 ms (= milliseconds, or thousandths of a second). Although this seems a very short time, it is longer than many individual sounds take to utter, so auditory feedback cannot be used to monitor the production of individual sounds, for even with long segments, such as some vowels, the majority of the sound would be completed before any correction could be made. Such a problem is not present in features such as loudness, intonation and so on which take place over a stretch of segments; and, as already mentioned, these are the very features that cause post-lingually deafened speakers most problems.

Nevertheless, post-lingually hearing-impaired speakers do eventually suffer attrition to the accuracy of consonants and vowels as well as prosodic features. It appears, then, that whilst auditory feedback cannot monitor the production of individual segments it is used to monitor the overall accuracy of classes of vowel and consonant (by testing whether they 'sound' correct, presumably). Without it, the stored neuromuscular patterns will deteriorate over time and cannot be corrected even using the other monitoring strategies discussed below.

Another feedback mechanism for speech, and one that might help in monitoring individual segments, is the **tactile/kinaesthetic feedback** mechanism derived from the sense of touch, and the ability to sense movement. Both tactile and kinaesthetic receptors are found throughout the vocal tract: tactile receptors are responsible for information about touch and pressure; the kinaesthetic ones inform us about the movement and position of vocal organs. The feedback from these receptors, therefore, can help speakers monitor the accuracy of the movement and placement of the articulators, and this in turn informs them about the accuracy of the execution of the neural commands for speech.

The tongue has a large number of tactile and kinaesthetic receptors, and this helps us to monitor the placement of the tongue: most important for a majority of individual speech sounds. Other parts of the supralaryngeal vocal tract are not so well endowed with receptors: for example, the palate does not have many. This is not a drawback, however, as when the palate is the **passive articulator** for a speech sound, the tongue is the **active articulator**, and so accuracy of articulation can still be monitored by the latter.

The importance of tactile/kinaesthetic feedback has been demonstrated through the examination of speakers who lack this mechanism due to an impairment to the receptors (this can be congenital). Alternatively, through the use of local anaesthetic, the feedback mechanism can be temporarily 'turned off' in experimental subjects and their speech can then be investigated. Such studies show that the lack of this monitoring route results in speech errors, generally in the articulation of individual speech segments. The tactile/kinaesthetic feedback loop is clearly shorter than the auditory one (*see* Figure 1.6), but even so it is still too long for monitoring the fine muscle activity required for the correct production of certain speech sounds or parts of speech sounds. We still need to find a quicker route.

Such a very fast feedback system requires that we examine the in-built feedback mechanism found with muscle activation (including, of course, muscle activation for speech). This feedback mechanism has been termed **proprioceptive** or **gamma-loop**, and is derived from the study of the physiology of the neuromuscular system. If we simplify this somewhat, we can state that neural impulses originating at higher levels of planning are transmitted via alpha and gamma motor neurons to the muscles. The resultant movement of the muscle is sensed in the 'muscle spindle', and impulses are sent back from the muscle spindles via the gamma system to impinge on the alpha motor neurons again. The returning gamma signal is compared via an automatic process with the intended outgoing signal and changes made to any deviations.

This comparison and emendation process takes place in an area of lower neural activity, and so is a quasi-automatic system, that does not need to be mediated by higher neural functions (unlike the two previous feedback mechanisms discussed). This results in an extremely rapid monitoring procedure, that we assume must be fast enough to control accuracy for even the most rapid and finest articulator movements in speech production (*see* Figure 1.6).

Our discussion of feedback mechanisms in speech allows us to propose a simple model of speech production and monitoring. In Figure 1.6 we show a diagram of this model. The model consists of series of boxes representing different stages in speech production (in reality, we have collapsed several stages into one in many of these boxes). The first of these we term **higher neural planning**, which represents the neural activity required to devise a message, organize it into phonological units needed for speech, and plan the ordering of neural impulses necessary for the final phonetic effect. Both auditory and tactile/kinaesthetic monitoring feedback fit

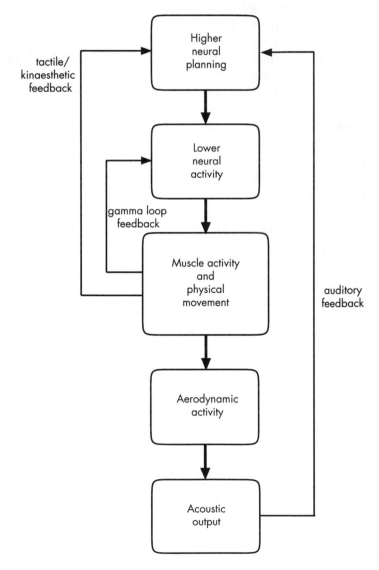

Figure 1.6 Model of speech production and feedback (adapted from Ball, 1993)

into this area, as they have to be decoded before any changes can be implemented.

Lower neural planning concerns the area where the actual nerve impulses are sent and, as mentioned above, where gamma loop feedback operates. The result of action in this box is **muscle activity** and the **physical movement** of articulators and other vocal organs. This is the source of both gamma loop feedback and the tactile/kinaesthetic systems, but as the figure shows they have different destinations. **Aerodynamic activity** is the result of vocal organ activity (*see* Chapter 2), leading to **acoustic output** (i.e. the speech sounds themselves). This last stage of the speech production process is the source of auditory feedback, and the model demonstrates the long path back to higher neural planning (via the hearing system, not included in the diagram) of this monitoring system.

Further reading

Readers wishing more detail on the anatomy and physiology of speech should consult Culbertson and Tanner (1997), Kent (1997b), Seikel et al. (1997) for recent texts; Kahane and Folkins (1984) and Perkins and Kent (1986) are excellent longer established texts.

Short questions

1 What organs make up the vocal tract?
2 How are the lungs made up?
3 What are the parts of the larynx most important for speech?
4 What controls the movement of the vocal folds and in what directions can they move?
5 What are the supralaryngeal resonating chambers?
6 How is entry to the nasal cavity controlled?
7 How can the oral cavity be modified?
8 What are the feedback mechanisms used to monitor speech?

Essay questions

1 Using library resources, discuss how the vocal tract changes from birth to adolescence, and comment on the effects these changes have on the ability to produce speech.
2 Review the literature on the effect of the lack of auditory feedback on the speech of hearing-impaired speakers, distinguishing between pre- and post-lingual hearing loss.

2 Initiation of speech

Introduction

In Chapter 1 we discussed the structures that make up the vocal tract, and pointed briefly to some of their functions as adapted for speech. For speech to occur, however, we must have a moving body of air through the vocal tract, or part of the vocal tract. Sound waves are created by modifying this moving body of air: the modifications being caused by the movements of various vocal organs, singly or in combination. What do we need to do to create this moving **airstream**? A variety of devices can cause air to flow: for example, a bellows-like pump can draw air in and then push it out creating an alternate inward and outward airflow. Also, a piston travelling up and down within its casing draws air alternately upwards and downwards.

What causes the air to flow when we use bellows-like or piston-like movements? The creation of an airstream depends on the exploitation of air pressure and changes in air pressure. There is a natural tendency to maintain equal air pressure throughout an aerodynamic system; if, therefore, there is an increase of pressure in one part of the system, air will flow away from that part to attempt to recreate equal pressure throughout (in other words to re-establish a balance in the system). If, on the other hand, there is a decrease of pressure in one part of the system then air will flow into that part, again in an attempt to return the pressure to a balance. Devices such as bellows or a piston cause changes in air pressure when they are used. For example, when bellows are squeezed together, the air pressure in the bags of the bellows is clearly greatly increased (as the bag volume is decreased so the same amount of air inside must be under greater pressure); this causes the air to flow outwards to aid in equalizing the air pressure with that of the outside. Conversely, when the bellows are opened out, the volume within the bags increases, so the air pressure is lower. This will cause air from the outside to flow into the bellows: again to equalize pressure.

Something similar occurs when we use a piston. If a piston moves upwards within a sealed cylinder then any gas (such as air) above the piston is subjected to positive pressure (i.e. the pressure increases). If an outlet to the outside is available above the piston, then the air in the cylinder will flow outwards to achieve pressure balance. Conversely, if the piston is pulled downwards in the cylinder, then any air above it will be subjected to negative pressure (air pressure reduces), and this time air from outside flows into the cylinder.

So, for speech purposes, we need to exploit vocal organs that can act like bellows or pistons to create air pressure changes and so airflow. Obviously, the lungs can be thought of as the equivalent of bellows, whereas the larynx moving up and down in the trachea acts in a piston-like manner. As we will see, these structures are responsible for most of the airstream types found in natural language, although other mechanisms can be used to produce speech sounds and extra-linguistic sounds. We noted above that both positive and negative pressure can cause airflow. With airstream mechanisms used for speech production, we find that positive pressure creates outward airflow, termed **egressive**, whereas negative pressure creates inward airflow, termed **ingressive**. Phoneticians sometimes use the terms 'positive pressure' and 'negative pressure' (or 'rarefactive pressure') to describe the direction of the flow, but we will use the more usual 'egressive' and 'ingressive' labels.

Airstream mechanisms

There are three airstream mechanisms used for speech initiation in natural language, but not all the egressive and ingressive possibilities are utilized. In Table 2.1 we list the location of each of them, with their names, and the direction of the airflow. In this last case, we note which directions are found in natural language through italics.

It should be noted that while the italicized airstream types are all found in natural language, not all languages use all types. Indeed, the majority of the languages of the world use only the pulmonic egressive airstream (as we do in English). Even when languages do use another type of airstream mechanism, the great majority of the sounds of the language are normally said on the pulmonic egressive airstream, with other sound types less common and inserted in a stream of otherwise pulmonic egressive sounds. (This is not so strongly the case with some of the Khoisan 'click' languages, which we return to later.)

Table 2.1 Airstream types

Mechanism location	Pressure (direction of air flow)	
	Negative	**Positive**
Lungs	Pulmonic (ingressive)	Pulmonic (egressive)
Larynx	Glottalic (ingressive)	glottalic (egressive)
Larynx + lungs (mixed)	Glottalic (ingressive) plus	pulmonic (egressive)
Mouth	Velaric (ingressive)	Velaric (egressive)

Note: Glottalic is sometimes termed 'laryngeal', velaric is sometimes 'oralic'.

Table 2.2 Sound types

Airstream	Sound type
Glottalic egressive	Ejectives
Glottalic ingressive	Voiceless implosives
Glottalic ingressive plus pulmonic egressive	(Voiced) implosives
Velaric ingressive	Clicks

Phoneticians have given names to the sound types made with the different airstreams. The wide range of consonant and vowels that can be made on the pulmonic egressive airstream are described in the following chapters. However, a smaller range of sound types is evident with the other mechanisms, and we can introduce these names here and use them as a shorthand for the full name of the airstream type. These sound types are all basically consonant-like; Table 2.2 shows their names.

Pulmonic egressive airstream

Pulmonic egressive speech has sometimes been referred to as 'modified breathing'. This is only partly true, in that speech on a pulmonic airstream is almost exclusively egressive (though see the section 'Pulmonic ingressive airstream' below), and so we are mainly interested in the modifications to the expiratory part of the breathing cycle; though, as we shall see, speech does require modifications to the relation between the inspiratory and expiratory parts of this cycle. First, therefore, we will look briefly at normal, quiet breathing.

Normal breathing consists of two phases: *inspiration* when air is drawn into the lungs, and *expiration* when it is expelled from them. As we noted above, these flows of air result from air pressure changes in the aerodynamic system, and these air pressure changes in the case of lung air are brought about through the expansion or contraction of the lungs. Finally, lung size is controlled mainly through muscular activity (see further below). As we noted in Chapter 1, inflation of the lungs is effected by means of the external intercostal muscles of the rib cage. Deflation, on the other hand, is partly the result of gravity, in that the full lungs collapse under their own weight; but this is aided by the internal intercostal muscles.

The respiratory cycle has been termed **tidal**, and the volume of air used in ordinary breathing is termed the **tidal volume**. Naturally, the amount of air making up this tidal volume will differ according to circumstances: for example, whether an individual is exerting themself or at rest. Quiet tidal breathing will require a low tidal volume (which has been termed the **resting expiratory level**); on the other hand, exertion will require a higher tidal volume. The limits to the amount of air we can breathe in and out, beyond the tidal volume, are anatomically and physiologically set; they are termed the **inspiratory** and the **expiratory reserve volume**: these volumes will differ from time to time depending how much air is being used in the tidal volume. As we noted in Chapter 1, the lungs can never be fully emptied, so even after the expiratory reserve volume has been expelled, there is still a **residual volume** left.

These are not the only volumes that can be measured however. If we add the tidal volume to the inspiratory reserve volume we get the **inspiratory capacity,** while the **vital capacity** is the maximum volume of air that can be expelled after a maximum inspiration. Vital capacity is the sum of the tidal volume and the inspiratory and expiratory reserve volumes. The **functional residual capacity** is worked out by adding the residual volume and expiratory reserve volume: this measure tells us how much air is in the lungs at the minimum of the tidal volume. Finally, all these measures allow us to work out the **total lung capacity** for any speaker.

In Table 2.3 we show all these measures worked out in litres of air for a healthy young adult male speaker. In working out such information, we also need to know the posture of the speaker and the prevailing atmospheric pressure: in this case we have the speaker standing upright, at sea level.

To understand pulmonic egressive speech, we also need to know something about different air pressures that can be measured in the vocal tract. We have already mentioned **atmospheric pressure**: that is the pressure of the 'outside air' that surrounds the speaker at any one time. This differs according to one's height above sea level, as well as due to the prevailing weather system. We can also measure the air pressure in the lungs (the **pulmonic pressure**), and the air pressure in the mouth (the **intra-oral pressure**).

Table 2.3 Lung volumes*

Lung volume type	Capacity (litres)
Tidal volume	0.5
Inspiratory reserve volume	2.5
Expiratory reserve volume	2.0
Residual volume	2.0
Inspiratory capacity	3.0
Vital capacity	5.0
Functional residual capacity	4.0
Total lung volume	7.0

* (*Source:* Laver, 1994: 165; after Hixon, 1973)

These pressures are clearly related, though the intra-oral pressure is also related to the position and type of articulatory constriction in the oral cavity and to phonatory activity. The term **subglottal pressure** is also encountered frequently in the phonetics literature. This refers to the pressure immediately below the larynx (and so, usually, equates to the pulmonic pressure). Subglottal pressure is proportional to perceived loudness, and is also an important measure in the examination of voiced plosive consonants (*see* Chapter 4).

We also need to know about **relaxation pressure**. This is the pressure in the subglottal vocal tract which holds when the respiratory muscles (referred to earlier) are relaxed, i.e. the pressure produced by non-muscular forces. This pressure is related to the amount of air that is currently in the system: therefore, if the respiratory muscles are relaxed and at the same time there is a large volume of air in the lungs and the lungs are expanded, then egressive airflow will result. This is because non-muscular relaxation forces (derived from elastic and mechanical recoil factors inherent in the lungs, rib cage and diaphragm) will compress the lungs back towards the resting level. Conversely, if the respiratory muscles are relaxed and at the same time there is a low volume of air in the lungs and the lungs are compressed, then ingressive flow will result. This is because the non-muscular relaxation forces will now allow expansion of the lungs back towards the resting level. Normal quiet breathing then, is at least partly controlled by an automatic system, although of course actions of the intercostal muscles can override the automatic nature of the cycle, and alter it if necessary. Figure 2.1 illustrates pressure changes involved with pulmonic egressive speech.

In speech on a pulmonic egressive airstream we usually do need to use muscular activity to alter this quasi-automatic respiratory system. To speak for more than a very brief moment we normally need to use a greater tidal volume than in quiet breathing. However, more importantly, we need

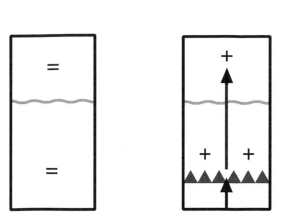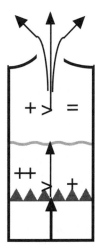

Figure 2.1 Pressure changes involved with the pulmonic egressive airstream (for a voiced plosive).

Key to Figures 2.1–2.5

+ positive pressure	———— closed glottis
– negative pressure	～～～ vibrating vocal folds
= equal pressure	↑ direction of airflow
	▲▲▲▲▲▲ pressurized air from lungs

to slow down the expiratory part of the cycle, but keep the inspiratory part short. To slow down expiration, speakers use muscular control (via the external intercostals) as a brake to slow down the outward flow of air, switching eventually, if necessary, to a pushing action (with the internal intercostals) to override the relaxation pressure within the system which would otherwise tend to cause inspiration to recommence. In this way, expiration can be made to last a relatively long time (up to about 25 seconds with some speakers), with speech on one exhalation normally lasting between two and 10 seconds.

This means that pulmonic egressive air flow is especially suited for speech, as we can produce long strings of sounds before having to repeat the modified respiratory cycle. As we will see, other airstream mechanisms used for speech normally only allow very short stretches to be uttered at any one time.

Pulmonic ingressive airstream

Speech is possible on a pulmonic ingressive airstream. However, we are not as able to slow down the inspiratory part of the breathing cycle as the expiratory, therefore we have only a small amount of air to use for speech.

Further, the vocal folds are well suited to air flowing through them from below (see phonation, later in this chapter), but are not so well adapted for pulmonic ingressive air flow. The result is that speech on such an airstream tends to sound harsh.

Nevertheless, pulmonic ingressive speech is sometimes encountered in natural language. For example, in rapid counting speakers sometimes alternate between egressive and ingressive airstreams for each numeral uttered (e.g. 'one, ↓two, three, ↓four', where ↓ stands for ingressive speech). It has also been noted for several languages that responsives such as 'yes' and 'no' (or their equivalents in the language concerned) may be uttered on a pulmonic ingressive airstream. This usage has sometimes been interpreted as having semantic function, for example, Laver (1994) reports that in some Scandinavian languages this usage conveys sympathy, whereas for English ingressive 'yes' has been taken to suggest reluctant compliance. However, we have noted for English that rapid ingressive 'yes' can be characteristic of simple back-channel behaviour (i.e. the supporting sounds made by a listener to someone else who is currently speaking), and have relatively little semantic content.

Pulmonic ingressive speech has also been reported as a means of disguising the voice from different areas. Perhaps the best-known case is that of 'Fensterle': a Swiss–German custom whereby a boy would talk to his sweetheart through the window of her room using ingressive speech so as to disguise his voice from her parents (it is unclear whether such a use is still required in modern Switzerland!). A disguising function is also reported in Greece and in the Philippines (for the Hanunóo language).

Finally, there is some evidence that this airstream may be used linguistically in the language Tsou spoken in Taiwan (*see* Laver, 1994). A speaker of a regional form of this language (the Punguu accent of the Tfuea dialect) used the ingressive forms [↓f] and [↓h] in certain phonological contexts. Certain other speakers investigated did not share this usage, so it is unclear whether it is purely idiosyncratic or whether it represents a sub-variety of this accent.

Glottalic airstreams

As we noted above, piston-like mechanisms can be used to create pressure changes and so air flow within an aerodynamic system. For a glottalic egressive airstream, the speaker needs to have a tightly closed glottis (achieved by bringing together the vocal folds) and then use the extrinsic laryngeal muscles to jerk the larynx upwards. Assuming there is also an articulatory stricture in the oral cavity, this movement of the larynx increases the intra-oral air pressure such that air flows outwards on the release of the articulatory stricture (*see* Figure 2.2). Only a small amount

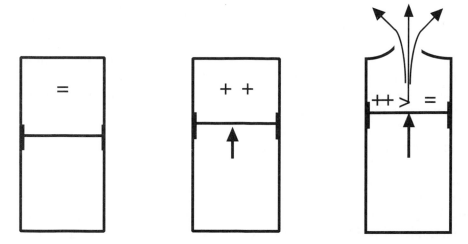

Figure 2.2 Pressure changes involved with ejectives

of air is involved here (the amount between the larynx and the place of articulation), so only a single sound can be made with any one larynx movement. This means that ejectives are normally encountered embedded in speech using lung air. The impression gained with this airstream that sounds are being 'jerked' out is the reason for the name 'ejective' that is used for them. We discuss ejectives in more detail in later chapters.

To produce a glottalic ingressive airstream we need to reverse the above actions. The tightly closed glottis is jerked downwards thus rarefying the intra-oral air pressure. On release of the articulatory stricture the air pressure differences are equalized through the rushing in of air to produce what

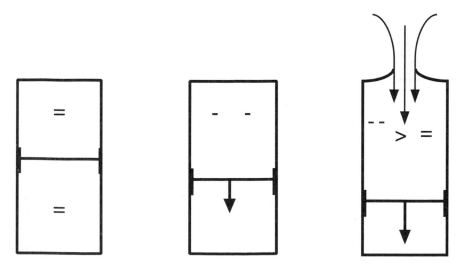

Figure 2.3 Pressure changes involved with voiceless implosives

is termed a 'voiceless implosive' (or a 'reverse ejective'). This set of events is illustrated in Figure 2.3. Voiceless implosives are very rare linguistically, possibly due to the fact that the sounds are difficult to produce with sufficient volume to render them on a par with pulmonic egressive sounds. More common are implosives produced with vocal fold vibration (i.e. voiced implosives), but these are the result of mixed airstream mechanisms, and we cover these in the next subsection.

Glottalic ingressive plus pulmonic egressive airstream

Glottalic ingressive sounds can be made louder (and thus more prominent) by adding an amount of pulmonic egressive airflow through the larynx at the same time as producing ingressive airflow into the mouth: the resultant sounds are termed 'voiced implosives'. This is done by modifying the closure of the glottis: instead of keeping it tightly closed, the vocal folds are only held together lightly. This means that as the larynx is lowered, pulmonic air below the larynx can pass through the glottis causing the vocal folds to vibrate and produce voice (see phonation, later in this chapter). Figure 2.4 illustrates how this can happen.

Clearly, to produce this mixed airstream, the pulmonic positive pressure must not be too much to overcome the intra-oral negative pressure, or no ingressive airflow will result. In carefully produced voiced implosives, Catford (1977) suggests that positive pulmonic pressure is not needed, but that the lowering larynx simply moves over a static mass of lung air. Laver (1994), however, feels that implosives used in natural, pulmonic egressive, speech may well need varying amounts of pulmonic activity to

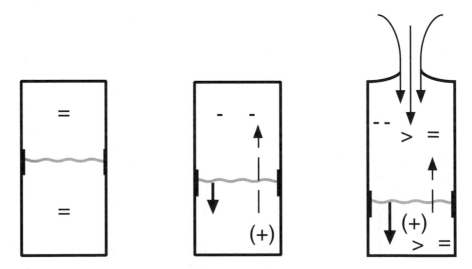

Figure 2.4 Pressure changes involved with voiced implosives

be produced. As with ejectives, voiced implosives are normally found surrounded by speech sounds made with the pulmonic egressive airstream; though one can produce short syllables implosively.

It is worth pointing out that certain sounds made with a pulmonic egressive airstream (voiced plosives; *see* Chapters 3 and 4) require a slight, gradual lowering of the larynx during production to retain the pressure differentials between the sub- and supra-glottal parts of the vocal tract. Voiced implosives differ from these pulmonic egressive sounds mainly in the timing, speed and amount of larynx lowering.

Velaric airstreams

A velaric airstream is initiated within the oral cavity, through actions of the tongue. To produce a velaric ingressive airstream, the back of the tongue makes a firm contact with the soft palate (or velum; hence velaric). Another part of the tongue is also used to make an articulatory contact (for example, the tongue tip against the alveolar ridge). This means that a small pocket of air is trapped between the back and front of the tongue. The air pressure in this pocket can be rarefied by expanding the size of this pocket. This can be done by lowering the centre of the tongue, or pulling the tongue tip back along the roof of the mouth, or combinations of these actions. On release of the articulatory closure (usually just before the velic closure), air flows into the mouth to equalize the pressure differences (*see* Figure 2.5).

As noted above, click sounds are normally made with two tongue contacts. However, one type is produced with an articulatory closure between the two lips. Here, the pocket of air is clearly larger, as it stretches from the velum to the lips. It is still possible to rarefy the pressure in this pocket by lowering the tongue body from a mid, neutral position.

Finally, we should note that clicks involve an even smaller amount of airflow than do ejectives and implosives, and so only single clicks can be produced at any one time, embedded in an otherwise pulmonic egressive stream of speech. Clicks can be modified in many ways, however, and we discuss these in later chapters.

Velaric egressive sounds are possible to produce (through making the air pocket smaller rather than larger), but these sounds (termed 'reverse clicks') are not found in natural language.

Other airstream mechanisms

Other mechanisms can be used to produce an airflow for speech, though none of these are used normally for natural language. Oesophageal and tracheo-oesophageal speech can be learned by speakers whose larynxes

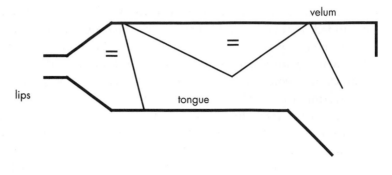

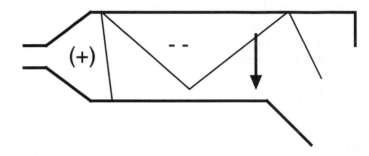

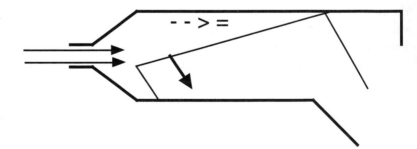

Figure 2.5 Pressure changes involved with clicks

have been removed (e.g. because of cancer of the larynx), whilst various other oral mechanisms (using the cheeks or tongue) have been used to produce non-linguistic or pathological speech sounds.

Oesophageal speech involves the use of a moving column of air from the oesophagus, which causes a vibration at the sphincteric pharyngo-oesophageal junction (acting as a pseudo-glottis). The resultant air stream is then modified by the supraglottal articulators and resonators in the normal way. Lung air is not available for speech, as following the removal of the larynx, the trachea now ends in a stoma in the throat. A variety of air-intake techniques are used by oesophageal speakers, but voice quality in oesophageal speech will clearly differ from that in pulmonic speech; one major difference lies in the amount of air available. With oesophageal speech the air reservoir is in fact the upper portion of the oesophagus, holding about 15 ml of air for each air-charge, approximately 100 times less than that used in normal speech. Apart from the shorter breath units, the use of the pseudo-glottis at the pharyngo-oesophageal junction instead of the normal glottis results in a voice quality normally deemed unnatural.

In tracheo-oesophageal speech the surgery leaves a slightly different result than that noted above for oesophageal speakers. Here, while the trachea still terminates with a stoma in the throat, a puncture is made between the trachea and the oesophagus just at the level of the tracheal opening. The intention is that lung air can still be used for speech by redirecting exhaled air from the trachea, through the tracheo-oesophageal puncture and into the oesophagus, from whence it will flow into the pharynx and upper vocal tract. To produce a more natural type of voice, artificial valves of different types may be fitted into the puncture, but the vibration for voice still occurs at the pharyngo-oesophageal junction. Although it is possible to use normal pulmonic egressive airflow with this voice type, thus increasing the length of the breath units, the voice quality is still markedly different from that of normal speech, but is generally deemed more acceptable than that of simple oesophageal speech.

On a lighter note, certain extralinguistic sounds may be made on airstreams produced within the oral cavity (other than the velaric). These require a glottal closure to create a resonating chamber within the mouth, and then pressure from the cheeks can push the air within the oral cavity outwards. This 'buccal egressive' airstream is used in certain varieties of the sound normally referred to as a 'raspberry'. Alternatively, the lips or teeth may be struck together percussively thereby causing a slight pressure change and then airflow. Another type of percussive involves the striking of the underside of the tongue blade against the lower alveolus (the floor of the mouth). With a closed glottis this also produces what we can call a 'resonating percussive'. These percussives can be found in pathological speech, and involve what we will term as 'bilabial-oral', 'bidental-oral' and 'sublaminal-oral' airstream mechanisms.

Phonation

As noted earlier, most speech in natural language involves a pulmonic egressive airstream. This air flows upwards from the lungs, through the larynx and then into the pharynx, oral and/or nasal cavities. 'Phonation' is the term we use to describe the range of modifications to this airflow as it

Table 2.4 Basic phonation types

Voiceless		Voiced			Whisper	Glottal closure
Breath	Nil-phonation	Modal voice	Creak	Falsetto		
V̥, n̥, l̥, h	s, p	V, z, b, a	C, a̠	F	W, a̠	ʔ

passes through the glottis within the larynx. As we described in Chapter 1, the glottis is the space between the vocal folds, and the folds themselves can be pulled together, kept apart, and subject to varying degress of tension. These points will all be important when we consider different phonation types.

When describing phonation, phoneticians have often set up two categories: four or five basic phonation types, and a number of combinations of these types. However, as Laver (1994) points out, the basic types themselves may best be thought of as falling into three classes. Table 2.4 shows a possible classification of these basic phonation types, with phonetic symbols used to transcribe them.[1] In most cases, there is a capital letter symbol, which is used with braces to indicate that a whole stretch of speech is uttered with a particular phonation type (or where the relevant sounds in that stretch are so uttered), and in some cases there are individual segment symbols. These segment symbols may represent sounds that are inherently voiced or voiceless, or – when used with an added diacritic – sounds that are uttered with creak, whisper etc. For glottal closure, the segmental symbol (for a glottal stop) only is used.

Voicelessness

With **voicelessness** the glottis is open, resulting from abduction of the vocal folds (*see* Figure 2.6). The glottis is open at between 60% and 95% of its maximal opening, and the pulmonic egressive air flows relatively freely through the larynx. If the flow of air has a low volume-velocity (Catford (1977) suggests below approximately 200–300 cc/sec for an adult male) then the air flow is laminar (i.e. smooth). This kind of airflow is termed **nil-phonation**. Nil-phonation is used for many voiceless speech sounds, such as [f, s, ʃ] in the English words 'feet, seat, sheet'.

On the other hand, if the volume-velocity is above the 300 cc/sec then turbulence will occur as the air flows through the glottis. This is termed

---

[1] Phonetic symbols are gradually introduced in this and the following chapters. The current International Phonetic Alphabet chart is reproduced in Appendix 1. See IPA (1989, 1993, 1995, 1999) for descriptions of the current version of the alphabet.

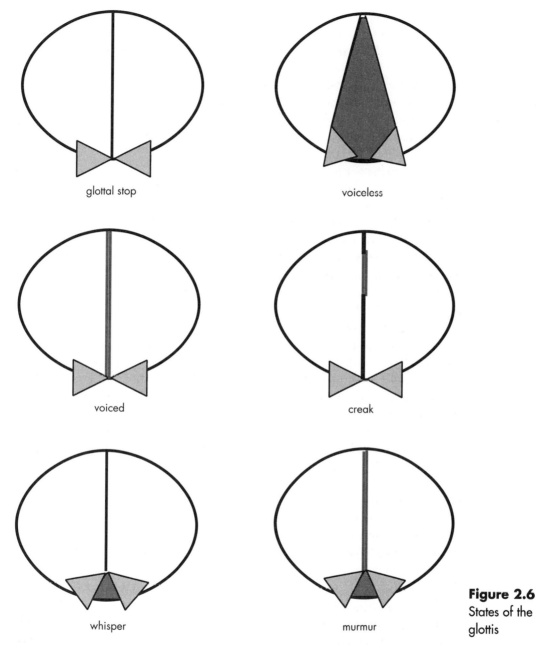

Figure 2.6
States of the glottis

breath, and is found in the sound [h] and, in those languages that use them, in voiceless vowel sounds.

Normally, phoneticians do not need to distinguish between these two varieties of an overall voiceless category, as they are not used contrastively in natural language. We will in future, therefore, only refer to voicelessness when discussing the phonatory aspects of sound segments. As we describe in Chapters 4 and 5, not all sound types occur equally commonly with voicelessness. Consonants termed 'obstruents' are commonly found voiceless; in English we have the following voiceless obstruents: [p, t, k, tʃ, f, θ, s, ʃ, h]. ([tʃ] is the sound of 'ch' in 'chin'; [θ] the sound of 'th' in 'thin'; [ʃ] the sound of 'sh' in 'shin').

As can be seen from the above, voicelessness is normally an inherent part of a particular symbol in the case of obstruents. However, with the other type of consonant (sonorant) and with vowels, voicelessness is rare, and so specific voiceless phonetic symbols do not exist. To show these sounds, a special **diacritic** (or mark) is added beneath or above the symbol (the choice depends on the symbol shape) to denote that the sound is, in fact, said without voice. Examples include [m̥, n̥, l̥, ɹ̥, i̥]. ([ɹ̥] is the voiceless 'r' sound found in English 'prim'.) Finally, the V̥ symbol can be used to mark an entire stretch of speech where the speaker is only using voiceless sounds (perhaps due to a voice disorder), rather than adding the voiceless diacritic to each voiced symbol in turn.

Voice

Voiced phonation is produced through the vibration of the vocal folds. The vibratory cycles of the vocal folds are repeated on average about 120 times per second in an adult male speaker, and about 220 times per second for an adult female (these frequencies are expressed as 120 Hz and 220 Hz, where Hz stands for Hertz or cycles per second). However, these frequencies may be increased or decreased by speakers when they raise and lower the pitch of their voices (*see* Chapter 6). Voiced phonation, then, involves a pulsing action that expels short puffs of air very rapidly, and this action creates a humming noise at the larynx that adds to the perceptual salience of voiced sounds. If you compare a voiced to a voiceless sound (for example, a sustained [z] as compared to [s]), you can feel the vibration of the vocal folds within the larynx used with [z] if you hold your fingers against your Adam's apple.

The vibration of the vocal folds are produced with the co-operation of both muscular and aerodynamic forces, with the balance of these forces altering subtly during the vibratory cycle. If we consider how one such cycle might operate, we can illustrate the interplay of what have been termed the **aerodynamic–myoelastic** forces. We will commence with a closed (or nearly closed) glottis, with contact between the edges of the two vocal folds. The vocal folds are brought together through the action of the adductor muscles of the larynx which control the position of the arytenoid cartilages. This adduction of the folds will form a barrier to the pulmonic egressive airflow that is being pumped upwards from the lungs. This barrier will result in a build-up of air pressure in the sub-glottal area, and eventually the aerodynamic force of this pressure will overcome the muscular force holding the vocal folds together. Eventually, therefore, the folds are pushed apart through the action of air pressure, and an amount of air will flow rapidly through the parted folds. According to Catford (1977), the speed of this jet of air is between 2000 and 5000 cm per second, and this is partly due to the sub-glottal pressure, and partly due to an aerodynamic effect (the Venturi effect) which accelerates any gas forced through a narrow constriction. Another aerodynamic effect (the Bernoulli effect) is responsible for a pressure drop in the area of the glottal constriction resulting in the sucking together of the vocal folds. This is combined with the elastic tension of the laryngeal muscles, and together these two forces are enough to overcome the falling sub-glottal pressure and so re-establish glottal closure. Then, of course, the cycle recommences. Figure 2.6 (p.31) shows the glottal shape for voice; Figure 2.7 illustrates the voicing cycle.

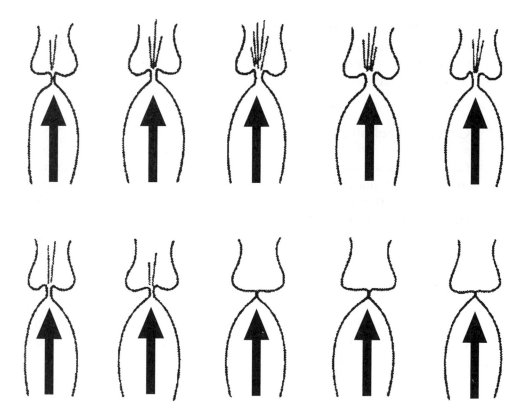

Figure 2.7 The voicing cycle

All languages have both voiceless and voiced sounds contrasting in their phonological systems (which is why we have dealt with these two types first). In English, for example, all vowels are voiced, as are the following consonants: [b, d, g, dʒ, m, n, ŋ, v, ð, z, ʒ, l, ɹ, w, j] ([dʒ] is the 'j' sound in 'jam', [ŋ] is the 'ng' sound in 'sing', [ð] is the 'th' sound in 'then', [ʒ] is the 's' sound in 'treasure', [ɹ] is the 'r' sound in 'red', and [j] is the 'y' sound in 'yellow'). English, therefore, has more voiced than voiceless sounds, and analyses of sample spoken texts of English reveal that voiced sounds are in general three times more common than voiceless ones. Similar ratios are found in many European languages, but it should be noted that other languages may have ratios that are more balanced, or even show voiceless sounds as occurring more often than voiced in sample texts.

As we have just illustrated, voiced sounds normally are denoted by dedicated symbols in phonetic transcription without the need to add diacritics. **Modal** (or normal) voice can be indicated for a stretch of speech by the simple use of V, perhaps to distinguish it from stretches of speech where the speaker uses another phonation type (such as **creak**). In such instances, of course, voiceless symbols would still stand for voiceless sounds. The diacritic for voice is sometimes needed (for example, to illustrate a combined phonation type such as **diplophonia** described later in this chapter). This diacritic resembles a small 'v' beneath the symbol: [s̬] (in this case denoting a sound with the force of an 's', but with added voicing).

Creak and Falsetto

Creak, which is also termed 'glottal fry' or 'vocal fry' (especially in the American literature) is similar to modal voice that we have just looked at, in that it consists of pulses of air passing through the glottis, but differs primarily in the frequency of these pulses. Creak has low sub-glottal pressure and low volume velocity airflow; and the frequency of vocal fold vibration can be in the region of 30–50 Hz. There is some debate as to vocal fold behaviour during the production of creak; for example, Catford (1977) suggests that this takes place at the anterior end of the vocal folds, with air being emitted through a small gap in the folds. Others, as noted in Laver (1994), feel that a full glottal location is used at least by some speakers. Figure 2.6 illustrates the glottal position for creak.

Creak (and creaky voice) are often used by English speakers extra-linguistically (replacing modal voice), where it can be used to suggest boredom, or authority. In other languages creak has a contrastive function (e.g. in Hausa, a language of Nigeria), or occurs with low tones in tone languages (*see* Chapter 6). Creak can be transcribed phonetically by adding a subscript tilde to individual sounds (e.g. [ɑ̰]), or by using capital C to mark that an entire stretch of speech is said using creak rather than modal voice (such usage assumes that voiceless sounds are unaffected).

Falsetto also is a phonation type with pulsed emission of air. With this phonation type the vocalis muscle is relaxed and the thyroarytenoid muscle contracts to leave the edge of the vocal folds (the vocal margin) thin. The glottis is kept slightly open and sub-glottal pressure is somewhat lower than in modal voice. The resultant phonation is characterized by very high frequency vocal fold vibration (between 275 Hz and 634 Hz for an adult male). Falsetto is not used linguistically in any known language, but has variety of extra-linguistic functions dependant on the culture concerned. Falsetto is transcribed by marking the relevant stretch of speech with capital F – again we assume that falsetto only applies to sounds that would ordinarily be voiced.

Whisper

Whisper requires a glottis that is narrowed to about 25% of its maximal opening, and this needs the vocal folds to be closer together than for voicelessness. It seems that normally for whisper the anterior portion of the folds are close together while a triangular-shaped opening is made at the posterior end (*see* Figure 2.6); an alternative full glottal form of whisper is possible but probably not as common.

With whisper, airflow is strongly turbulent, producing the characteristic hushing quality. This phonation type is used contrastively in some languages, but we are more used to thinking of whisper as an extra-linguistic device to disguise the voice, or at the least to reduce its volume. When whisper phonation is used in this way, speakers transfer voiced sounds to whisper, but maintain voiceless sounds as voiceless (to avoid the loss of contrast between the two groups). Whisper is transcribed by adding a single subscript dot beneath the relevant symbol (as [ɑ̣]), or by attaching a capital W to a stretch of speech.

Glottal closure

Although not technically a phonation type, this state of the glottis can be noted here. If the vocal folds are brought together we have 'glottal closure'. By holding them together with enough muscular action to overcome the sub-glottal pressure, the result is a **glottal stop**. A glottal stop is usually treated as an individual segment, and like other stops (*see* Chapter 3) may last for approximately 50–60 ms before it is released, and the pressurized sub-glottal air released. Further, glottal stops may be used in some languages (e.g. Arabic) as an individual sound, with a letter assigned to it in the relevant alphabet. In other languages (e.g. English) it is not usually recognized as being part of the sound system, even though it may often occur prosodically (e.g. in English as a hiatus blocker or pause marker), or segmentally (e.g. in English as a realization of /t/ post-vocalically). Glottal stops are transcribed with the symbol [ʔ].

Combinatory phonation types

As we can see in Table 2.5, various combinations of these basic phonation types are possible, and we will describe briefly the most important of these. **Breathy voice** (V^h) has a glottal opening wider than for 'whisper' but narrower than for 'voicelessness'. The vocal folds vibrate in the high volume-velocity airflow through this gap, but as the air is soon exhausted because of the high rate of flow, this phonation type cannot be maintained for long. 'Slack voice' is a term that has been applied to this phonation type. Unfortunately, 'breathy voice' has also been applied to a phonation type we term **whispery voice** (V̰, a̰) (or 'murmur'). Here, we have relaxed yet vibrating vocal folds combined with whisper through a gap at the posterior portion of the folds. This type of phonation is used linguistically in languages such as Hindi, Shona and Zulu to contrast with modal voice. This terminological mix-up between breathy voice and whispery voice also means that transcriptions can be ambiguous. Here, we follow Laver (1994) and use subscript double dot to represent whispery voice/murmur, as this is used frequently by phoneticians dealing with those languages which use this phonation contrastively. An alternative symbol is V with a subscript single

Table 2.5 Combined phonation types

	Breath	Voice	Creak	Falsetto	Whisper
Breath		V^h			
Voice			V̰		V̰ a̰
Creak				F̰	C̣
Falsetto					F̣
Whisper					
Whispery creaky		WV̰		WF̰	

dot (V̪); although this is a logical combination, it cannot be used on individual symbols.

Creaky voice (V̰) has proved difficult to define, but may well consist of creak phonation at the anterior part of the vocal folds, with voice at the posterior. Alternatively, what we hear as a combination of creak and voice may simply be due to slight variations in creak vibration from cycle to cycle. Languages that have creak phonologically, never contrast it with creaky voice, so many phoneticians tend to treat the two as basically the same. 'Stiff voice' has been applied to a phonation type that involves a slight degree of 'creaky voice' (or 'laryngealization'). **Whispery creak** (C̰) is similar to murmur, with a lower frequency vibration of the vocal folds. Creak and whisper may also be combined separately with falsetto (F̰, F̣) – these combinations being similar to creaky voice and whispery voice except for the special setting of the vocal folds; and the whispery creak combination itself may also co-occur with voice (WV̰) and with falsetto (WF̣). None of these types is known used linguistically.

Location and larynx setting

We have noted that certain phonation types occur with the entire vocal folds, the anterior portion or the posterior (or cartilagenous) portion. If necessary, the International Phonetic Alphabet (IPA) diacritics for advanced and retracted can be added to the phonation symbol to make these differences clear: e.g. W̠ for posterior whisper, V̟ for anterior modal voice (sometimes termed 'tense' voice or 'pressed phonation').

However, there is another location we have not yet referred to: the false vocal folds, or ventricular bands (*see* Chapter 1). These are situated above the vocal folds, and can be used by themselves to produce voice (and indeed a variety of phonation types as noted in Catford, 1977), or can be used simultaneously with the vocal folds (**diplophonia**, or 'double voice'). Ventricular phonation has a harsh quality, and the VoQS symbol system denotes harsh voice produced from the vocal folds with V!, and ventricular phonation as V!!. Diplophonia is transcribed with V̰!!. These phonation types are not used linguistically, but are found paralinguistically in certain types of jazz singing ('scat singing') and, for example, in the chanting of Tibetan monks.

Finally, we should note that larynx setting also affects voice quality. The extrinsic laryngeal muscles can be used to raise or lower the larynx slightly from its normal setting. With a lowered larynx we have a slightly increased length of the supraglottal vocal tract, resulting in a lower pitch to the voice. Conversely, a slightly raised larynx will result in a higher pitched voice. The pitch changes required for intonation are normally regulated through increasing or decreasing vocal fold vibration rates, therefore raised and

Table 2.6 Phonation types used segmentally

	Plosives	Nasals	Approximants	Vowels
Creaky voice	*Fula* [o ḍaːnike] 'he slept'	*Jalapa Mazatec* [m̬e] 'dies, kills'	*Montana Salish* [l̬láts] 'red raspberry'	*Jalapa Mazatec* [ja̰] 'he wears'
Stiff voice	*Korean* [p*ul] 'horn'	–	–	*Mpi* [s*iɹ] 'seven'
Slack voice	*Javanese* [ḅaku] 'standard'	–	–	–
Murmur	*Hindi* [b̤al] 'forehead'	*Hindi* [kumʱar] 'potter'	*Sindhi* [l̤ʊl̤i] 'fat'	*Gujerati* [bạr] 'outside'
Whisper	–	–	–	*Malagasy* [maso̤] 'eye'

lowered larynx settings will be independent of intonation: they are part of a speaker's overall voice quality. Using IPA diacritics, lowered larynx is symbolized by L̞ while raised is L̝ .[2]

Examples of phonation types in natural language

In the following chapters we restrict most examples to voiced and voiceless segments, but we include here a short set of words from a variety of languages using other phonation types. These are shown in Table 2.6, and include a variety of consonant types and vowels. The description of these different types is given in Chapter 3.

Further reading

Airstream initiation is dealt with in detail in Kent (1997b), but most standard phonetics texts deal with this topic. Among those recommended are Catford (1977, 1988), Clark and Yallop (1995), Ladefoged (1993) and Laver (1994). Speech aerodynamics are described in detail in Shadle (1997), whereas Zajac and Yates (1997) look at instrumental analysis of speech aerodynamics. Phonation is also dealt with in the main texts noted above, and Hirose (1997) and Ní Chasaide and Gobl (1997) provide more detailed accounts of laryngeal physiology and the acoustics of voice production. Abberton and Fourcin (1997) describe instrumental approaches to the examination of phonation.

---

[2] Although languages do use many of the phonation types listed above contrastively, in the following chapters we concentrate mainly on the voiced–voiceless distinction. Some examples are given in Table 2.6, but readers wishing to find more should refer to Laver (1994) and Ladefoged and Maddieson (1996).

Short questions

1 What do you understand by the term initiation?
2 What direction of airflow do we normally get with pressure initiation, and with rarefactive initiation?
3 What airstreams are used in natural language?
4 What are the names given to sounds made on the non-pulmonic airstreams?
5 What are the main phonation types? Use glottal diagrams to illustrate your answer.
6 Name any four combined phonation types. Use glottal diagrams to illustrate your answer.
7 How is diplophonia produced?
8 What is a glottal stop?

Essay questions

1 Describe how the four main airstreams used in natural language are produced. Illustrate your answer with appropriate diagrams.
2 What is phonation? Illustrate the production of the main phonation types of natural speech and their combinations.

3   Speech articulation

Introduction	Prolongability
Consonant and vowel	Manner of articulation
State of the velum	Place of articulation
Direction of airflow	Three-term labels
Force of articulation	

Introduction

Once an airstream has been set in motion, speech can be 'articulated' through the movements and settings of the supraglottal vocal organs (for example, the tongue and the lips). These settings can create long term characteristics of speech (such as voice quality), and these characteristics, together with aspects of speech controlled at the initiation and phonation stages of speech production, are termed **suprasegmental** aspects; we return to look at these in detail in Chapter 6. Shorter-term aspects of speech are usually termed **speech segments,** and it is these that are dealt with in this and the following two chapters.

At this stage, we can consider speech segments to be the individual consonants and vowels that go to make up syllables (and, of course, words). Later, in Chapter 7, we return to this topic, and will point out that speech segments do not, in fact, have strict boundaries and to some extent merge one into another. For now, however, we adopt the usual phonetic practice of assuming that we can describe segments in a discrete manner. To this end, we will continue introducing the symbols of the International Phonetic Alphabet (IPA) to illustrate specific sounds: these symbols are always placed within square brackets to show they represent sounds not spellings. The entire IPA Chart is included in Appendix 1, and the most recent version described in IPA (1989, 1993,

1995, 1999). We look in more detail at transcription into phonetic symbols in Chapter 8.

It is difficult to offer a strict definition of segments simply because, as we have just noted, the features that go to make up segments (and which we are exploring in this chapter) do not all share the same boundaries. However, as Laver (1994) for example points out, we would normally expect the feature of degree of **stricture** (that is how close together the articulators are) to remain the same throughout a segment, even if other features (such as **voicing**, or **lip shape**) stretch over shorter or longer periods of time. We use the term segment in this book therefore to mean a period of time (anything from 30 ms to 300 ms depending on the sound concerned) during which the degree of stricture is maintained.

There are a number of ways we can group speech segments, and we discuss these here. We go on to illustrate the categories of speech sounds in some detail in the next chapters. The classifications we examine here are: consonant and vowel; state of the velum; direction of airflow; force of articulation; prolongability; manner of articulation; place of articulation.

Consonant and vowel

These two terms can, unfortunately, be used with a variety of meanings and we must be clear how they are to be employed in this book. First, they are in everyday use to refer to orthography: that is, writing. So, people talk about our alphabet having five vowels and 21 consonants. This is in reality a complicated distinction in that it does not refer to anything inherent in the letters. By this we mean that just looking at the shapes of the letters called **vowels** there is nothing that distinguishes them from the shapes that are called **consonants**. (It is true that lower-case vowel letters lack descenders or ascenders – parts of letters that go below the line, or above the main body of the letter – but there are consonant letters that are like this as well.) 'Consonants' and 'vowels' in this meaning in reality should be understood something like 'letters that normally represent consonant sounds and letters that normally represent vowel sounds'. Note the use of the word 'normally' here. Even among the 21 consonant letters we use to write English there is one ('y') that often stands for a vowel sound (compare 'yes' with 'by'). We term this approach the **orthographic usage**.

This mixing of writing and speech is one of the main problems with this usage. Because we have five vowel letters, for example, there is a perception that we have only five vowel sounds in English. This is far from the truth and, while the number varies from region to region in the English-speaking world, one can state that most accents of English have approximately 20 contrastive vowel units (including both monophthongs and diphthongs: single and double vowel sounds). Similarly, most accents of English have approximately 24 contrastive consonant sounds, although we only have 21 consonant letters.

The distinction between consonant and vowel letters may well vary from language to language even though they may share the same Latin-based alphabet. For example, in Finnish 'y' is always thought of as a vowel letter, and in Welsh 'w' is also counted among the vowels. Writers of languages that use different writing systems may not even have the same concept of the vowel–consonant distinction as just described. Some writing systems (such as Arabic and Hebrew) are primarily consonant-based, and symbols for vowels may normally be omitted as the context will inform the reader which vowel is intended. Writing systems based on the syllable (e.g. Japanese kana systems) will have a single symbol that combines a consonant sound with a vowel sound, and so the distinction between the two (in the orthographic usage) disappears. In this book we avoid the orthographic usage of the terms 'consonant' and 'vowel' because it mixes writing and sound, and is language-specific.

A second usage that is sometimes encountered is based on how consonants and vowels can be uttered. It is claimed that vowels can be spoken by themselves, whereas consonants have to be spoken with a vowel after them. We term this the **utterance usage**. It is, however, inaccurate, and so no more helpful than the first usage just described. Although it is true that certain sounds traditionally termed consonants do seem to need a short vowel after them (such as [p], [b], [t], [d], and [k]), many others do not. Try, for example to say a long 's' sound without adding a vowel at the end. It should sound a bit like a hissing snake, and is quite easy to produce without a vowel. Similarly, a long 'm' sound will be like a humming noise and does not require a vowel. Some languages even have words that consist simply of a consonant sound: the sound [v] in Russian is a preposition meaning 'in' (written in the Cyrillic alphabet as в).

The utterance usage also will be avoided in this book therefore. However, it is an advance in that it moves us away from writing and towards sound as a definition of these terms. Our next two definitions are often found in the phonetics and phonology literature, and are best considered together. We will terms these the 'phonetic' and the 'phonological usage', and they derive from attempts by speech scientists to define the terms strictly. One such definition looks at how speech sounds are produced. Some speech sounds are articulated with a relatively free flow of air through the mouth, in that the airflow remains smooth and does not become turbulent. Others are made with a narrowing in the oral cavity (produced by movement of the tongue towards the roof of the mouth, for example). In these cases, airflow is likely to become turbulent, or be blocked altogether for a while. In phonetic usage, the sounds with a free passage of air are termed 'vowels' and those with a blocked or turbulent airflow are called 'consonants'.

The phonological definition looks at how sounds work in syllables rather than how they are made. All syllables require a nucleus (or central portion) that is sonorant (referring to the sound's inherent loudness, and roughly meaning clearly perceptible), and optionally beginning and end portions that are less sonorous. Individual languages have different constraints as to whether these beginning and end portions ('onset' and 'coda') are optional and what precise sounds can go into these three positions. The nucleus position is occupied by vowels, and the onset and coda by consonants under this usage system.

These two approaches to defining consonants and vowels overlap in the majority of cases. However, there some instances where they do not. Sounds like [w] in 'went' and [j][1] in 'yes' are clearly consonants under the phonological usage (they can be onsets but not nuclei in syllables); however, they are produced with a relatively free passage of air and no turbulence and so would appear to be vowels under the phonetic usage. This is reflected in some of the names these sounds are given in phonetics texts: semi-vowels (older usage, semi-consonants). The same problem is often claimed to occur with sounds like [l] in 'light' and [ɹ][2] in 'right', as they too have a relatively free passage of air.

Finally, there are sounds that can be both peripheral to the syllable and central. [l] for example is clearly a syllable onset in 'light' and a coda in 'bell'. In 'bottle', however, it is the nucleus of the second syllable of this word in most accents of English (some accents, such as South Wales, do allow a short vowel between the [t] and the [l] of the second syllable). This would mean that [l] can be both a consonant and a vowel under the phonological definition.

To try to avoid the problems of these two competing definitions in speech science, some writers (e.g. Pike, 1943) have adopted the terms 'contoid' and 'vocoid' to capture the phonetic distinction, and retained 'consonant' and 'vowel' for the phonological one. (Though, note that in Laver (1994) the author uses contoid and vocoid with a slightly different meaning.)

In this book we have decided not to use contoid and vocoid despite the mainly phonetic focus of the text. This is primarily because they only have limited currency in the phonetics literature. However, this does mean we have to be clear on our use of consonant and vowel. We will be grouping true consonants (i.e. in the contoid meaning), together with semi-vowels and other 'approximants' (see below for this term) that can be syllable onsets and codas, as 'consonants'. True consonants are often called

---

[1] [j] is the phonetic symbol for the consonant we normally write as 'y' in English.
[2] [ɹ] is the phonetic symbol for the variety of 'r' found in the majority of accents of English.

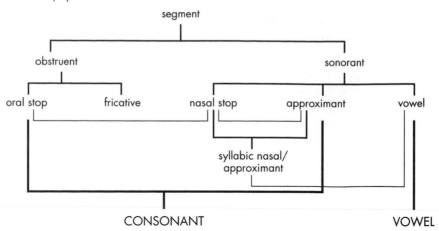

Figure 3.1
Consonants
and vowels

'obstruents', whereas 'sonorants' can be applied to other consonant types. 'Vowels' will encompass only those sounds that can be syllable nuclei. Sounds like [l] and [n] that are normally considered to be consonants, will be termed 'syllabic consonants' in words such as 'bottle' and 'button', and can be thought of as being linked to both categories. The chart in Figure 3.1 demonstrates how these sounds are divided (some of the terms are defined later in this chapter).

State of the velum

In Chapter 1 we noted that the velum (or soft palate) was the flexible extension to the hard palate, and that it could be raised or lowered by muscle activity and thus separate the oral from the nasal cavity, or link the two together. In Chapter 2 we saw that the velum had a part to play in the initiation of the velaric ingressive airstream mechanism that is employed to produce click sounds. The velum is also important in terms of speech segments. Later in this chapter and in Chapters 4 and 5 we will see how it is used as a place of articulation for consonants, but before that we need to note a major distinction between different sound types that is controlled by the velum.

As we have just noted, the velum can be raised or lowered. If the velum is raised then the airflow (in egressive sounds, which is what we will concentrate on here) will pass through the oral cavity only. Such sounds are termed 'oral' sounds, and the majority of both vowels and consonants in the world's languages are oral sounds. If the velum is lowered and, at the same time, the airflow through the oral cavity is blocked by, for example, closing the lips or pressing the body of the tongue up onto the hard palate then the the air will flow out through the nasal cavity alone. Such sounds are termed 'nasal' sounds (more precisely 'nasal stops', see below), and the majority of the world's languages have a number of such nasal sounds (as, for example, [m] and [n] in English).

However, a third possibility exists. The velum may be lowered and at the same time airflow through the mouth is not blocked. This means that the egressive air will flow out through the mouth and the nose together, giving a mixture of oral and nasal airflow. Such sounds are termed 'nasalized sounds'. Nasalized vowels are quite common in the languages of the world: French and Portugese, for example, have nasalized vowels as contrastive sounds. Even in English, vowels can be nasalized through part of their articulation when followed by or preceded by nasal stops, though in this case the resultant partially nasalized vowels do not constitute separate, contrastive, vowel sounds. Nasalized vowels are written in IPA as, for example, [ɛ̃, ɑ̃, ɔ̃, œ̃], where the 'tilde' over the symbol denotes nasal airflow.

It is not only vowels that can be nasalized, however. Any consonant that does not involve a complete blockage in the oral cavity can be pronounced with added nasal airflow. This means that we can have nasalized [s̃], or [l̃], or [w̃] and so on. We may well find that such consonants, when followed by a nasal consonant, become nasalized through all or part of their articulation. An example from English is the nasalization that is commonly found in the [l] in the word 'elm'. It is comparatively rare to find nasalized consonants as contrastive sounds in languages, but they are reasonably frequent as positional variants.

Can sounds such as [p], [b], [t] and [k], which involve a complete blockage in the oral cavity be nasalized? As noted above, if there is a complete blockage in the oral cavity, and the velum is fully lowered, then we get nasal sounds such as [m] and [n]. This is because, as we describe in more detail below, [p], [b], [t], [k] and so on require a build-up of air pressure in the mouth before the blockage in the oral cavity is removed. If the velum is fully lowered, that build-up of air pressure is impossible, as the air escapes through the nasal cavity. However, it is possible to produce [p̃] and [ɓ̃] etc. with the velum lowered slightly so that a certain amount of air pressure can still build up in the mouth. Such slightly nasalized sounds can often be found in speakers with an inability (for a variety of reasons) to raise the velum completely. Figure 3.2 illustrates the different states of the velum.

Direction of airflow

As we noted in the previous chapter, airflow initiated in the lungs is the most common airstream for speech. This airflow is, of course, egressive, and flows upwards through the larynx and then through the oral cavity (and/or the nasal cavity). For air flowing out of the oral cavity there is a

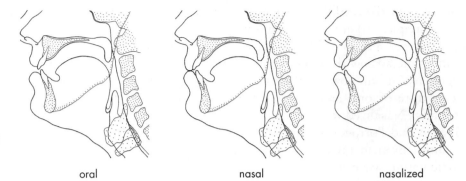

Figure 3.2
States of the
velum

oral   nasal   nasalized

further parameter we can consider: that is whether the air moves centrally
out of the mouth, or is directed by the tongue laterally (i.e. sideways).

The majority of the sounds we make are central. So, for English, all vowels, the obstruent consonants and most of the sonorant consonants are pronounced with central flow of the air. One sonorant consonant (the
approximant [l]) has lateral airflow. If you try pronouncing [l], and making
the [l] sound continue as long as possible, you should be able to feel that
the tip of your tongue remains on the roof of your mouth just behind the
upper teeth. This means that the airflow cannot escape centrally, as your
tongue tip is blocking it. Instead, it goes down one side or the other (for
some speakers down both sides at once), and so escapes laterally. See
whether you can discover which side of the tongue air is escaping when you
pronounce [l]: the terms 'dexter lateral' and 'sinister lateral' are sometime
encountered to classify right and left lateral air escape respectively.

Not only approximants can be found with lateral air escape. One type
of obstruent consonant, the fricative (see below) can also be pronounced in
this way. Lateral fricatives are not found in English but are, for example in
Welsh and in Zulu. We will return to these in more detail in the next
chapter. It is also possible for obstruents of the stop variety (e.g. [t] and
[d]) to have the build-up of air released from the mouth laterally rather
than centrally. Because it is only the release of air that is lateral, these
sounds are usually considered to be combinations of a central stop sound
and a lateral approximant sound. We will consider these further as well in
the next chapter.

Force of articulation

Traditionally, phoneticians have divided consonants between the stronger
or **fortis** types, and the weaker or **lenis** ones. Voiceless sounds are generally
fortis, and voiced are lenis. But what are the phonetic characteristics that
distinguish fortis from lenis sounds? A traditional account would claim
that fortis sounds have a greater muscular tension throughout the vocal

tract than lenis. This has proved difficult to measure objectively, so some authorities are wary of using the distinction. However, one result of greater muscular effort should be that fortis sounds should have a longer duration than lenis ones (as more air is being pushed out of the lungs). This does seem to be borne out, not only for stops, but also for fricatives. We will therefore use the terms fortis and lenis as well as voiced and voiceless in this book.

Similar distinctions have been claimed to occur for vowels, where the terms **tense** and **lax** are often found. Here, tense vowels are claimed to be articulated with greater muscular effort and consequently to be longer in duration and nearer the periphery of the vowel area (*see* Chapter 5). Lax vowels, on the other hand, are shorter in duration and more likely to be centralized. Although this distinction may be a helpful generalization, there are of course many vowels in natural language that fall between these two extremes.

Prolongability

Sounds may also be classified in terms of whether they are prolongable or not. Most sounds (including all vowels) can be prolonged by the speaker as long as she or he has breath. Of course, in natural language, the duration of a prolongable sound depends on the environment of the sound, and whether the language makes contrastive use of length differences. In English, for example, some vowels (such as [i] in 'seat') are always longer than others (e.g. [ɪ] in 'sit'), though the contrast in length here is only part of how these two vowels differ: the tongue position is somewhat different as well.

In English also, the [i] in 'seat' is shorter than the [i] in 'seed'. In this instance, this is purely a positional variant determined by the consonant that follows the vowel: [t] is always preceded by a slightly shorter vowel than is [d].

There are also sounds that are not prolongable. Some of these are obstruent type consonants and some are sonorant type consonants, and these will be described in some detail in the following section. The 'tap' obstruent consonant type (as found in some old-fashioned British English pronunciation of 'r' in a word like 'Harry', or American English pronunciation of 't' in 'better'), cannot be prolonged, as it requires a very swift contact between the tip of the tongue and the roof of the mouth. If it is held more than a few milliseconds at this position the sound would change, and be heard as a [d]. The semi-vowel approximant type of sonorant consonant (e.g. [w] and [j]), if pronounced for more than a very brief period will sound like a vowel (for example [w] will sound like [u] in 'bl*ue*'). This is because the articulators are in the position for the relevant vowel, and the semi-vowel itself is a rapid movement from this vowel position to the position of the following sound.

Manner of articulation

Having considered the path of the airflow through the oral and/or nasal cavities, whether the air escapes centrally or laterally, and whether sounds can be prolongable, we need now to examine how the individual sounds are made. In the production of individual sounds we are often interested in the articulators that are used. Normally, any sound can be thought of as being produced by the coming together of two articulators: one is often passive (e.g. the roof of the mouth) while the other is active (e.g. the tip of the tongue). In some instances both articulators may be active (e.g. the two lips). We are also interested in how close together the articulators come, and this is termed the **degree of stricture**.

Two parameters can be employed to look at how sounds are articulated: the sound type (manner of articulation), and the sound position (place of articulation). We will examine manner of articulation in this section. Unless otherwise stated, a pulmonic egressive airflow is assumed in the following descriptions. Also, sound types should be assumed prolongable, unless it is noted that they are momentary. Figure 3.3 illustrates different manners of articulation: both prolongable and momentary.

Categories of manner of articulation are based on the size of the air passage during the production of the sound. Looked at in another way, this corresponds to the degree of stricture between the articulators concerned. When the articulators are brought close together so that they make firm contact and the airflow in the oral cavity is completely blocked, the resultant manner of articulation is termed a **stop** (because the flow of air is stopped). This manner of articulation is often considered to be the strongest on a hierarchy of sound types. Clearly, if we go back to our discussion on consonants and vowels, this type of sound must be a consonant (as there is no relatively free passage of air, and these sounds are always peripheral in syllables), and the oral stops fall into our subcategory of obstruents, or true consonants.

Stops are divided into two types: oral stops, or **plosives**, and nasal stops or **nasals**. Plosives are formed by creating a complete closure somewhere in the upper vocal tract, for example by making a firm contact between the tip and blade of the tongue and the alveolar ridge. This stoppage of the airflow seems short to us (approximately 40–150 ms), but it still results in a build-up of air pressure behind the closure so that, when the articulators part (e.g. when the tongue tip and blade are lowered from the alveolar ridge) the air bursts out with a characteristic popping sound which is why the term 'plosive' is used. Plosives are prolongable in that the stage of their production

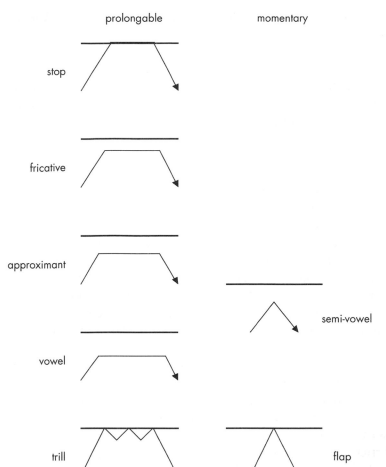

Figure 3.3 Manners of articulation: prolongable and momentary

where the articulators are together may be prolonged, though clearly not the stage where the air is released (though see also 'affricates' below). Plosives are found in all known languages, and while more commonly occurring voiceless, voiced plosives are not unusual. In English we have six plosives: [p, b, t, d, k, g[3]]. We examine plosives in more detail in Chapter 4.

Nasal stops have a complete closure in the oral cavity, but (as noted above) air is allowed to escape freely through the nasal cavity because the velum is lowered. This means that no build-up of air pressure occurs, and so these sounds do not have plosion. In fact, while there is stoppage in the oral cavity there is a relatively free passage of air through the nasal cavity. Because of this, these sounds are normally classed as part of the sonorant group of consonants and, indeed, they may well take on the role of syllabic consonants in some languages (e.g. the [n] in 'button'). As with most

---

[3] The symbol [g] always stands for a plosive as in 'get', never for the sound in 'gin'.

sonorants, nasal sounds can be prolonged for as long as the speaker has sufficient air. English has three nasals: [m, n, ŋ⁴]. The nasal release of oral stops is looked at in the next chapter, and we return to nasals in Chapter 5.

The next strongest manner of articulation is the **fricative**. Fricatives are pronounced with the articulators close together, but not so close as to block the airflow completely. There has to be a small channel left open for the air to flow along (the precise size and shape of this channel differs from sound to sound, and we look at this in more detail in Chapter 4). Because the air is being forced through this small space, it becomes turbulent (this is what happens when any gas is forced along a narrow channel), and we hear this turbulence as the rough sound quality associated with fricatives. Phoneticians terms this quality 'friction' or 'frication'. Because these sounds lack a relatively free passage of air, and because they normally are only peripheral to the syllable, we classify them as part of the obstruent group of consonants. They are prolongable, again for as long as the speaker has air. In English we have six pairs of fricatives, both voiceless and voiced: [f, v, θ, ð, s, z, ʃ, ʒ⁵]. Added to this, we have the sound [h], which many phoneticians regard as a fricative, with the stricture being between the two vocal folds. Some writers, however, prefer to classify this sound as a 'voiceless approximant'.

A combination of the oral stop manner and the fricative manner is found in the category of **affricate**. We return to these in more detail in the following chapter, but we can note here that affricates are formed like oral stops with a complete closure somewhere in the oral cavity. However, instead of a quick release stage as in plosives, the articulators part only very slightly to leave a narrow channel. The air flowing out from the released closure is therefore forced along a narrow channel and so becomes turbulent. The release of the affricate, therefore, sounds like a fricative. As these sounds have a dual nature (starting like a plosive and finishing like a fricative), writers have disagreed as to whether they should be treated as single sounds or as combinations. We will return to that point later, but for now we can note that English has two contrastive affricates (one voiceless and one voiced): [tʃ, dʒ], as found in the first and last sounds of 'church' and 'judge' respectively. Affricates are classed here as obstruents, and are prolongable both in the closed stage of the stop part, and in the release stage of the fricative part.

The next strongest manner of articulation is the **approximant** (the term 'frictionless continuant' is often encountered in older accounts). With these consonants there is a much wider passage of air so that the airflow for

---

⁴ The symbol [ŋ] stands for the 'ng' sound as in English 'sing'.
⁵ [θ, ð] stand for the two 'th' sounds in 'thin' and 'then' respectively; [ʃ, ʒ] stand for 'sh' in 'shop' and 's' in 'treasure' respectively.

voiced approximants remains laminar (smooth), and does not become turbulent. Voiceless approximants are rare in the languages of the world, but when they do occur the airflow is usually somewhat turbulent. Because of this, it is not always clear whether such sounds should be classed as voiceless approximants or voiceless fricatives.

Approximants can be central (e.g. [ɹ], the most common variety of 'r' in English), or lateral (e.g. [l]). These two sounds are also prolongable approximants, but as noted above the semi-vowel approximants (such as [w] and [j]) are momentary. These four sounds are the only approximants found in English, but many languages have a variety of lateral approximants, for example. In phonological descriptions, the terms 'liquid' (for prolongable approximants) and 'glide' (for semi-vowels) may be encountered.

The weakest manner of articulation is termed **resonant**, or **vowel**. Strictly speaking, these two labels do not mean quite the same, as some of the vowels we pronounce high in the oral cavity (such as [i] in 'bee', and [u] in 'boo') are often classed as being in the approximant category, because if they are pronounced without voice the airflow becomes slightly turbulent. The definition of resonant is that both voiced and voiceless airflow is laminar. However, as vowel sounds hardly ever occur other than voiced in natural language, the distinction between these high vowels and other vowels is somewhat academic. Therefore, rather than divide the vowel category between approximants and resonants, we will ignore the distinction, and stick to the term 'vowel'.

Vowels will also be dealt with in more detail in Chapter 5, but we need just to note one major division here: the difference between 'monophthongs' and 'diphthongs'. **Monophthongs** (or 'pure vowels') maintain the same articulator positions throughout the sound, and so the sound quality which we perceive is steady (for example, like the long [ɑ] sound in the word 'spa' in most accents of English). On the other hand, **diphthongs** are vowels where the tongue position moves during the production of the vowel, so that we perceive two different qualities of sound (in reality, as the tongue may move quite a way, we may hear a slide from one sound quality to another). An example of this would be the vowel in the word 'toy', where the tongue changes from a lowish back position to a highish front position, and the shape of the lips also changes from a rounded to an unrounded shape. In this book, we use the term diphthong only to refer to such vowel changes which take place within a single syllable (this is the normal usage in phonetics). A word which has two neighbouring vowels in two different syllables (e.g. the word 'naïve') would not be classified as containing a diphthong. Please note, diphthong refers only to sound; we are **not** referring here to spellings using two vowel letters (e.g. 'tea') or two letters joined together (e.g. 'œuvre').

Finally, we can consider two manners of articulation that are related to the stop category we examined earlier. The **trill** (or 'roll') type of consonant involves the rapid repetition of one articulator striking another (or both articulators striking each other in the case of the two lips). For example, if we imagine the first part of the production of the plosive [d] – the placing of the tip and/or blade of the tongue against the alveolar ridge, and then we remove the tongue from the alveolar ridge almost immediately (before any air pressure build-up), and then repeat these actions again two or three times, we have a trilled sound. This sort of trill can be found in English 'r' in certain regional accents (e.g. some Scottish accents), and in formal, rhetorical styles of speech sometimes encouraged in stage acting or singing. These consonants will be classed with the obstruents, and are prolongable in that the number of contacts between the articulators can be increased or decreased as the speaker wishes. In natural languages two or three contacts seems to be the norm, however. Trills produced with incomplete contact between the active and passive articulators thus allowing turbulent airflow to pass through are termed **fricative trills**.

A momentary variant of the trill is the **tap** (or 'flap' or 'flick'). The tap involves a single rapid contact between one articulator and another without repetition. As we noted above, the contact between the articulators cannot be prolonged beyond a few milliseconds, or else air pressure will build up and the sound will then become a plosive. Taps can involve an active articulator striking a passive one, and then returning to its place of rest: for example, the tip of the tongue striking the alveolar ridge. This is the type of tap found in American English, where it is used for 't' in words like 'better', or in older forms of British English for 'r' in 'Harry'. Alternatively, the active articulator may strike the passive one while the active articulator is moving from one position to another: in this case, this can be termed a 'flap' or 'transient flick'. A transient flick is the form of tap used in a number of languages of India.

In our discussion of the above manners of articulation we have restricted ourselves to looking at pulmonic egressive sounds. As we saw in Chapter 2, other airstreams can be used to make sounds as well. Ejectives (glottalic egressive consonants) can be made as oral stops, fricatives and affricates, and all these types can be found in natural language. Other types of sound are technically feasible, but as ejectives are always voiceless, attempts at nasal stops, approximants and vowels generally result in barely perceptible segments.

Implosives, as the name suggest, are always of the oral stop type in natural language. However, being voiced, all the consonant and vowel types described above can in fact be said on the glottalic ingressive airstream. Finally, clicks are generally classified as being stop type consonants, though they are able to be modified in a wide variety of ways which we look at in Chapter 4.

Place of articulation

The final parameter we need to consider when describing individual sound segments is the place within the vocal where the articulators form a stricture. As we noted above, most sounds are made with one active and one passive articulator, or in some instances with two active articulators. It is usual, when describing the place of articulation, to note these articulators. However, when the tongue is the active articulator and the roof of the mouth the passive one, it is common to refer only to the part of the roof of the mouth concerned. This is because if we know which part of the roof of the mouth is involved, we can usually be confident which part of the tongue is used to make the stricture. There are exceptions to this, however, especially concerning the tip and blade of the tongue. Because of this, we do include in brackets for some of the places below, the term used to denote the part of the tongue involved which, when used, is prefixed to the passive articulator. We use the following terms: **apico-** (tongue tip), **lamino-** (blade), **dorso-** (tongue body), and **radico-** (tongue root).

Sounds can be made anywhere from the very front of the oral cavity using the two lips, back through the oral cavity and into the pharynx, and as far down as the glottis. It is usual in the phonetics literature to list these places from the front to the back (though there is no theoretical reason for this), and we will follow this practice here. The names of the places of articulation are derived from the divisions of the vocal tract (including the divisions of the roof of the mouth and of the tongue) that were introduced in Chapter 1. We show the tongue divisions in Figure 3.4, and the places of articulation labels in Figure 3.5.

We also need to note that most phoneticians do not utilize the same set of place labels to describe vowels as they do with consonants (though some have attempted this). This is because the air channel with vowels is so wide, it is not always easy to associate the tongue position with any specific part of the roof of the mouth. Traditionally, therefore, different approaches have been adopted, and these are dealt with in Chapter 5. We list below, then, those terms that have normally been restricted to consonants.

Articulations made with the two lips are termed **bilabial**. In these

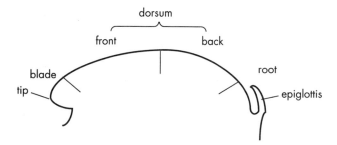

Figure 3.4 Divisions of the tongue

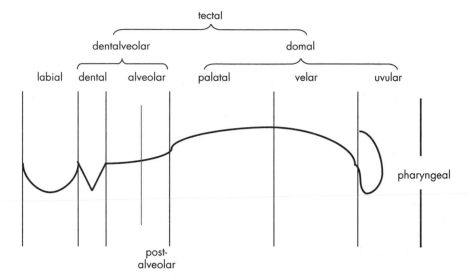

Figure 3.5
Places of
articulation

articulations the upper and lower lips are brought together: in the case of bilabial stops they form an air-tight seal producing the plosives [p, b][6] or, if the velum is lowered, the nasal [m]. If a narrow channel is left between the lips, the fricatives [ɸ, β] are produced; these are not found in English, but the voiceless bilabial fricative occurs, for example, in modern Greek, whereas the voiced one is found in Spanish. Bilabial approximants do occur in some languages, but in many they are combined in a double articulation (*see* Chapter 7) with some other place. In English, [w] is an approximant with bilabial and velar place of articulation. The bilabial trill, [ʙ], is rare linguistically, though many of us make it as an extra-linguistic noise to express that we are feeling cold.

Labio-dental articulations are produced with the lower lip approximating to the underside of the upper front teeth. Some speakers tend to curl the lower lip inwards so that it is the outside of the lower lip that makes the contact or the near contact ('exolabial' contact); others simply raise the lower lip upwards so that it is the inside surface that makes the contact ('endolabial'). These differences may also be related to specific languages; however, they make little difference to the quality of the resultant sound. Oral and nasal stops can be made at this place of articulation although they are not common in the world's languages. The IPA only provides a symbol for the labio-dental nasal: [ɱ]; this sound is often used as a positional variant of [m] before [f] by English speakers, in words such as 'comfy'. The labio-dental fricatives are [f, v], and the labio-dental approximant [ʋ] has been termed 'the politician's r' in common parlance, as it is often used as a substitution

---

[6] When pairs of phonetic symbols represent sounds of the same manner at the same place of articulation, they should be read as *voiceless* on the left and *voiced* on the right.

for [ɹ] in adult speech (and is a pronunciation found in a surprisingly large number of politicians!). Bilabial and labio-dental places of articulation are sometimes grouped together under the cover term 'labials'.

A place of articulation straddling the divide between lip types and tongue types is **linguolabial**. In these sounds the tip or blade of the tongue is placed on the upper lip. Whilst a range of sound types can be made in this fashion, they are very unusual sounds, and found mainly in certain languages of the Pacific. They are transcribed with a special diacritical mark added to alveolar symbols: [t̼, d̼, n̼].

Dental fricatives occur in English as pronunciations of the 'th' spellings. The voiceless dental fricative, [θ], is the sound of 'th' in 'thin', whereas its voiced counterpart, [ð], is the sound of 'th' in 'then'. These sounds are sometimes termed **interdental** to reflect the common slight protrusion of the tip of the tongue between the upper and lower teeth used by, for example, many English speakers. Dental plosives and nasals also occur in many languages, but the IPA has a common set of symbols for dental, alveolar and post-alveolar plosives and stops, with diacritics (small markings) that are added to the symbol to show whether it is dental or post-alveolar (unmarked symbols are assumed to be alveolar). Therefore, we use the symbols [t̪, d̪] and [n̪] to transcribe these sounds. Dental approximants can also be made, though there is no special symbol to denote them. (In this case, as with the bilabial approximant, the fricative symbol with an added diacritic is used to show the air channel is wider: [ð̞].) Dental sounds are generally apical, though laminal versions may be used by some speakers.

Alveolar sounds are common in English, where we find alveolar plosive stops, [t, d], a nasal stop, [n], fricatives, [s, z], and an approximant, [l]. These sounds are all formed by raising the tip and/or blade of the tongue up to the alveolar ridge to form a contact or near contact. The terms 'apico-alveolar' and 'lamino-alveolar' are used to denote the tip/blade distinction. In transcription, we can add the tip or blade diacritic to the alveolar symbol to show the difference: [d̺, d̻]. The choice between tip and blade appears to be personal and the difference is not easy to hear. (Tip and blade distinctions can also be made at the dental and post-alveolar positions.)

In the case of [l], of course, the tongue maintains its contact at the alveolar ridge while the air escapes laterally down the side of the tongue. Lateral fricatives also occur at the alveolar position; in fact the alveolar [ɬ, ɮ] are the only two lateral fricatives to occur at all regularly in natural language. The trill [r], and the tap [ɾ] are also alveolar and, as noted above, sometimes occur in English. **Denti-alveolar** is sometimes used to apply to sounds where the contact straddles the dental and alveolar regions.

If the place of articulation is right at the back edge of the alveolar ridge, just before its boundary with the arch of the hard palate, we term the sounds **post-alveolar**. Fricatives made here, with the blade of the tongue (and so, are 'lamino-post-alveolar'), have their own symbols, [ʃ, ʒ], and are the sounds of English 'sh' in 'shop' and 's' in 'treasure'. Until recently these sounds were termed 'palato-alveolars' and this usage may still be encountered. Post-alveolar affricates, [tʃ, dʒ], are the sounds of English 'church' and 'judge' respectively.[7] The central approximant produced at this position is the [ɹ] sound: the most common variant of 'r' in English (this is generally considered to be 'apico-post-alveolar'). Other than these, post-alveolar oral and nasal stops are transcribed using the alveolar symbols with a diacritic to mark retraction (i.e. back from alveolar place): [t̠, d̠, n̠].

The label **alveolo-palatal** is applied to a pair of fricatives [ɕ, ʑ] which, while comparatively rare, do occur in Polish. With these sounds, the blade and front of the tongue are raised up towards the roof of the mouth to form a stricture at the front part of the palate and the post-alveolar area. Not all authorities agree on the precise definition of this place, and how it differs from the traditional term palato-alveolar.

Traditionally, the next place of articulation is termed **retroflex**. However, this is a term that describes the tongue's shape rather than its place of articulation. It may well be more precise therefore to use the term 'sublaminal (pre)palatal' suggested by Catford (1988). This term tells us that it is the underside of the blade of the tongue that articulates with either the very front or the main part of the hard palate (depending on the language). Retroflex sounds are very common in the languages of India, and we can find retroflex stops, fricatives, central and lateral approximants, and a tap: [ʈ, ɖ, ɳ, ʂ, ʐ, ɻ, ɭ, ɽ]. Some of these sounds may occur in some varieties of English; for example, some speakers use a retroflex approximant as their realization of 'r', and if they pronounce final 'r' in words like 'reader' and then add a plural ending to this, the final sound may well be [ʐ]. Languages using these sounds differ as to the extent of tongue retroflexion. This can be recognized be specifying the part of the roof of the mouth the underside of the tongue blade actually articulates against. Using this approach, we can divide this category into **sublamino-post-alveolar** and **sublamino-pre-palatal** (Laver (1994) prefers the term **subapical** in each case). The IPA diacritics for advanced and retracted can be employed if this distinction needs to be transcribed.

Some languages do seem to use a type of retroflex tongue shape where the underside of the tongue is not brought into play, but the tongue tip articulates against the rear of the alveolar ridge and the front of the palate. These **apical-alveolo-palatals** do not have separate symbols, but Laver (1994) suggests they can be transcribed with a subscript dot beneath the alveolar symbol.[8]

---

[7] Affricates can be made at most of the places of articulation where both plosives and fricatives occur, but these are the only contrastive affricates in English. Details of other affricates are given in Chapter 4.

[8] Note that this can be confused, however, with the diacritic for *whisper* introduced in Chapter 2.

The next set of places all involve the body of the tongue ('dorsum'), so the prefix **dorso-** may be added.

Palatal is the first of the dorsal places of articulation. Here, the front of the tongue dorsum is raised up to the hard palate. Palatal stops [c, ɟ, ɲ], fricatives [ç, ʝ], central approximant (semi-vowel) [j], and lateral approximant [ʎ] can all be found. English has [j], for example the 'y' in 'yes', whereas [ʎ] denotes the 'gl' in Italian 'tagliatelle', [ɲ] the 'ñ' in Spanish 'España', and [ç] the 'ch' in German 'ich'. An approximant with both bilabial and palatal place of articulation is [ɥ], found for example at the beginning of the French word 'huit'. The terms 'pre-palatal' and 'post-palatal' may sometimes be encountered for border areas of the palatal region.

With the **velar** position the back of the tongue dorsum is raised up to the soft palate (or velum). The plosives and nasal are found in English: [k, g, ŋ], but none of the other velar sounds are. The fricatives are [x, ɣ] ([x] is found for example as 'ch' in the German surname 'Bach'), the central approximant is [ɰ], and the lateral approximant is [ʟ]. An approximant with both bilabial and velar place of articulation is [w], as in 'wet'. Velar sounds are especially prone to being influenced by neighbouring sounds (e.g. vowels), and can therefore be pronounced at the front or the back of the velar area dependent on context (sometimes termed the 'pre-velar' and 'post-velar' regions). Examples of this can be heard in English, where the [k] of 'key' is pronounced at the front of the velar area (it is almost palatal in fact) while the [k] of 'cool' is pronounced at the back of the velar area. To show these advanced and retracted varieties in transcription we use plus and minus diacritics respectively: [k̟, k̠].

Uvular sounds are made by raising and retracting the back of the tongue to the uvula. None of these sounds occur in English, but the voiced uvular fricative and trill are both varieties of 'r' in standard French. The uvular plosives and nasal are [q, ɢ, ɴ], the fricatives [χ, ʁ], and the trill [ʀ]. No symbols are provided for central or lateral approximants at this place of articulation, but the former at least is possible to make.

If the back and root of the tongue are retracted into the upper pharynx, the resultant sounds are termed **pharyngeal** (or 'radico-pharyngeal'). Traditionally, pharyngeal fricatives are the only sounds given IPA symbols: [ħ, ʕ] (sounds common in Arabic, for example). However, there is some debate as to whether **epiglottal** sounds are possible as a separate place of articulation (retraction of the epiglottis into the pharynx), or whether, indeed, all pharyngeal sounds also involve epiglottal activity. The current IPA recognizes a voiced epiglottal plosive [ʡ], but there is some debate as to whether a voiceless epiglottal plosive is found (Laver (1994) states that it is possible to produce); Laufer (1991), however, suggests that the voiced epiglottal plosive is aerodynamically impossible, and gives examples of the voiceless version from Hebrew and Arabic. With epiglottal stops the epiglottis is retracted to make a closure against the rear pharynx wall. Epiglottal fricatives [ʜ, ʢ] are also noted as occurring in some languages, but, as we have noted, it is unclear how much these differ from their pharyngeal counterparts, mainly because if one retracts the tongue root into the pharynx, the epiglottis automatically retracts as well. A voiced pharyngeal central approximant can be made, but has no IPA symbol (though could be symbolized by adding a diacritic to the fricative symbol: [ʕ̞]).

The final sub-category of places of articulation has no tongue involvement. It comprises the single place of **glottal**, and with these sounds the two articulators are the vocal folds. If these are held together and closed, blocking off the airflow, we have a glottal stop [ʔ], which we described in Chapter 2 when discussing states of the glottis. This segment (we cannot call it a sound, as a glottal stop is of course a short period of absolute absence of sound) is relatively common in many English varieties; used, for example, for 't' in 'better' in London accents. Glottal fricatives [h, ɦ] can also be thought of as phonation types: breath and breathy voice. No other types of glottal sound can be produced, and it is possible to argue that the glottal place of articulation should actually be thought of as a group of glottal settings used at the segmental level rather than than the suprasegmental. Figure 3.6 illustrates some of the places of articulations we have discussed, showing oral stops.

We have not included non-pulmonic sounds in our illustrations of place of articulation. Ejective plosives and fricatives can be made at all the positions noted for voiceless pulmonic plosives and fricatives above, e.g. [p', t', k', f', s']. Of course, languages that have ejectives will not use every possible place. Implosives are given the following phonetic symbols by the IPA: [ɓ, ɗ, ʄ, ɠ, ʛ] (for bilabial, alveolar, palatal, velar and uvular), though again, this does not mean that all of these will be found in any one language. Clicks occur

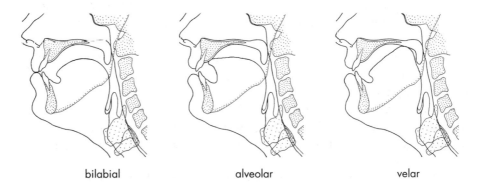

bilabial   alveolar   velar

Figure 3.6 Examples of different places of articulation

in a total number of six places, but most languages using clicks have only a subset of these: [ʘ, |, !, ǂ, ǁ] (for bilabial, dental, (post-)alveolar, palatoalveolar, alveolar lateral, respectively).

Three-term labels

In this and the preceding chapter we have seen how a range of parameters can be used when we describe individual segments. We can list some of these:

(a) airstream mechanism
(b) direction of airflow
(c) phonation type and location
(d) state of the velum
(e) centrality versus laterality
(f) force of articulation
(g) prolongability
(h) place of articulation
(i) manner of articulation.[9]

Using these parameters we could label an individual sound such as [z] in the following way: 'a pulmonic egressive full glottal voiced oral central lenis prolongable alveolar fricative'.[10] This is clearly much too great a mouthful for ordinary usage! Fortunately, many of these parameters have values which we can term 'default'. That is to say, if the usual value of a parameter is employed in a sound, we need not mention it – we would only mention it if an unusual value were employed.

The vast majority of the sounds used in language are pulmonic egressive, so parameters (a) and (b) are usually not included in our description of individual segments. Similarly, most sounds are oral and central, so parameters (d) and (e) are normally excluded. Force of articulation is normally derivable from voicing status, so in common usage (f) is omitted, though some authorities prefer to keep (f) and exclude (c). Finally, prolongability is also derivable from manner of articulation in most instances, so category (g) is seldom needed. The phonation parameter (c) does not usually need the location included, as such differences in phonation due to location appear to have only extra-linguistic usage.

Therefore, our description of [z] can be simplified to what is traditionally called its 'three-term label', phonation, place and manner: 'a voiced alveolar fricative'. The following list of consonants gives further examples

---

[9] In Chapter 5 it is noted that vowels require the parameters of height, anteriority and lip-shape instead of place and manner.
[10] As we will see in the next chapter, fricatives may need an extra parameter to describe the channel shape employed.

of three-term labels: in a few instances you will note extra labels are added if any of the parameters listed above are not set to their default values.

- [p] voiceless bilabial plosive (stop)
- [ŋ] voiced velar nasal (stop)
- [ʃ] voiceless post-alveolar fricative
- [ɮ] voiced alveolar lateral fricative
- [ʀ] voiced uvular trill
- [ɾ] voiced alveolar tap
- [j] voiced palatal (semi-vowel) approximant
- [ɭ] voiced retroflex lateral approximant
- [z̃] voiced nasalized alveolar fricative
- [t'] (voiceless) alveolar ejective stop
- [ɓ] voiced bilabial implosive.

Further reading

Speech articulation is covered in the main phonetics texts such as Abercrombie (1967), Brosnahan and Malmberg (1970), Catford (1977, 1988), Clark and Yallop (1995), Ladefoged (1993) and Laver (1994). Perkell (1997) gives a recent summary of the area, whereas Ladefoged and Maddieson (1996) provide a summary of how different articulation types are represented in the languages of the world.

Short questions

1 What definition of consonant and vowel is used in this book?
2 What three categories of sound are dependant on the state of the velum?
3 How is strength of articulation labelled by phoneticians? Illustrate with sounds from English.
4 List with examples the manners of articulation of consonants.
5 List with examples the places of articulation of consonants.
6 Which sounds are prolongable, and which momentary?
7 Give the three-term labels for the following sounds: [b, s, ɳ, ʌ, r, ʊ].
8 Give the symbols for the following three-term labels: voiced alveolar implosive; voiceless dental fricative; voiced uvular nasal; voiceless palatal plosive; voiced uvular fricative; voiceless bilabial fricative.

Essay questions

1 What are the different ways in which the terms 'consonant' and 'vowel' have been defined by phoneticians and phonologists? Outline the strengths and weaknesses of the different approaches.
2 Illustrate how phoneticians have used articulatory parameters to classify consonants.

4 Segments of speech: obstruent consonants

Introduction	Ejectives
Stop production	Implosives
Fricatives	Clicks

Introduction

In the previous chapter we introduced the main divisions of manner and place in the description of consonants. In this and the following chapter, we are going to examine the consonant types in more detail, and look also at the description of vowels. We will look at other aspects of segmental production, including double and secondary articulation, in Chapter 7.

Stop production

Oral stops, or plosives, are described as having three stages in their production. As we noted in the previous chapter, these consonants involve a complete closure in the oral cavity, to block off the airflow. To achieve this, the articulators involved move together to make this closure, and this is termed the **shutting** (or 'approach') stage of the stop. The articulators are then held closed for a period (about 40–150 ms), during which air pressure builds up behind the closure: this is called the **closure** phase. During this closure stage there is, in fact, silence if the stop is voiceless, or the buzzing of the vibrating vocal folds if the stop is voiced (this voicing may not last for the whole closure period in many English 'voiced' stops). Finally, when the articulators move apart, we have the **release** stage, which is normally accompanied by the outrush of compressed air, which gives plosives their characteristic 'popping' quality. This popping noise is often termed 'plosion', or the 'plosive burst'.

To illustrate this, let us consider the production of a [b] plosive, in the word 'abbot'. Towards the end of the first vowel, the upper and the lower lip (the articulators) move closer and closer together, until they form an airtight closure. For a period of 40–150 ms they maintain this closure, and all that can be heard is the buzz of voice, caused by the vibrating vocal folds. At the end of this closure stage, the lips part and the compressed air rushes out to make the popping noise we hear as [b]. During the closure stage, the tongue moves from the position it took up to produce the first vowel, to that needed for the second one, and the release of the stop is followed by the production of this vowel.

These three stages are illustrated in Figure 4.1, where the upper and lower portions of the line represent the upper and lower lips (they could of course also represent any of two articulators used to produce stops). The nonsense word [ɑbɑ] is used to illustrate the three stages of the stop. Table 4.1 illustrates plosives from a range of languages.

For a consonant to be classed as an oral stop, the central closure stage must be present. However, both the shutting stage, and the release stage may be modified in stops in many languages (including English), and we will examine next the ways in which this can happen.

Stops and velic action

One way in which we can modify stops is to transfer either the approach stage or the release stage to velic action. To explain what this means, we will examine what is termed the 'nasal release' of stops first. In our original example, we considered the production of a [b] sound; this time we will look at another stop: [t]. During stage 1, the tip and/or blade of the tongue (the precise choice appears to be speaker-specific) is raised upwards to the

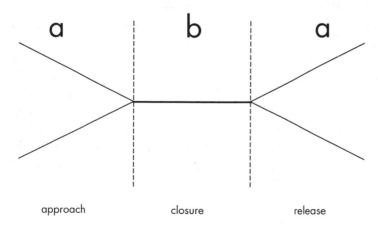

approach   closure   release

Figure 4.1 Three stages of the stop

Table 4.1 Plosives

	Voiceless*	Voiced
Bilabial	p	b
	French [pã] 'bread'	*French* [bã] 'bath'
	Hindi [pal] 'take care of'	*Hindi* [bal] 'hair'
Dental	t̪	d̪
	North Welsh [t̪o] 'roof'	*North Welsh* [d̪o] 'yes' (past)
	French [t̪y] 'you' (sg)	*French* [d̪y] 'of the' (m)
Alveolar	t	d
	English [ten] 'ten'	*English* [den] 'den'
	Isoko [útí] 'sugar cane'	*Isoko* [údí] 'drink'
Post-alveolar	t̺	d̺
	English [t̺ɹeɪn] 'train'	*English* [d̺ɹeɪn] 'drain'
	South Welsh [t̺ɹʊm] 'heavy' (m)	*South Welsh* [d̺ɹɔm] 'heavy' (f)
Retroflex	ʈ	ɖ
	Hindi [ʈal] 'postpone'	*Hindi* [ɖal] 'branch'
	Malayalam [kuʈːi] 'child'	*Tamil* [ʋaɳɖɪ] 'cart'
Palatal	c	ɟ
	Turkish [cel] 'bald'	*Turkish* [ɟel] 'come'
	Hungarian [cuk] 'pen'	*Hungarian* [ɟur] 'to knead'
Velar	k	g
	German [kɛʀn] 'kernel'	*German* [gɛʀn] 'willingly'
	Swahili [taka] 'to want'	*Swahili* [taga] 'to lay eggs'
Uvular	q	ɢ
	St Lawrence Yupik	*Farsi* [ɢar] 'cave'
	[atəχtoq] 'he goes down'	*Kwakw'ala* [ɢaɢas]
	Quechua [qaʌu] 'tongue'	'grandparent'
Glottal	ʔ	
	Hawaiian [haʔa] 'dance'	
	Gimi [rahoʔ] 'truly'	

* The 'Voiceless' column includes both aspirated and unaspirated plosives, and the 'Voiced' column both fully and partially voiced. These distinctions are discussed further below.

alveolar ridge.[1] There, it makes an airtight closure to produce stage 2 (the closure stage). In a [t] with an oral plosive release, of course, this would be followed by the release stage where the tongue is lowered to allow the compressed air to rush out. However, if stage 3 is transferred to velic action,

[1] In the following examples, we assume that [t] and [d] are alveolar, as they are not marked with either the dental or the retracted diacritic. However, we recognize the ambiguous nature of the symbolism in this area, as unmarked symbols can also be read as standing for basic apical or apico-laminar sounds irrespective of exact place of articulation.

then the tongue remains at the alveolar ridge, but the soft palate (the velum) is lowered. If this happens, the compressed air will flow out through the nasal cavity, producing what is sometimes termed 'nasal plosion'. The articulators remain in place within the oral cavity while the air is released, and then move apart to assume the position required to make the following sound (*see* Figure 4.2, where the line beneath the articulator lines represents the raising or lowering of the velum).

Nasally released stops sound like plosives followed immediately by a nasal stop at the same place of articulation without any intervening vowel sound. In English, for example, the usual pronunciation of 'button' ends with a nasally released [t], while 'hidden' ends with a nasally released [d] (both of which in these cases are also syllabic-n's). Nasal release can also occur across syllable boundaries, and in English we have examples with [t] and [d] as follows: 'partner' 'midnight'. Examples with bilabial stops are also found: 'submarine', 'apeman'.

We can transcribe nasal release in IPA through the use of superscript [^{n}], as in [t^n], [d^n]. However, it is usual to transcribe a nasally released plosive by use of the plosive symbol followed by that of the homorganic (i.e. same place of articulation) nasal stop, as in: [tn], [dn], [bm], and so on. If the nasal element in these stops is also syllabic (as in 'button' and 'happen' in English), we can add a diacritic to the nasal to show this: [n̩].

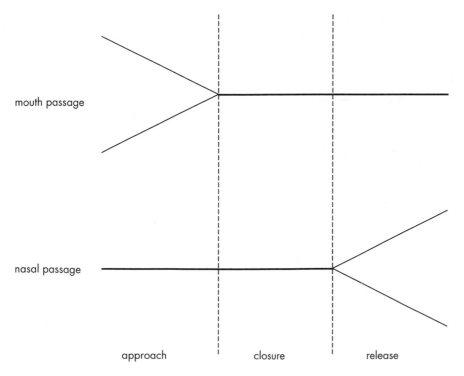

mouth passage

nasal passage

approach closure release

Figure 4.2
Nasal release

We can transfer the approach stage of a stop to velic action as well. In this case, the articulators take up the position to make the oral closure (e.g. the tip of the tongue to the alveolar ridge), but during this time the velum is lowered. This means that air continues to flow out through the nasal cavity for a period. Then, stage 2 is achieved by the raising of the velum, so that air can no longer flow through the nasal cavity, and the closure in the oral cavity means that air pressure builds up ready for the normal oral release of plosion (*see* Figure 4.3). This can be termed the 'nasal approach' to a stop, and sounds, of course, like a nasal stop followed immediately by an oral stop, and this is how we transcribe them: [mp], [nt], [nd], [ŋk] etc. Examples from English include: 'lamp', 'lumpy', 'hint', 'wanting', 'land', 'handy', 'monk', 'conker'.

Finally in this section, we can consider stops where both stage 1 and stage 3 are transferred to velic action: that is stops with both nasal approach and nasal release. Here, the articulators move together to produce the oral closure while the velum is in a lowered position, allowing nasal air flow. Then the velum is raised to produce stage 2: complete stop to airflow. This stage lasts, of course, for the normal stop period of 40–150 ms or so, and is then followed by the lowering of the velum again allowing air to be released nasally (*see* Figure 4.4). In effect, these stops sound like a nasal with a brief interruption of silence (if the stage 2 is

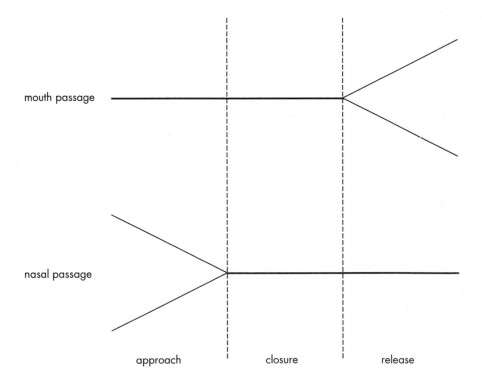

Figure 4.3
Nasal
approach

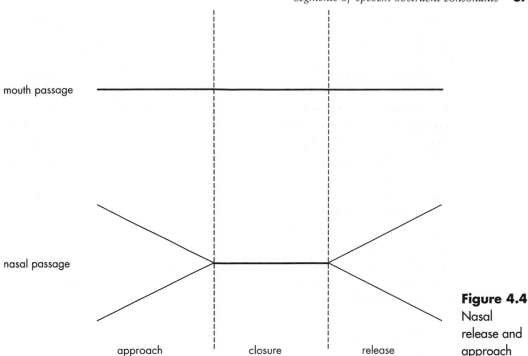

Figure 4.4 Nasal release and approach

mouth passage

nasal passage

approach   closure   release

voiceless) or of the voicing buzz part way through. They are normally transcribed as a sequence of nasal, plosive, nasal: [pmp], [ntn] etc. and examples from English include: 'lampman', 'Saint Ninian'.

Laterally released stops

Another way in which we can modify stage 3 of a stop is to release the compressed air laterally instead of centrally. If we consider again the production of a [t] stop, and look in detail at the release stage, we will remember that in ordinary oral plosives this is achieved by the lowering of the tip and blade of the tongue. In a laterally released stop, the tip of the tongue is kept pressing against the alveolar ridge, but one or other of the side rims of the tongue (or both in some speakers) is lowered. This means that the air rushes out of the oral cavity down the side of the tongue, and so is lateral rather than central release.

This lateral release of the air can be either fricative or approximant in nature. The fricative release is often classed as a lateral affricate (see the example given in Table 4.2 p. 70). This depends upon whether the movement of the tongue rims opens a narrow or a wide channel for the release of the air. In English, we have approximant release in our laterally released stops. They sound like a stop followed immediately by a lateral approximant with no intervening vowel, and can be either voiced, as in 'middle', or voiceless, as in 'little'. In the latter case, the lateral segment usually lacks voicing at least for the first part of the sound.

The examples from English happen to include laterals which are also syllabic. Just as with syllabic-n above, we can transcribe syllabic-l with a special diacritic: [l̩]. However, laterally released stops can also occur across syllable boundaries in English, for example 'at last', 'midline', 'hotly', 'badly', and initially in some languages (e.g. Welsh [tlus] 'pretty'). We can denote a laterally released stop by adding a superscript diacritic after the stop: [tˡ, dˡ]; however, normally we simply write the stop symbol followed by the lateral: [tl̥, dl].

We have described laterally released [t] and [d], but laterally released stops can occur at any place where it is possible to produce both a stop and a lateral (i.e. any of the lingual consonants). As English only has alveolar laterals, we do not encounter any lateral release at any other place of articulation. Nevertheless, lateral release of, for example, retroflex, palatal and velar stops is possible to produce: [tl̺, dl̺, cʎ, ɟʎ, kʟ, gʟ].

Affricated release

Another way we can modify the release stage of oral stops is to control the parting of the articulators so that only a narrow channel is opened for the release of the compressed air. This results in a turbulent airflow, similar to that found in fricatives, and this is termed 'affricated release' (*see* Figure 4.5). Some authorities contrast stops with affricated release with affricates (*see* Chapter 3, where affricates were classed as a separate consonant category). It is not clear how easy it is in reality to make a distinction here, but it would appear to be based on whether the portion of the sound with frication (i.e. the affricated release portion) is brief (in which case we might call it a stop with affricated release), or longer so that it has a similar duration

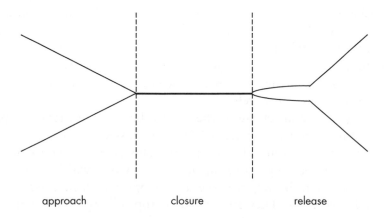

Figure 4.5 Affricated release

approach   closure   release

to that of the stop part (in which case we might call the whole combination an affricate, or more clearly, a full affricate).

This distinction can be reflected in transcription too. A voiceless affricated stop at the post-alveolar place of articulation can be transcribed [tˢ], but if we want to show a voiceless alveolar affricate we would use [t͡ʃ]. In the first instance, the superscript [ˢ] indicates that we are to understand that the fricative element in this sound is brief, or less important than the stop part. However, the second example shows by the linking curve over the two symbols that they are to be considered of equal importance. (Alteratively, the two symbols can be joined together, as in [tʃ].)

A question that arises here is whether a full affricate differs from a stop followed by a fricative. Clearly, affricates are stop–fricative combinations where the two elements are homorganic (i.e. articulated at the same place), whereas stops can be followed by fricatives at other places of articulation: 'caps', 'lacks', 'length' and so on. Normally, phoneticians suggest that where we have two separate sounds (homorganic or not), the duration of the fricative element is longer than in any kind of affricate, or affricated release.

English has voiceless and voiced post-alveolar affricates in words such as 'church', 'catches', 'judge' and 'cadges', and these sounds operate as contrastive units in the sound system (as we can see from the examples, they can be both word-initial, word-medial and word-final). As it is typographically easier, these sounds are often transcribed in books on English phonetics as [tʃ, dʒ], but are normally treated phonologically as single units. Other affricate combinations are regularly used in English, however, including the initial sounds of 'train' and 'drain'. Phonetically, the 'r' element here has a narrower channel than the normal approximant-r, which means that the [t] and [d] are released with an affricated airflow. We can transcribe these as [t͡ɹ̝, d͡ɹ̝] but, as they only occur syllable-initially, phonologists normally treat them as sequences of stop + 'r'.

Affricates at a range of places of articulation can be found in other languages, and Table 4.2 lists some of these. For example, German has both [p͡f] and [t͡s]; Polish has [t͡ɕ], and [k͡x] occurs for [k] in some varieties of Liverpool English. Table 4.2 also includes a lateral affricate, and an aspirated affricate. Most of the examples are full affricates, but we also include a couple of stops with affricate release.

Incomplete stops

Oral stops can also have their stage 3 modified so that no audible release occurs. These incomplete stops can come about in two different ways: through **overlap** where release occurs but is inaudible, and through **suppression** of audible release.

Table 4.2 Affricates

	Voiceless	Voiced
Labiodental	p͡f	
	German [p͡faɪfən] 'to whistle'	
Dental	t͡θ	d͡ð
	Chipewyan [t̪͡θʰe] 'pipe'	Chipewyan [d͡ðɛθ] 'hide'
Alveolar	t͡s	d͡z
	Nupe [t͡sa] 'to choose'	Italian [d͡zona] 'zone'
Laminar post-alveolar	t͡ʃ	d͡ʒ
	Sundanese [ŋahant͡ʃa] 'to work'	Turkish [had͡ʒɨ] 'pilgrimage'
Apico-post-alveolar	t̠͡ɹ̝̊	d̠͡ɹ̝
	English [t̠͡ɹ̝̊eɪn] 'train'	English [d̠͡ɹ̝eɪn] 'drain'
Alveolo-palatal	t͡ɕ	d͡ʑ
	Chinese [t͡ɕa] 'to add'	Croatian [lĕ:d͡ʑa] 'back' (n)
Palatal	c͡ç	ɟ͡ʝ
	Sherpa [c͡ça:n] 'north'	Hungarian [ɟ͡ʝa:r] 'factory'
Velar	k͡x	
	Liverpool English [kˣeɪkˣ] 'cake'	
Uvular	q͡χ	
	Skagit [qˣəp] 'foolish'	
Lateral affricate	t͡ɬ	d͡ɮ
	Nitinaht [t͡ɬʊɬ] 'good'	Tlingit [d͡ɮaa] 'settle (of sediment)'

Overlap occurs in some languages when there is a sequence of two stop consonants, either within a word or often across word boundaries as well. With languages, such as French, which avoid overlap, the first stop is released audibly before the closure for the second stop takes place (*see* Figure 4.6(a)). An example might be in the French word 'acte', where we hear the release of the [k] before the closure for the [t]. In other languages, such as English, the articulatory closure for the second stop is put in place just before thc release of the closure for the first stop. So, while a release of the first stop occurs (in that the articulators move apart), this is inaudible because a second closure is now in place within the oral cavity (*see* Figure 4.6(b)). An example might be the English word 'act', where we do not hear the plosive burst for [k] because the closure of [t] overlaps it. These incomplete stops can be marked in a transcription through the use of a diacritic, e.g. [t̚].

The other type of incomplete stop is the 'unreleased' or 'unexploded stop' (confusingly, both this type and the overlap type are sometimes called 'unreleased'). These are common in English in utterance-final position (though they occur in other languages as well). In this instance the articu-

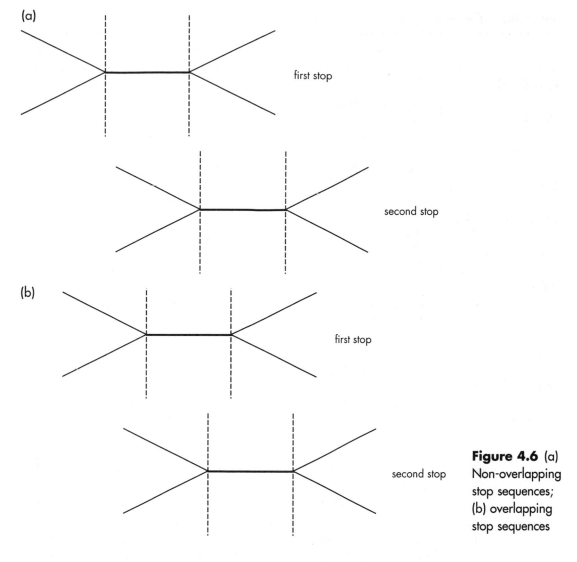

Figure 4.6 (a) Non-overlapping stop sequences; (b) overlapping stop sequences

lators do not part immediately, and the compressed air is released slowly and inaudibly through the nasal cavity (and possibly also the oral cavity after the eventual parting of the articulators) as part of normal breathing. An example in English would be an unreleased [t] in the phrase 'give me my hat'. This type of incomplete stop is transcribed with the same diacritic as above: [t̚].

These unexploded stops in English only occur with the voiceless (or fortis) plosives, and they are often 'reinforced' through the simultaneous use of a glottal stop. Such double articulations (*see* Chapter 7) can be transcribed as, for example, [ʔ͡t̚].

Stops and phonation

In this section we will examine the relationship between the three phases of stop production and phonatory activity: in other words the co-ordination of voicing with plosives. Perhaps the most straightforward case involves fully voiced plosives. If we return to the example in Figure 4.1 (reproduced as the top example in Figure 4.7), it can be noted that the line representing vocal fold vibration remains unchanged from the vowel before the stop to the vowel following it. Fully voiced stops, of course, do need a continual flow of air through the glottis to maintain the voicing; at the same time we have the complete blockage within the oral cavity that constitutes the stop. This closure, as we have noted before, allows the build-up of air pressure needed to produce plosion. There comes a point, however, where the air pressure behind the closure is as great as the sub-glottal air pressure which forces the pulmonic egressive air past the vibrating vocal folds. This results in fully voiced stops being usually of shorter duration than voiceless ones, as the closure stage cannot be maintained so long. Alternatively, a certain amount of devoicing may occur, so that only part of the closure stage is voiced, the remainder being voiceless. Languages may have both fully voiced stops in some positions within the word, and partly voiced ones in other positions (such as English), although fully voiced stops may be found in all positions in other languages.

Voiced stops, as we have just noted, may be subject to a certain amount of loss of voicing (i.e. voicelessness, often termed 'devoicing') during their production. This is common in English, for example, in word-initial and

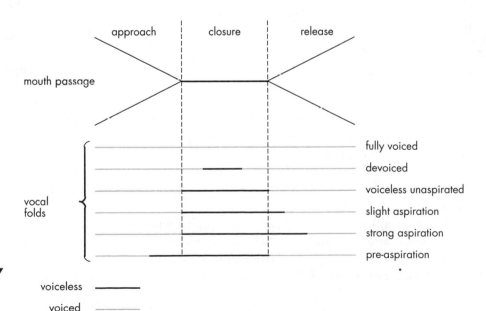

Figure 4.7
Stops and voicing

word-final positions. We can have both word-initial and wordfinal devoicing. In the word-initial case, we see that the voicing is only started some time into the closure stage and then continues into the following vowel. In the word-final case, we see that voicing from the preceding vowel lasts into the closure stage of the stop, but then ceases before the end of that stage. In some languages (such as Welsh) even inter-vocalic voiced stops may be partly devoiced (i.e. voicing occurs only right at the start and right at the end of the closure stage), or indeed wholly voiceless. Indeed, in English, word-initial and word-final voiced stops for some speakers may be totally devoiced. How these can be distinguished from voiceless stops will be discussed below, but we can note here that devoiced stops can be transcribed by use of the IPA voiceless diacritic: [d̥]; if we wish to show that the devoicing is initial or final, the diacritic can be set off to one side: [̥d], [d ̥].

When we turn to voiceless stops, we can investigate the relationship between the stages of the stop and the phasing of phonation. Assuming the stop is followed by a voiced sound (such as a vowel), then the voicing for the vowel can commence immediately on the release of the stop (*see* Figure 4.7). In English, this is what we do for voiceless stops following [s], as in 'spot', 'stop', 'scot'; whereas in French, for example, all syllable-initial voiceless stops behave this way. This type of voiceless stop is termed 'voiceless unaspirated', and is represented by a plain stop symbol, or a diacritic can be added to denote unaspirated: [t], or [t⁼].

If, however, the voicing is not commenced for a period after the release of the stop (for approximately 30–40 ms, for example), then we hear a short burst of voicelessness before the buzz of voicing. This delay in 'voice onset time' produces what we call **aspiration**, and such sounds are called 'voiceless aspirated stops' (*see* Figure 4.7). In English, most syllable-initial stops (apart from those following [s]) are aspirated. Syllable-final stops may be aspirated too, or unreleased. Aspirated stops can be transcribed with a diacritic: [tʰ]. Languages differ in the amount of aspiration that occurs (i.e. the length of the voice onset time), and languages such as Thai and Scots Gaelic are noted as having strongly aspirated stops.[2]

Pre-aspiration can also occur. Here, the voicing of the preceding segment ceases even before the closure stage of the stop is achieved (*see* Figure 4.7). We hear, therefore, a brief stretch of voicelessness ('breath') before the silent period of the closure stage. This feature does not appear to be very common in the world's languages, but has been noted in Icelandic and Lappish among others. It can be transcribed by use of the aspiration diacritic to the left of the symbol (extIPA recommended usage), or by using

---

[2] Voiceless aspirated fricatives are rare, but do occur in some languages (see Laver, 1994). Here there is a brief period of breath following the end of the fricative and before the vowel begins.

the voiceless diacritic to the left of the symbol, or by transcribing the preceding vowel as voiceless: [ʰt], [ˌt], [ḁt].

Finally, we can consider the so-called 'voiced aspirated' stops. In reality, these are voiced sounds that are followed on their release stage by a short burst of breathy voice, and this can be interpreted as the following sound (often a vowel) starting with a short breathy voice component. Nevertheless, it has become traditional to transcribe them with a superscript diacritic in the shape of the so-called 'voiced glottal fricative' (in Chapter 3 we noted that this was, in fact, breathy voice under another name): [bʱ]. These sounds are common in Hindi/Urdu, Gujerati, Sindhi, Marathi and Bengali in northern India.

Earlier in this section we asked what the difference might be between a fully 'devoiced' voiced stop and a voiceless stop. The term devoiced is ambiguous in that it is not always clear whether it is being used to denote a partial or complete absence of voicing. If we are referring to fully devoiced sounds, however, why not simply call them voiceless? The reason may be partly phonological. Assuming that these devoiced sounds derive in some way (i.e. are positional variants) from a sound that is voiced, we may wish simply to keep that relationship overt. However, there may be phonetic differences in any case. As we noted in Chapter 3, phoneticians have divided consonants between the stronger or fortis types, and the weaker or lenis ones. Voiceless sounds are generally fortis, and voiced are lenis. Therefore, a devoiced stop (whether fully or partially) is still lenis, whereas a voiceless stop is fortis. One result of greater muscular effort claimed for fortis sounds should be that they should have a longer duration than lenis ones (as more air is being pushed out of the lungs). This does seem to be borne out, not only for stops (where the problem of sub-glottal and intra-oral air pressure referred to above plays a part) but also for fricatives. We can see that devoiced lenis stops may still be distinguished from voiceless fortis stops if the length difference is maintained.

Fricatives

Fricatives can be found in many places of articulation, and apart from illustrating these, here we will examine channel shape in fricatives (one of the reasons why we have such a range of possible fricative consonants), and lateral fricatives. First, we will look in Table 4.3 at some fricatives from a range of languages. Retroflex fricatives (as with other retroflex sounds) may have different degrees of tongue retroflexion, but we do not mark this distinction (*see* Laver (1994) for examples).

Table 4.3 Fricatives

	Voiceless	**Voiced**
Bilabial	ɸ	β
	Ewe [ɸu] 'bone'	*Ewe* [βu] 'boat'
	Pedi [ɸoɸa] 'to fly'	*Isoko* [iβe] 'sacrifice'
Labiodental	f	v
	Portuguese [faka] 'knife'	*Portuguese* [vaka] 'cow'
	Ewe [fu] 'feather'	*Ewe* [vu] 'to tear'
Dental	θ	ð
	English [mauθ] 'mouth' (n)	*English* [mauð] 'mouth' (v)
	Greek [exθros] 'enemy'	*Kikuyu* [ðovu] 'soup'
Alveolar	s	z
	English [sil] 'seal'	*English* [zil] 'zeal'
	Isoko [ési] 'horse'	*Isoko* [ezi] 'period of time'
Post-alveolar	ʃ	ʒ
	Portuguese [ʃa] 'tea'	*Portuguese* [ʒa] 'already'
	Kurdish [ʃin] 'blue'	*Kurdish* [ʒin] 'life'
Retroflex	ʂ	ʐ
	Northern Irish English [kɔɹʂ] 'course'	*Northern Irish English* [kɔɹʐ] 'cores'
	Chinese [ʂa] 'to kill'	*Chinese* [ʐaŋ] 'to assist'
Palato-alveolar	ɕ	ʑ
	Polish [baɕa] 'Barbara' (dim)	*Polish* [baʑa] 'catkin'
	Ubykh [ɕaɕa] 'mother-in-law'	*Ubykh* [ʑawa] 'shadow'
Palatal	ç	ʝ
	Margi [çà] 'moon'	*Margi* [ʝàʝàɗè] 'picked up'
	Greek [çoni] 'snow'	*English* [ʝist] 'yeast' (var)
Velar	x	ɣ
	Urhobo [exa] 'dance'	*Urhobo* [aɣa] 'broom'
	Welsh [xi] 'you' (pl)	*Greek* [laɣa] 'to purify'
Uvular	χ	ʁ
	Kwakw'ala [χasa] 'rotten'	*French* [sɔʁ] 'fate'
	Tlingit [χeːt] 'multiply'	*Portuguese* [ʁatu] 'mouse'
Pharyngeal	ħ	ʕ
	Agul [muħ] 'barn'	*Agul* [muʕ] 'bridge'
	Hebrew [ħor] 'hole' (var)	*Hebrew* [ʕor] 'skin' (var)
Epiglottal	ʜ	ʢ
	Hebrew [ʜor] 'hole' (var)	*Hebrew* [ʢor] 'skin' (var)
	Agul [mɛʜ] 'whey'	*Arabic* [ʢallama] 'he taught' (var)
Glottal	h	ɦ
	Hungarian [hoː] 'snow'	*Igbo* [áɦà] 'name'
	Palantla Chinantec [háa] 'so, such'	*Dutch* [ɦut] 'hat'
Labio-velar	ʍ	
	Scottish English [ʍɛn] 'when'	

Channel shape

Fricatives are produced with a narrow channel through which the airflow is forced, thus becoming turbulent and producing what we perceive as frication. However, the shape of the channel in fricatives can differ between different fricative types. Channel shape differences are considered to occur only with central fricatives made with the tip and blade of the tongue; labial fricatives, on the one hand, and dorsal fricatives (i.e. those made with the main body of the tongue) are not produced with noticeable differences in channel shape. The names we apply to channel shape are derived from an imaginary cross-section of the channel from left to right looking at the front of the speaker's face (a transverse section), whilst we have normally labelled place of articulation from front to back of a sideways cross-section of the supraglottal vocal organs (a sagittal section).

A **grooved** fricative is one where the channel for the airflow is extremely narrow, thus producing a rather high-pitched quality to the friction. The most common grooved fricatives are [s] and [z] (*see* Figure 4.8), and many of us will have encountered speakers who make such a narrow channel for these sounds that a whistled variety results. These two fricatives are made at the alveolar place of articulation, though [s] and [z] can be articulated somewhat further forward to give dental versions, and retracted to give post-alveolar ones.

Fricatives with a wider and flatter channel shape are usually termed **slit** fricatives, though the actual shape of the channel will differ somewhat from sound to sound. Among the slit fricatives are dental [θ, ð], which have a wide, flat-shaped channel (*see* Figure 4.8), and post-alveolar (also termed palatoalveolar) [ʃ, ʒ] which have a narrower, slightly deeper channel shape.

However, another variety of slit fricative occurs at the alveolar place: the so-called 'slit-t'. This sound occurs in some varieties of Hiberno–English (i.e. the English spoken in Ireland) as a realization of 't' in certain contexts. Although it is normally pronounced as a fricative, it differs from the grooved [s]. The channel shape appears to be more like that for [θ], though placed at the alveolar ridge rather than behind the upper front teeth. In a recent account by Pandeli et al. (1997), it is suggested that this sound is best transcribed as [θ̲].[3] We can see in Table 4.4 the range of slit and grooved fricatives described here.

It is technically possible to produce retroflex fricatives with slightly different channel shapes, which does affect the resultant sound quality. How-

---

[3] The double underline diacritic is taken from the extIPA system, and denotes an alveolar place of articulation. The Pandeli et al. (1997) article lists a large number of other suggestions for the transcription of this sound.

Figure 4.8
Fricative
channel shapes   wide slit channel: [θ]   grooved channel: [s]   narrow slit channel: [ʃ]

Table 4.4 Slit and grooved fricatives

Grooved fricative	Slit fricative	
Dental	[s̪] [z̪]	[θ] [ð]
	Polish [kos̪a] 'scythe'	*English* [mæθ] 'math'
Alveolar	[s] [z]	[θ̠] [ð̠]
	Toda [koːs] 'money'	*Hiberno–English* [maθ̠] 'mat'
Post-alveolar	[s̠] [z̠]	[ʃ] [ʒ]
	Toda [poːs̠] 'milk'	*English* [mæʃ] 'mash'

ever, as there are no IPA diacritics to distinguish slit from grooved fricatives, we have not included them in the table.[4]

Bilabial and labiodental fricatives, and palatal fricatives and further back do not come into the slit-grooved dichotomy. However, a division of fricatives in terms of their sound quality is often encountered, and this includes a wider range of places of articulation. **Sibilant** fricatives are those with a higher pitch and greater acoustic energy than non-sibilant fricatives. Sibilants include [s, z, ʃ, ʒ, ʂ, ʐ, ç, ʑ] while non-sibilants include [ɸ, β, f, v, θ, ð, ç, ʝ, x, ɣ, χ, ʁ, ħ, ʕ]. Phonologists often divide fricatives into 'strident' and 'non-strident' (that is to say, greater versus lesser acoustic noise), with [θ, ð] in the non-strident group and [f, v, s, z, ʃ, ʒ] in the strident group. Phoneticians do not all agree with this last analysis, as it cuts across both the production and perception divisions of slit/grooved and sibilant/non-sibilant described earlier.

Lateral fricatives

As we noted in Chapter 3, fricatives can be pronounced with both central and lateral airflow. The fricatives we have described up to now have been all central, but both voiced and voiceless alveolar lateral fricatives are relatively common sounds in natural language. As noted in Chapter 3, a lateral fricative is formed when there is a closure made between the central part of

---

[4] One might use the apical diacritic to denote grooved, and the laminal to denote slit, as the use of the tip of the tongue would probably be required to get a narrow grooved channel, whereas the blade would no doubt come into play with a wider slit one.

the tongue and the roof of the mouth (e.g. the tip of the tongue and the alveolar ridge), but air is allowed to escape down one or other side of the tongue (and for some speakers both sides of the tongue). However, this lateral gap for the air to flow through is kept narrow, so that the air escapes with turbulence. Lateral fricatives can be both voiceless and voiced, and may be part of laterally released affricates. They are most common at the alveolar place of articulation, though unofficial symbols exist for both palatal and velar lateral fricatives (*see* Table 4.5).

Trills and taps

Trills and taps can be considered as varieties of stops, but they have traditionally been listed as separate classes of obstruents. As we noted in the previous chapter, trills require the repeated, rapid striking of an active articulator against a passive one (except in bilabial trills, where both articulators can be considered as active), whereas taps are made with a single such strike.

Trills are recorded as occurring at three main places of articulation: bilabial (where the upper and lower lip both take part in trilling action); alveolar (the tip of the tongue against the alveolar ridge); and uvular (where the uvular trills within a channel formed at the back of the tongue). However, variations do exist, so that in Malayalam (a Dravidian language of south India), for example, apical trills occur both at a pre-alveolar position and a post-alveolar position with tongue retroflexion. In connected speech, trills rarely exceed two to three contacts, though in emphatic usage large numbers of contacts may be made. Trills are normally voiced, but voiceless alveolar trills (often found with aspiration between the final contact and the beginning of voicing) are reported reasonably often (*see* Table 4.6).

Taps and flaps are generally voiced, and consist of the active articulator striking rapidly and singly against the passive one. The term flap is nor-

Table 4.5 Lateral fricatives and affricates

	Voiceless	**Voiced**
Alveolar	ɬ	ɮ
	Welsh [ɬɛu] 'lion'	*Xhosa* [umɮalo] 'game'
	Zulu [ɬuːpha] 'trouble'	*Zulu* [ukuɮa] 'to eat'
	Navajo [tsitɬɛɬi] 'match'	*Warja* [ɮaɮa] 'eight'
Palatal	ʎ̥	
	Bura [ʎ̥ela] 'cucumber'	
Velar	ʟ̥	ʟ̬
	Archi [k͡ʟ̥an] 'hole'	*Archi* [naʟ̬dor] 'home'

Table 4.6 Trills, taps and flaps

Bilabial trill	ʙ
	Kele [mbʙuen] 'its fruit'
Dental trill	r̪
	Hungarian [r̪oː] 'to carve'; *Farsi* [sir̪i] 'satiety'
Alveolar trill	r
	Spanish [karo] 'cart'; *Tigre* [kərɐʃ] 'stomach'
Voiceless alveolar trill	r̥
	Welsh [r̥es] 'terrace'; *Ingush* [vwɔr̥] 'seven'
Uvular trill	ʀ
	Southern Swedish [ʀas] 'breed'; *French* [ʀuʒ] 'red'
Retroflex flap	ɽ
	Gbaya [eɽe] 'hen'; *Warlpiri* [ɽupa] 'windbreak'
Alveolar tap	ɾ
	Spanish [kaɾo] 'expensive'; *Slovene* [riːti] 'to dig'
Alveolar fricative trill	ɼ or r̝
	Czech [ɼad̪] 'order'

mally given to such a sound when the active articulator is moving from one position to another and strikes the passive one in passing. The sound that fits into this category is the retroflex flap, where the tongue tip strikes the alveolar ridge as it moves from a retroflex shape, held just behind the alveolar ridge forward to a non-retroflex shape, and into position for the following sound. Taps, on the other hand, involve the active articulator striking the passive one, and returning to the same or similar position (clearly, the final position will be influenced by the following sound). The alveolar tap is the one most often found in natural language, though dental taps are also reported. Uvular taps may occur as varieties of uvular trills in some languages, though taps at other places of articulation are not reported (*see* Table 4.6).

Fricative trills, flaps and taps are reported for some languages. In the case of the taps and flaps, the fricative nature of the sounds is brought about through an incomplete closure at the 'striking' stage, i.e. the active articulator does not make a brief, but complete, closure, but rather leaves a narrow channel where small amounts of turbulent air are forced through. With a fricative trill (or 'trilled fricative') the articulation is somewhat different. Normally in a trill the airflow is smooth (laminar) during the inter-strike periods (i.e. the periods of time between the repeated strikes of one articulator against another). However, if the air pressure is great enough, or if the space left by the moving articulator is small enough, the airflow in these inter-strike periods will become turbulent, and we will hear this as friction. An alveolar fricative trill is found in Czech (this is probably the best known fricative trill), and in Table 4.6 this is represented with the pre-1989 IPA symbol; in the current system it is recommended that all fricative varieties of trill, taps and flaps be represented by the normal symbol with the diacritic for a more open articulation (as fricative type articulations are more open than stop types). Languages (such as French) that use a so-called uvular-r often use a fricative version of this rather than a simple uvular trill. If this variety occurs, it is best thought of as a fricative trill, though uvular fricatives always seem to have a tendency to produce some trilling of the uvular. There are no separate symbols to distinguish uvular fricatives from uvular fricative trills.

Ejectives

As we noted in Chapter 3, ejectives can be produced as stops, fricatives and affricates. Due to the airstream mechanism employed (the glottalic), ejectives are made without voice, and the manners of articulation found are, of course, exactly those obstruents where voiceless segments are common in pulmonic egressive speech. It is technically possible to produce other voiceless sounds with a glottalic egressive airstream, but voiceless sonorant consonants and vowels made in this manner are so faint as to be hardly perceptible.

Table 4.7 demonstrates a range of possible ejectives, with examples from languages that use these sounds; ejective stops and affricates occur more frequently than ejective fricatives.

Implosives

Voiced implosive (or simply implosive) is the term generally applied to stops made on the glottalic ingressive airstream mixed with a voiced pulmonic egressive one as described in Chapter 2. Languages that use this mixed airstream only have oral stops on it; however, it is quite possible to make the whole range of voiced consonants and vowels on the airstream, and it is quite likely that vowels preceding and following implosives (especially if the vowel is 'framed' by two implosives) may well be pronounced on the mixed airstream on occasions by speakers.

Although rare, in a few languages stops may be produced on a glottalic ingressive airstream alone, without the added voiced pulmonic egressive air: these we will term 'voiceless implosives'. We include below the symbol devised for a voiceless bilabial implosive at the Kiel convention of the IPA in 1989, although subsequently recognition was withdrawn from this and similar symbols for other places of articulation (presumably because the sounds are so rare linguistically). Instead, voiceless implosives should now be transcribed by adding the voiceless diacritic to the symbols for the voiced sounds.

Table 4.7 Some ejectives

Ejective stops	
Bilabial	p′
	Kalispel [p′ɔχʷp′ɔχʷotʰ] 'old'; *Skagit* [qˣəp′] 'bird landing'
Alveolar/dental	t′
	Amharic [t′ərrəgə] 'he swept'; *Tigre* [ʃariːt̪′] 'line'
Velar	k′
	Hausa [k′aːɽàː] 'to increase'; *Xhosa* [uk′uχula] 'to tow'
Ejective fricatives	
Labiodental	f′
	Kabardian [fəzef′] 'good woman'
Alveolar	s′
	Amharic [s′afə] 'he wrote'; *Hausa* [s′ara] 'contemporary'
Velar	x′
	Tlingit [x′aːt] 'file'
Uvular	χ′
	Xhosa [uχ′ot′i] 'bravery'
Ejective affricates	
Alveolar	t͡s′
	Hausa [t͡s′aːɽàː] 'to arrange'; *Salish* [t͡s′aɬt] 'it's cold'
Post-alveolar	t͡ʃ′
	Amharic [t͡ʃ′ərrəsə] 'he finished'; *Chipewyan* [t͡ʃ′oɣ] 'quill'
Alveolar lateral	t͡ɬ′
	Chipewyan [t͡ɬ′uli] 'rope'; *Salish* [t͡ɬ′aq′] 'hot'

Table 4.8 Some implosives

	Implosives
Voiceless bilabial	ɓ̥ (or ƥ)
	Lendu [ɓ̥áɓ̥á] 'attached to'; *Uzere Isoko* [oɓ̥a] 'rooster'
Voiced bilabial	ɓ
	Uduk [ɓàʔ] 'back of neck'; *Sindhi* [ɓəni] 'field'
Voiced alveolar	ɗ
	Hausa [harɗòo] 'Fulani man'; *Sindhi* [ɗinu] 'festival'
Voiced palatal	ʄ
	Sindhi [ʄətu] 'illiterate'
Voiced velar	ɠ
	Lendu [ɠǒ] follow'; *Sindhi* [ɠənu] 'handle'

Implosives at various places of articulation are possible, and examples of both voiceless and voiced implosives are given in Table 4.8.

Clicks

Clicks are all of a basic stop manner of articulation. However, as well as the variety of places of articulation that they can occur in, there is a set of click combinations that are found in most languages that have clicks. Because click sounds are made with a velaric airstream mechanism, the vocal tract below the velic closure can still be used to produce sound. Therefore, voicing can be maintained during click production, as air can be passed through the vibrating vocal folds; if the velum is lowered, air can flow through the nasal cavity during click production; click release can be accompanied by aspiration; and by affrication (i.e. velar affrication caused by a slow release of the velar closure); and by glottal stop. A wide variety of other combinations (such as voiceless nasal airflow, that in some instances appears to be ingressive; and various phonatory settings) can also be found, and readers should consult Laver (1994) and Ladefoged and Maddieson (1996) for further information.

It is becoming current practice to recognize that all clicks involve some kind of combination of articulation. The so-called simple clicks do, in fact, involve a combination between a velar closure (i.e. [k]) and the click place of articulation: although of course the [k] is not heard as it is overlapped by the click sound itself. In other instances, the accompaniment is heard. In transcribing click sounds therefore it is now usual to combine the [k] with the click symbol for a 'simple click' (using the tie-bar diacritic to show simultaneous articulation; *see* Chapter 7), and relevant other symbols for other combinations. Some of these can be seen in Table 4.9.

Khoisan languages in particular can show a very large number of possible click combinations, and so to illustrate click use in language, we restrict ourselves to just some examples from !Xóõ as displayed in Table 4.10 (analysed by Traill, reported in Ladefoged and Maddieson, 1996). The account of ǀGui given by Nakagawa (1996) also demonstrates how complex click systems can be.

Table 4.9 Some click combinations

	'Simple'	Voiced	Nasal	Aspirated	Affricated	Glottal stop
Bilabial	k͡ʘ	g͡ʘ	ŋ͡ʘ	k͡ʘʰ	k͡xʘ	ʔk͡ʘ
Dental	k͡ǀ	g͡ǀ	ŋ͡ǀ	k͡ǀʰ	k͡xǀ	ʔk͡ǀ
Alveolar	k͡ǃ	g͡ǃ	ŋ͡ǃ	k͡ǃʰ	k͡xǃ	ʔk͡ǃ
Palatal	k͡ǂ	g͡ǂ	ŋ͡ǂ	k͡ǂʰ	k͡xǂ	ʔk͡ǂ
Lateral	k͡ǁ	g͡ǁ	ŋ͡ǁ	k͡ǁʰ	k͡xǁ	ʔk͡ǁ

Table 4.10 Clicks in !Xóõ

	Bilabial	Dental	Alveolar	Lateral	Palatal
1	ɡʘòõ	ɡǀáã	ɡǃàã	ɡǁàã	ɡǂàã
	type of worm	'work'	'accompany'	'beg'	'exploit'
2	kʘôõ	kǀàa	kǃàã	kǁāã	kǂàã
	'dream'	'move off'	'wait for'	'poison'	'bone'
3	kʘʰoũ	kǀʰáa	kǃʰàn	kǁʰàã	kǂʰàa
	'ill fitting'	'be smooth'	'inside'	'other'	'stamp flat'
4	ɢʘòo	ɢǀáa	ɢǃáã	ɢǁàa	ɢǂàa
	'be split'	'spread out'	'brains'	'light up'	depress'
5	qʘóu	qǀàa	qǃàe̞	qǁáã	qǂâa
	'wild cat'	'rub with hand'	'hunt'	'thigh'	'conceal'
6	ŋʘọ̀õ	ŋǀ āa	ŋǃàã	ŋǁáã	ŋǂàa
	'louse'	'see you'	'one's peer'	'grewia berry'	'peer into'
7	ŋʘâʔã	ŋǀûʔi	ŋǃâʔm	ŋǁâʔm	ŋǂûʔã
	'be close together'	'be careful'	'evade an attack	'be damp'	'be out of reach'
8	ʔŋʘâje	ʔŋǀàa	ʔŋǃàn	ʔŋǁàhã	ʔŋǂâũ
	'tree'	'to suit'	'lie horizontal'	'amount'	'right side'
9	ŋʘʰòõ	ŋǀʰáa	ŋǃʰài	ŋǁʰáa	ŋǂʰ àa
	'smeared with dirt'	'look for spoor'	'fall'	'carry'	'ahead'
10	kʘˣóõ	kǀˣâã	kǃˣáa	kǁˣàa	kǂˣáa
	'walk slowly'	'dance'	'go a distance'	'scrape'	'mind out'
11	ɡʘkxàna	ɡǀkxáã	ɡǃkxàn	ɡǁkxáʔn	ɡǂkxáʔã
	'make fire with sticks'	'soften'	'splatter water'	'calf muscle'	'sneeze'
12	kʘʼqʼóm	kǀʼqʼàa	kǃʼqʼáa	kǁʼqʼâã	kǂʼqʼàû
	'delicious'	'hand'	'spread out'	'grass'	'neck'
13	ɡʘqʼóõ	ɡǀqʼàã	ɡǃqʼáã	ɡǁqʼáã	ɡǂqʼàa
	'fly'	'chase'	'cry incessantly'	'tumor'	'ground to powder'
14	ɡʘhòõ	ɡǀhâa	ɡǃhàa	ɡǁhàã	ɡǂháa
	'sp. bush'	'stale meat'	'thorns'	'bone arrow tip'	'cut'
15	kʘʔòo	kǀʔâa	kǃʔáã	kǁʔàa	kǂʔāa
	'be stiff'	'die'	'be seated' (pl)	'not to be'	'shoot you'
16	qʘʼûm	qǀʼán	qǃʼàma	qǁʼúɲa	qǂʼàn
	'close mouth'	'small'(pl)	'stickgrass'	'turn one's back'	'lay down'(pl)
17	–	ɢǀhàô	ɢǃhâɲa	ɢǁhâẽ	–
		'put into'	'grey haired'	'push away'	

Further reading

Again, we recommend phonetics texts such as Abercrombie (1967), Brosnahan and Malmberg (1970), Catford (1977, 1988), Clark and Yallop (1995), Ladefoged (1993) and Laver (1994) for an examination of obstruents, with Laver (1994) providing the most detailed account. Ladefoged and Maddieson (1996) illustrate a wide range of obstruents in different languages.

Short questions

1   What consonants count as obstruents?
2   What are the three phases of the stop? Illustrate with diagrams.
3   Describe nasal and lateral release of stops with examples from English.
4   Describe the main ways in which fricatives can be sub-divided.
5   What is aspiration? Comment on stops and phonation.
6   How do trills and taps/flaps differ?
7   Describe the sequence of events needed to produce affricates.
8   How can click consonants be combined with other articulatory events?

Essay questions

1   Describe the three stages of stop production and the range of modifications that can take place at these stages. Illustrate your answer with relevant diagrams.
2   How are fricatives produced? Describe the main divisions of fricatives in terms of central/lateral and channel shape. Use diagrams to illustrate your answer.

5

Segments of speech: sonorant consonants and vowels

Introduction	Approximants
Nasals	Vowels

Introduction

In this chapter we will look at the different types of sonorant consonants (nasals and approximants, including lateral approximants and semi-vowels), and the vowels. This will then conclude our examination of the articulation of the segmental aspects of speech.

Nasals

As we noted in Chapter 3, nasal stops can occur at a large number of places of articulation. However, in this section we will be concerned with two main areas of interest: nasals and phonation, and nasal–oral stop combinations. Nasals are hybrids in some respects in that, while they are made with a complete closure in the oral cavity (and so are stops), they have a comparatively free passage of air through the nasal cavity (and so are like approximants). That is why, although they were classed together with stops in Chapter 3, they are categorized as sonorants here. This reflects a difference between articulatory classifications and perceptual ones: terms such as 'stop' and 'approximant' refer to the way a sound is produced, while terms such as 'sonorant' refer to the sound quality we perceive.

Although pulmonic egressive obstruents can occur both voiced and voiceless, sonorants are much more commonly found voiced. As we will see, some languages do use voiceless sonorants contrastively (and devoiced sonorants may occur as positional variants), but because of the lack of turbulence in such sounds they lack acoustic power and are therefore much quieter sounds than their voiced counterparts. This is true of nasals as well as approximants. Nevertheless, some languages do make use of voiceless

Table 5.1 Nasal stops

Bilabial	m
	Irish [ma] 'good'; *Dyirbal* [midin] 'possum'
Dental	n̪
	French [n̪ɔt̪ʁə] 'our'; *Tigre* [n̪ebit̪] 'wine'
Alveolar	n
	Burmese [nǎ] 'pain'; *Oaxaca Chontal* [panta] 'bag'
Voiceless alveolar	n̥
	Burmese [n̥ǎ] 'nose'; *Oaxaca Chontal* [pan̥ta] 'he will go and stay'
Retroflex	ɳ
	Tamil [ʋaɳɖɪ] 'cart'; *Margany* [wakaɳ] 'crow'
Palatal	ɲ
	Sundanese [ɲokot̪] 'to take'; *Jalapa Mazatec* [ɲa] 'we'
Velar	ŋ
	Walmatjari [ŋapa] 'water'; *Burmese* [ŋâ] 'a fish'
Uvular	ɴ
	Japanese [daɴdaɴ] 'gradually'; *Inuit* [saaɴɴi] 'his bones'

nasals, and some examples are given in Table 5.1. The rest of the table illustrates a range of voiced nasal stops in a number of different languages.

In Chapter 4 we looked at how sequences of oral and nasal stops can occur and at how, when they do, the nasal stop can take the place of either the approach or release stage of the plosive. In these instances, therefore, we have two contiguous sounds with an overlap. However, there are also instances where a single segment can have both nasal and oral aspects within it. This can occur, for example, when a basically oral stop might have a brief nasal portion at the beginning of the closure stage: this can be termed a **pre-nasal oral stop** (the terms in this section are taken from Laver, 1994). Conversely, a basically oral stop might have a brief nasal portion at the end of the closure stage, just before the release (this is what distinguishes this sound from a nasally released stop): this can be termed a **post-nasal oral stop**.

Furthermore, we can find examples where the segment can be considered basically a nasal stop, with brief portion of oral closure either at the beginning or end of the closure stage. These sounds can be termed **pre-occluded nasal stops** and **post-occluded nasal stops**. Clearly, in all these types, the nasal and oral elements will share the same place of articulation: they will be what is termed 'homorganic' (though they may not share the same voicing type).

Laver (1994) suggests that these complex segments should be transcribed with a small raised symbol to denote the brief portion of the sound (i.e. either the oral or nasal portion). This device is commonly used in tran-

Table 5.2 Complex nasal and oral stops

	Bilabial	**Alveolar / retroflex**	**Velar**
Pre-nasal oral stop	^{m}b	^{n}d	^{ŋ}g
	Kikuyu [^{m}bura]	*Sinhalese* [ka^{n}da]	*Tiv* [^{ŋ}guhwar]
	'rain'	'trunk'	'leg/foot'
Post-nasal oral stop	p^{m}	t^{n}	k^{ŋ}
	Vietnamese [lɣ'p^{m}]	*Vietnamese* [bát^{n}]	*Vietnamese* [ɣák^{ŋ}]
	'grade'	'bowl'	'upper floor'
Pre-occluded nasal	^{p}m	^{t}ŋ	^{k}ŋ
	Arrernte [^{p}mwaɭə]	*Arrernte* [kə'ŋə]	*Arrernte* [a^{k}ŋə]
	'coolamon basket'	'top'	'carry'
Post-occluded nasal	m^{b}	n^{t}	ŋ^{g}
	Acehnese [ham^{b}a]	*Amuzgo* [n^{t}a]	*Zhongshan Chinese*
	'servant'	'our children'	[ŋ^{g}y] 'fish'

scription to mark a short or secondary characteristic. This would give us (using bilabial examples) [^{m}b] for a pre-nasal oral stop, [b^{m}] for a post-nasal oral stop, [^{b}m] for pre-occluded nasal stop, and [m^{b}] for a post-occluded nasal stop. The use of some of these types is illustrated in Table 5.2.

Laver (1994) suggests that if we wish to transcribe these complex segments without specifying whether the oral or nasal portion is dominant, then we can use [m͡b] and [b͡m].

Approximants

As we noted in Chapter 3, approximants can be divided into the non-prolongable semi-vowels and prolongable other approximants. These latter can be further divided into central and lateral approximants. We will therefore examine these different categories in turn. Approximants are normally voiced in natural language; where common voiceless versions are found this is noted.

Semi-vowels

Semi-vowels are glide-like movements from a tongue position equivalent to one of the high vowels (that is, a vowel with the tongue high in the mouth; see the following section), immediately away to the position for the following sound. If we try to prolong these sounds, what we actually hear is the equivalent high vowel.

The high vowels are found in the front (or palatal) region of the vowel area, and the back (or velar) region; further, they can be made with or without lip-rounding. This gives us four possibilities: front unrounded; front rounded; back unrounded; back rounded. Table 5.3 shows the relationship between the symbols for the high vowels and the semi-vowels.

As can be seen from the table, the high central vowels ([ɨ, ʉ]) can also have semi-vowel equivalents. The two central semi-vowel symbols are not officially sanctioned by the IPA, but are derivable by imitating the way that the central vowel symbols were established. The semi-vowels are normally given place of articulation labels similar to other consonants rather than to vowels. This means that rounded semi-vowels are considered to be double articulations (*see* Chapter 7), with both labial approximation and palatal or velar. The places of articulation of the semi-vowels are: [j] palatal, [ɥ] labio-palatal, [ɰ] velar, and [w] labio-velar. The central semi-vowels do not have official names, but we could term them: [ɟ] post-palatal-pre-velar, and [ɰ̈] labio-post-palatal-pre-velar. These awkward names clearly suggest that vowel terminology might be preferable with semi-vowels.

Semi-vowels can be followed immediately by their equivalent vowel; for example, in English we have [wu] combinations (e.g. 'woo'), and [ji] combinations (e.g. 'yield'). In these instances there is still a brief glide element before the vowel: with the [wu] example there is a slight weakening of the lip rounding as the speaker moves from the glide to the vowel (also a slight lowering and advancement of the tongue), and with [ji] there is a slight lowering and retracting of the tongue. Table 5.4 shows the use of some of the semivowels in different languages.

Table 5.3 Vowels and semi-vowels

	front unr.	front r.	central unr.	central r.	back unr.	back r.
Vowel	i	y	ɨ	ʉ	ɯ	u
Semi-vowel	j	ɥ	ɟ	ɰ̈	ɰ	w

r. = rounded; unr. = unrounded

Table 5.4 Semi-vowels

Unrounded	j	ɰ
	Welsh [jaɪθ] 'language'	Galician [atɰo] 'something'
	Chengtu Chinese [ji] 'one'	Korean [ɰiza] 'doctor'
Rounded	ɥ	w
	French [ɥit] 'eight'	English [weit] 'weight'
	Chengtu Chinese [ɥỳ] 'rain'	Chengtu Chinese [wù] 'five'

Semi-vowels are normally voiced, but in some environments in certain languages they may become devoiced to a greater or lesser degree. A voiceless version of [w] occurs sufficiently often for the IPA to provide a symbol for the sound ([ʍ]); this is the sound of 'wh' in words such as 'when' in many varieties of English. However, because voiceless semi-vowels like this have a high degree of turbulent airflow, some phoneticians prefer to class them as fricatives (*see* Table 4.3).

Central approximants

Non-semi-vowel approximants can be made with either central or lateral air flow. The central approximants fall into two types: those that are weaker versions of voiced fricatives, and rhotic approximants.

Weak fricative approximants can be produced at all the places of articulation at which voiced fricatives occur. However, there is only one special symbol for this group: [ʋ] for the voiced labiodental approximant. Other weak fricative approximants are transcribed by use of the symbol for the voiced fricative and adding the diacritic that denotes a more open articulation (approximants of course have a wider or more open articulation such that the airflow does not become turbulent).[1]

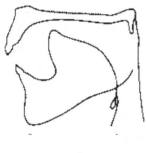

retroflex-r

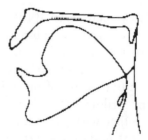

bunched-r

Figure 5.1 Bunched and retroflexed approximant-r

The term 'rhotic approximant' is used here to stand for apical-r types only. Two places of articulation for these are recognized on the IPA chart: post-alveolar and retroflex. For both types, the tongue tip is raised and points either directly upwards towards the rear of the alveolar ridge, or is bent backwards to a more retroflex position. There is a hollowing of the body of the tongue for both of these sounds, although it has been noted that some speakers produce a different tongue configuration for these rhotic approximants whereby the front of the tongue is bunched up in the mouth and the tip is drawn back into the body (Figure 5.1). The bunched-r sounds remarkably similar to the

[1] The difference between an approximant version of the voiced velar fricative [ɣ], and the velar semi-vowel [ɰ] is that the latter requires spread lips, and must have a slightly opener articulatory channel so that it becomes [ɯ] if prolonged.

Table 5.5 Central approximants

	Bilabial	Labio-dental	Dental	Velar
Weak fricatives	ß *Spanish* [aßoɣaðo] 'lawyer'	ʋ *Tamil* [ʋaz̺i] 'path'	ð̞ *Spanish* [aßoɣaðo] 'lawyer'	ɣ *Spanish* [aßoɣaðo] 'lawyer'

	Post-alveolar	Retroflex
Rhotics	ɹ *Edo* [áɹába] 'rubber' *London English* [ɹed] 'red'	ɻ *Hausa* [báɻà:] 'begging' *Plymouth English* [ɻed] 'red'

hollow-shape rhotics, and the choice between them appears to be speaker-specific. Laver (1994) suggests the symbol [ψ] for a bunched-r, but this is not IPA sanctioned.

Table 5.5 illustrates some of these central approximants in a variety of languages.

Whereas we have classed the rhotic approximants as separate from the weak fricative type, we must also recognize that these rhotics may also occur with fricative airflow in certain environments in some languages. For example, in English the [ɹ] following [d] (as in 'drain') is fricative. This is shown in IPA by use of the raising diacritic to denote a narrower channel for the airflow: [ɹ̝]. Indeed, rhotic approximants may also be found voiceless, either with or without friction. For example, in English the [ɹ] following [p] is devoiced, whereas following [t] it is both fricative and devoiced: [ɹ̥] in 'pray', and [ɹ̥̝] in 'train'.

Lateral approximants

Lateral approximants all have a closure between the tongue and the roof of the mouth, with air escaping smoothly through a channel at one or other (or both) sides of the tongue. This means that lateral approximants can only be made at those places of articulation where the tongue tip and body are the active articulators. It is of course possible to allow air to escape at the side of the mouth with an otherwise bilabial closure and so this might be thought of as lateral as well; however, such an articulation is not exploited linguistically, even if it may be a characteristic of some individual speakers.

Normally, lateral approximants, like other approximants, are voiced. Devoiced varieties may be encountered in some languages in specific envi-

Table 5.6 Lateral approximants

Dental	Alveolar	Voiceless alveolar	Retroflex
̪l	l	l̥	ɭ
Portuguese [l̪iʃu]	*English* [lif]	*Burmese* [l̥a]	*Tamil* [val̩]
'rubbish'	'leaf'	'beautiful'	'sword'
Watjarri [kul̪u]	*Watjarri* [kulu]	*Toda* [kal̩]	*Toda* [pal̩]
'sweet potato'	'flea'	'study'	'bangle'

Palatal	Velar	Flapped alveolar	'Dark-l'
ʎ	ʟ	ɺ	ɫ
Italian [fiʎʎɔ]	*Melpa* [raʟ]	*KiChaka* [iɺaa]	*English* [fiɫ]
'son'	'two'	'to dress oneself'	'feel'
Spanish [ʎɔɾo]	*Mid-Waghi* [aʟaʟe]		*Marshallese* [ɫaɫ]
'I weep'	'dizzy'		'knock'

ronments (e.g. [l̥] in English 'play'). Further, some languages have voiceless laterals as contrastive sounds; however, as with the voiceless semi-vowels referred to earlier, it is not always easy to determine whether these sounds should be classed as approximants or fricatives. A few languages use a lateral version of a flap, that can be termed an 'alveolar flapped lateral approximant'. In this sound, a very brief lateral configuration is made as the tongue tip flaps against the alveolar ridge. Table 5.6 illustrates a range of lateral approximants.

Vowels

Vowels are more difficult than consonants to describe articulatorily, because there is no contact or near contact between the articulators. Most phoneticians, therefore, have avoided the place of articulation labels used for consonants, although recently there has been a tendency to see whether descriptions for consonants and vowels can be brought further together. Vowels need to have a very wide articulatory channel (as compared to all consonant types), however, even with this wide channel there is a comparatively large area within the oral cavity within which the tongue can take position to make vowels. This 'vowel area' is shown in Figure 5.2. We can see from the figure that the vowel area is in the form of an ellipse, and that the tongue can move from a fairly high to a low position within it, and from a fairly front to a back position. If the tongue is raised above the upper, front or back boundaries of the vowel area the resultant sound will be approximant or fricative. Traditionally, therefore, phoneticians have attempted to

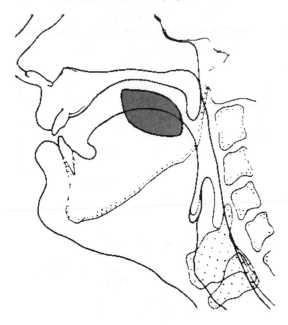

Figure 5.2 The vowel area

describe vowels in part by stating where within the vowel area the tongue is placed.

However, the tongue is, of course, a large articulator, and rather than describe where the tip, blade and dorsum all are, it has become standard to note only where the highest point of the tongue is during the production of the vowel. Normally, the tongue takes up a convex shape when making vowels (*see* 'secondary articulations' in Chapter 7 for an exception to this practice), and it is the highest point on the tongue arch that is used to describe the vowel position. It is assumed that the position of the rest of the tongue is derivable from the highest point.

Of course, the tongue can take up a myriad of slightly different positions within the vowel area, all of which will produce slightly different vowel sounds. We cannot hope, therefore, to produce a labelling system for vowels that can capture every possible tongue position. We could get near this if we took X-ray pictures (*see* Chapter 12) of someone making large numbers of slightly different vowel sounds, and then measured the tongue position on the X-rays. It is not practicable to do this normally, and so we have to make do with a manageable number of regions within the vowel area. We are helped in this by the fact that natural languages do not have vast numbers of contrastive vowel segments (though there can be well over 20).

Phoneticians normally make use of a stylized version of the vowel area, in the shape of an irregular quadrilateral (*see* Figure 5.3). Unfortunately they do not always agree as to the number of regions this quadrilateral should be divided into. To some extent this disagreement reflects geographical differences (British phonetics as opposed to American), and the different needs of phoneticians as opposed to phonologists. We adopt here a maximal labelling system, derived from both the phonetics and the British tradition. We consider that in terms of tongue height we should identify four degrees: **close** (the tongue is closest to the roof of the mouth yet still within the vowel area); **close-mid**; **open-mid**, and **open** (the jaw is fully open, and so the tongue is low in the mouth). These are plotted on Figure 5.3. (Older terms may well be found: close, half-close, half-open, open; high, half-high, half-low, low; high, mid, low.) If we think of vowels in English, we find that a vowel such as [i] in 'tea' is a close vowel (though usually not fully close), whereas the [ɑ] in 'spa' is an open vowel. The vowel in 'get' varies between close-mid and open-mid depending on local variety, and can be transcribed as either [e] or [ɛ].

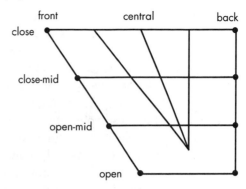

Figure 5.3 The vowel quadrilateral

In terms of **anteriority** (i.e. 'frontness–backness') we adopt a tripartite division into front, central and back, although other traditions divide solely into front and back. English [i] in 'tea' is a front vowel (though not always fully front), whereas English [ɔ] in 'paw' is a back vowel. An example of a central vowel in English might be the vowel [ʌ] in 'hut', though we do recognize that not all varieties of English have this vowel. Another example is the 'schwa' vowel which is made in the centre of the vowel area. This is found in many unstressed syllables in English, for example, '*a*gree', 'banan*a*', and 'phonetics'; it is transcribed [ə].

We also need to remember that it is not only a vowel's tongue position that needs to be described, but also its lip-shape. Lip shape is described normally as being either rounded or unrounded, although a slightly more detailed analysis gives us rounded, neutral and spread. These lip shapes are portrayed in Figure 5.4. In English, [i] is pronounced as a spread (unrounded) vowel, with [ʌ] having a neutral lip shape, and [ɔ] a rounded one. With lip rounded vowels the degree of lip rounding normally changes as we move from close to open tongue height. This is a result of progressively wider jaw opening: with an open jaw for an open vowel it is of course not possible to have a tightly rounded lip shape. Nevertheless, different degrees of closeness of rounding may need to be described to compare

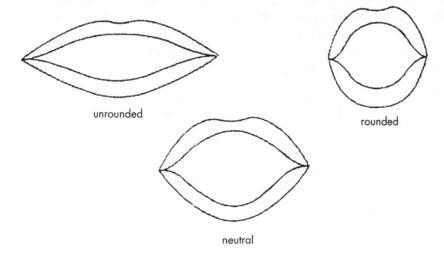

unrounded

rounded

neutral

Figure 5.4
Lip shapes

similar vowels between languages, or local accents (or even individual speakers): in this case we use the terms 'close rounded' and 'open rounded'.

Finally we can consider voiceless vowels. These are rare in the languages of the world, but some northern accents of French (e.g. of Brittany and Normandy) have devoicing of [i] and [y] (and occasionally other vowels as well) in word-final position for at least part of the vowel, e.g. [wi̥] 'yes'. In Japanese voiceless vowels regularly occur as positional variants between voiceless obstruents: [ku̥ʃi] 'comb'. Few languages appear to use voiceless vowels contrastively, however, Laver (1994) notes that in Comanche these vowels are not simply positional variants; for example, we have [pakḁ] 'arrow', although the language also allows final voiced vowels.

The Cardinal Vowel System

Labelling vowels from an articulatory standpoint proves problematic, as we noted above. Even a phonetician would find it difficult to be as precise describing the position of the articulators in their own production of a vowel compared to that of a consonant. This difficulty was addressed early in the twentieth century by Daniel Jones, one of the leading phoneticians of the British School. He decided to alter the approach to the problem of vowel description by concentrating on the perception of vocalic differences, rather than the production. To do this he devised the **Cardinal Vowel System** (first described in 1917). This system is at least partially derived from the cardinal points of the compass. Just as any direction can be recorded in terms of how close it is to the four cardinal points (North, South, East and West), so Jones thought up a system whereby any vowel quality heard by a trained phonetician could be recorded in terms of how close it sounded to a cardinal vowel quality. Clearly, these cardinal vowel qualities had to be learnt by the phonetician (and therefore had to be unchanging so that everyone would be using the same system); also there could not be too many of them, so that they would be easy to learn.

Jones decided to chose vowels that would be defined in terms of the vowel area, rather than vowels of a specific language: the Cardinal vowels, therefore, are language neutral. For the sake of consistency, he also decided that they should be peripheral vowels: that is to say they should be around the edge of the vowel area. It would be straightforward to ensure that these vowels, when produced, had the tongue on the edge of the area – it would be much more difficult to insist that some of them were pronounced at particular points within that area. Finally, he decided that the spacing between the cardinal vowels would be equal: but not physically equal (we have already commented on the difficulty of knowing precisely where the tongue is when making vowels), but auditorily equal. By this we mean that the movement from one cardinal vowel to the next should *sound* as if the spacings were equal. Auditory equidistance is much easier to produce for a well-trained ear than attempts at physical equidistance.

Jones constructed the Cardinal Vowel System in three main stages. First, he chose two anchor points which could be found physically in a straightforward manner. The first of these points was the highest frontest vowel that could be made without the sound becoming consonantal (i.e. the top left point of the vowel area in Figure 5.2). This he labelled 'Cardinal Vowel 1' (CV1). The second anchor point was the lowest backest vowel he could produce, without the sound becoming some kind of pharyngeal consonant (i.e. the bottom right point of the vowel area in Figure 5.2). This he labelled 'Cardinal Vowel 5' (CV5).

For his second stage, Jones fitted three more Cardinal vowels along the front periphery of the vowel area between CV1 and CV5. These five vowels were all auditorily equidistant from each other, and all were pronounced with unrounded lip shapes (CV1 has a fully spread lip shape, but as the jaws open progressively to go from CV1 to CV5 the lips adopt a looser spread and then almost neutral shape). In stage three, Jones added in three more Cardinal vowels between CV5 and CV1 along the back periphery of the vowel area. Again there is auditory equidistance between the vowels, but this time all three are pronounced with lip rounding, and this gets progressively tighter as we move up from CV6 to CV8. The Cardinal Vowel System is shown in Figure 5.5 displayed on the stylized vowel area quadrilateral, with the CV numbers and the symbols Jones associated with each vowel.

The system was to be used by the trained phonetician who would hear a vowel quality and classify it in terms of how close it was to a particular CV. This would be done by specifying whether it sounded higher, or more advanced (i.e. more front), or more retracted, or more/less rounded than the CV in question. Note that these descriptions concerned whether the vowel *sounded* higher etc. than the cardinal quality, there was no explicit claim that the tongue *was* physically higher. The vowel under investigation could be plotted onto a vowel quadrilateral and so the relationship with CV quality could be displayed visually. Also, a series of diacritics have been approved (for example by the IPA) over the years which can be added to vowel symbols to denote features such as 'advanced', 'retracted', 'higher' and so on.

While having only eight Cardinal vowels meant the system was easy to use, the asymmetrical split between rounded and

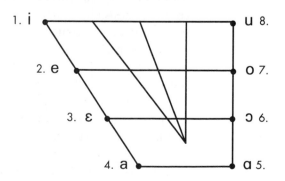

Figure 5.5 Primary Cardinal vowels

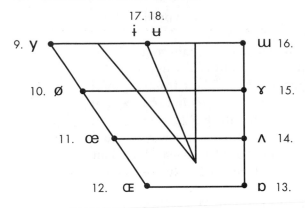

Figure 5.6 Secondary Cardinal vowels

unrounded vowels did cause something of a problem. The reason for this division probably reflects Jones's language background: English has front unrounded vowels and back rounded ones (more or less like the CV system). However, front rounded vowels are common (many European languages have them), and back unrounded vowels, though perhaps less common, are by no means unusual. There is also the fact that many languages have a range of central vowels. So all three of these features (front rounded vowels, back unrounded vowels and central vowels) can only be shown on a CV system through the use of diacritics.

To overcome this objection, Jones added to the eight **primary Cardinal vowels** a system of ten **secondary Cardinal vowels** (*see* Figure 5.6). CVs 9–13 have exactly the same tongue positions as CVs 1–5, but have rounded lip shape instead of spread (tight rounding for CV9 becoming progressively looser as you go to CV13). CVs 14–16, on the other hand, have unrounded lip shape, becoming fully spread at CV16. The final two CVs were an unrounded and a rounded central vowel midway between CV1/9 and CV8/16. Jones did not propose symbols for any opener central vowels, but such symbols have recently been adopted by the IPA, and we return to this area below.

The Cardinal Vowel System proved popular as a means of vowel descriptions within British phonetics (and to a lesser extent, European phonetics). It was never so popular in North America, however. Objections to the system were mainly to do with the difficulty in learning it (i.e. you need a good teacher, but also a 'good ear'); uncertainty as to whether its auditory basis could or should be translated into claims about the physical position of the tongue in vowel production; and oddities of the system such as the curious arrangement of rounded and unrounded vowels.

IPA vowel symbols

It is probably true to say that today a version of the Cardinal Vowel System is still in use in many phonetics training institutions. By this we mean that the values of the vowels are taught as a means of familiarizing students with a wide range of vowel sounds. However, the arrangement of symbols on a vowel chart and the choice of diacritics is likely to be from the 1989 and 1996 revisions to the IPA, and the tendency is probably to treat these as articulatory rather than audi- tory descriptions. The current arrange- ments of the IPA is shown in Figure 5.7, where it can be seen that the division into primary and secondary vowels is abandoned, replaced by a division between unrounded and rounded vow- els.. The list of diacritics that can be used with vowels is given in Table 5.7: many of these are to do with tongue position, but there also diacritics for lip shape, duration, and nasalization.

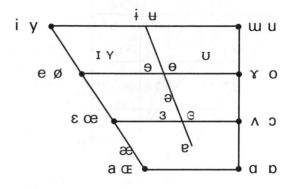

Figure 5.7 IPA vowel chart

The advanced and retracted tongue root diacritics refer to the fact that in some languages contrasts are made between vowels that have the same tongue position, but differ in the width of the pharynx (caused through advancing or retracting the root of the tongue). Such a distinction is present, for example, in Twi: a language of Ghana, and Igbo of Nigeria. In Igbo we can see the advanced and retracted vowels in [ọ́bị̀] 'heart', and [ụ̀bị̀] 'poverty of ability'. In English peripheral vowels (such as [i]) have a wider pharynx than lax vowels (such as [ɪ]). However, the tongue positions for such pairs of vowels are also dif- ferent, so advanced versus retracted tongue root is not contrastive in English.

As well as the diacritics, the diagram in Figure 5.7 also shows what are some times termed the 'spare vowel symbols', but more accurately can be called 'symbols for lax vowels'. These are symbols for vowel sounds in non- peripheral areas, and can be used for any vowel in a language that is made within the area concerned. Amongst these symbols is the central 'schwa' vowel we referred to above, but the 1996 IPA revision also includes sym- bols for the close-mid and open-mid rounded and unrounded central vowels.

Table 5.7 Vowel diacritics

Advanced	a̟	Mid-centralized	ŭ
Retracted	a̠	More rounded	ɔ̹
Raised	ɛ̝	Less rounded	o̜
Lowered	e̞	Nasalized	ã
Raised & lowered (former)	e̝ e̞	Long	iː
Advanced tongue root	e̘	Half-long	uˑ
Retracted tongue root	e̙	Short	ă
Centralized	ë	Non-syllabic vowel	i̯

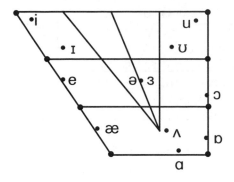

Figure 5.8 Vowel chart of the English monophthongs

To demonstrate the Cardinal Vowel System 'in action', we include here as Figure 5.8 a vowel quadrilatral with the monophthong vowels of southern British Standard English accent plotted on it. On the chart we mark each vowel phoneme (i.e. the most common allophone of the phoneme) with a filled circle, and use the normal simple symbol used in most phonological analyses of this variety of English. Examples of these vowels as CV symbols with diacritics are as follows: /i/ = [i̞-], /ɪ/ = [i̽], /ɑ/ = [ɑ̟], etc. Readers can match the diacritics to the position of the symbol on the diagram.

Diphthongs

In Chapter 3 we noted that vowels can be termed monophthongs (or 'pure' vowels) if they maintain a relatively stable tongue position throughout the segment. Diphthongs are vowel segments where the tongue position moves from one point to another during a single syllable. Triphthongs also seem to occur in some languages (with the tongue gliding from an initial to a medial position, and then changing direction to a third position), but like diphthongs they must be restricted to a single syllable. Diphthongs are transcribed by using the vowel symbol for the initial tongue position and that for the final one and, optionally, a tie-bar diacritic over the two to show they constitute a diphthong rather than a series of two vowels (i.e. in two syllables). Among the diphthongs of English are [a͡ɪ] as in 'sky', [a͡ʊ] in 'now', and [ɔ͡ɪ] in 'toy'. Southern British English (SBS) accents may have triphthongs in words such as 'fire' and 'tower' ([faɪə], [taʊə]), but in rapid speech they are often simplified to diphthongs through the omission of the second element. We chart in Figure 5.9 a selection of diphthongs from the SBS accent.

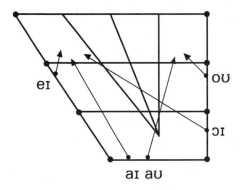

Figure 5.9 Vowel chart of English diphthongs

Diphthongs can be sub-divided in terms of whether the greatest intensity and duration lies at the initial or final stage, or in terms of the direction of tongue movement. For example, a diphthong such as English [aɪ] in 'sky' is termed a 'falling' diphthong because the initial element is longer and more intense than the final (in other words, the diphthong falls away). Conversely, if the greatest intensity and duration is found on the final element, as in Welsh [ɪu] in 'lliw' (colour), then this is termed a 'rising' diphthong. If necessary, we can add a diacritic to the less intense (or non-syllabic) part of the diphthong, as in [aɪ̯] or [ɪ̯u], or write this element as a semi-vowel: [aj], [ju].[2] Catford (1977) points out that this distinction may be too simplistic, as diphthongs may involve a smooth tongue glide from one position to another without noticeable differences in duration on any element, or they may move in a sequential fashion in which the tongue rests for a time at one location before moving rapidly to another.

If we classify diphthongs according to their direction then we find the term 'closing' to refer to diphthongs where the tongue moves from a lower to a higher position (i.e. becoming more close) as in [aɪ]; 'opening' for diphthongs where the tongue moves from a higher to a lower position (i.e. becoming opener) as in [ia] found, for example, in Catalan [iaia] 'grandma'; and 'centring' for diphthongs where the final position is in the centre part of the vowel area irrespective of initial position (e.g. [ɪə], [ʊə] of English 'pier' and 'poor' respectively). It is often noted that, in rapid speech, diphthongs may involve shorter tongue glides than in careful speech: for example, in English [aɪ] the tongue may not get above the close-mid position.

Articulatory description of vowels

We noted earlier that alternative labelling for vowels did exist that used many of the place of articulation labels normally found with consonants. Some of this work derived from X-ray studies of vowel production that showed that the highest point of the tongue arch could be linked to areas of the roof of the mouth traditionally used to classify consonants. Later, the phonetician Catford (1977) devised a new way of displaying the vowel area and his diagram, at least in part, might be thought to be closer in physical shape to the vowel area shown in Figure 5.2. We reproduce his diagram in Figure 5.10, and it can be seen from this that labels from palatal through to pharyngeal can be used to describe vowels, although the labels close, half-close, half-open, and open (or similar) still need to be retained. It is not clear, however, whether the vowel [a] counts as being both an open palatal and an open pharyngeal vowel at the same time.

Whilst it is possible that further instrumental work on vowel production (*see* Chapter 12) may still result in a major overhaul of how we describe vowels, at the moment the system adopted by the IPA (or slight variants of it) is still the dominant approach in articulatory phonetics.

---

[2] It is debateable whether glide+vowel or vowel+glide differ from a rising or falling diphthong. Certainly, there is a perceptible difference between English [kju], 'queue', and Welsh [kɪu], 'queue' which seems to be, at least partly, derived from the distinction between the glide and vowel elements respectively.

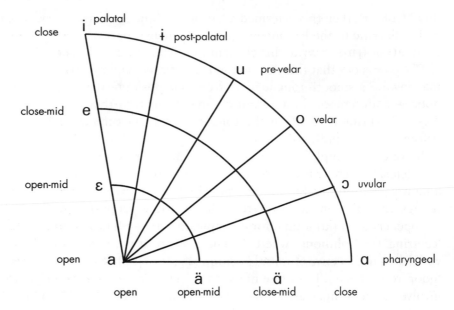

Figure 5.10
Articulatory
vowel diagram

Examples

Finally, we show in **Tables 5.8–5.10** a range of monophthongs and diphthongs illustrated in a number of different languages, including a few
examples of nasalized vowels. It should be noted, however, that the
example words given usually do not contain exact Cardinal values of the
vowels shown; they are, nevertheless, close to the Cardinal values.

Table 5.8 Monophthongs

i	*Italian* [ʌi] 'him' (dat)	u	*Lhasa Tibetan* [nuː] 'west'
e	*Thai* [ʔēn] 'ligament'	o	*Galician* [koro] 'I run'
ɛ	*Taba* [hɛn] 'turtle'	ɔ	*Amharic* [gʷɔrf] 'flood'
a	*Igbo* [tá] 'chew'	ɑ	*Hungarian* [hɑt] 'six'
y	*German* [mydə] 'tired'	ɯ	*Sc.Gaelic* [ɫɯɣ] 'calf'
ø	*Dutch* [bøk] 'beech'	ɤ	*Ngwe* [mbɤ] 'ivory'
œ	*French* [sœʁ] 'sister'	ʌ	*Korean* [bʌːl] 'bee'
ɶ	*Austrian German* [sɶː] 'rope'	ɒ	*Farsi* [nɒn] 'bread'
ɨ	*N.Welsh* [tɨ] 'house'	ʉ	*N.Irish Eng* [tʉ] 'two'
ɪ	*Irish* [ɪlə] 'all'	ʊ	*Sindhi* [sʊrə] 'tunes'
æ	*Hindi* [bæt] 'cricket bat'	ʏ	*Swedish* [nʏtta] 'use' (n)
ə	*Catalan* [blaβə] 'blue' (fem)	ɜ	*S.Brit Eng* [wɜd] 'word'
ɐ	*Palatinate German* [ʀidɐ] 'knight'	ɵ	*S.Walian Eng.* [bɵd] 'bird'

Table 5.9 Diphthongs

ai	*German* [ais] 'ice'	au	*Dutch* [lau] 'lukewarm'
ei	*Catalan* [rei] 'king'	ɛu	*Slovene* [lɛu] 'lion'
ɔi	*Cantonese* [sɔiˀ] 'gill'	ou	*Czech* [mouxa] 'fly' (n)
uɪ	*Welsh* [uɪ] 'egg'	ɪu	*Welsh* [ɪu] 'is'
ɪə	*S.Brit Eng* [pɪəd] 'peer'	ʊə	*N.Brit Eng* [pʊə] 'poor'

Table 5.10 Nasalized vowels

ĩ	*Sundanese* [mĩʔãsih] 'to love'	œ̃	*French* [œ̃] 'one, a'
ẽ	*Guaraní* [ʃẽ r̃ẽtã mẽ] 'my country' (acc)	ẽĩ	*Portuguese* [nuvẽĩ] 'cloud'
ã	*Hindi* [sãp] 'snake'	ɛ̃ũ	*Polish* [ʒɛ̃ũsa] 'eye-lash'
õ	*Tereno* [õw̃őⁿgu] 'his house'	ãũ	*Brazilian Portuguese* [kãũma] 'calm'
ũ	*Portuguese* [mũdu] 'world'	ɔ̃ũ	*Polish* [vɔ̃ũsci] 'narrow'

Further reading

As in the previous chapter, we recommend phonetics texts such as Abercrombie (1967), Brosnahan and Malmberg (1970), Catford (1977, 1988), Clark and Yallop (1995), Ladefoged (1993) and Laver (1994) for an examination of sonorants and vowels, with Laver providing the most details. Ladefoged and Maddieson (1996) illustrate a wide range of sonorants and vowels in different languages.

Short questions

1 What consonants count as sonorants?
2 In what ways are nasals hybrid sounds?
3 Describe the various ways in which nasal and oral aspects can co-occur in a segment.
4 Describe the main ways in which approximants can be sub-divided.
5 What is the vowel area? How can we determine its borders?
6 How have tongue height and anteriority traditionally been sub-divided?
7 List the eight primary Cardinal vowel symbols by placing them on the Cardinal vowel chart.
8 List the 10 secondary Cardinal vowel symbols by placing them on the Cardinal vowel chart.

Essay questions

1 Describe the Cardinal Vowel System, including how it was devised and how it is used. Discuss some of its strenghts and weaknesses compared to an articulatory approach. Illustrate your answer with relevant diagrams.

2 How are approximants produced? Describe the main divisions of approximants in terms of central/lateral and momentary and prolongable. Use diagrams to illustrate your answer.

6

Suprasegments of speech

Introduction	Syllable juncture
The importance of prosodic aspects of speech	Pitch
	Intonation
Stress	Voice quality
Length	Rhythm

Introduction

So far in this book, we have been dealing with the phonetic aspects of individual speech sounds or segments, and we have explained the IPA conventions for classifying these segments. In this chapter, we move on to examine non-segmental characteristics of speech, and suggest means for analysing and transcribing them.

It is clear that speech encompasses a broader range of phenomena than just strings of individual segments. In addition to producing a CVCV item as in 'coffee' [kɒfi] for instance, using the appropriate articulatory actions for each of the consonants and vowels, speakers must also indicate which syllable in the item will carry the stress, i.e. whether [kɒ] or [fi]. Sometimes, it is important to assign stress to particular syllables within certain words for the purpose of differentiating meaning. For example, the phonetic string [kɒnvɜ.ɪt] 'convert' has two possible meanings; when the stress falls on the first syllable, a noun is intended whereas when the stress occurs on the second syllable a verb is meant. Only when the location of the stress is specified (i.e. whether on the first or the second syllable) can the possible meanings can be disambiguated. Syllable length can also be responsible for fulfilling a disambiguating function, as in 'wood' and 'wooed', which are distinguishable from one another because 'wooed' [wʉːd] contains a longer syllable than 'wood' [wud].

Additionally, it may be important for speakers to produce a particular pitch pattern during their utterance. The word 'ready' [ɹɛdi] when spoken with a rising intonation, for instance, would tend to be interpreted as a question ('Are you ready?') whereas, if uttered with a falling intonation, would usually indicate a statement ('I am ready').

Furthermore, all speakers produce a characteristic voice quality during their utterances. We may notice, for instance, that a particular speaker's voice is usually rather high-pitched, or tense, or breathy. It may also be that speakers produce certain voice qualities only on a temporary basis, such as an excessively nasal quality where cold or flu is present.

Finally, some of the articulatory characteristics of any given segment are capable of influencing preceding and following sounds. For example, the first two sounds in 'sleigh' are, according to their IPA specifications, voiceless and voiced respectively but, when produced together in this context, the /l/ is articulated on a voiceless airstream (i.e. [sl̥ɛi]). This is because the voiceless-ness of the /s/ has effectively spilled over into the /l/, resulting in a supra-segmental phenomenon known as **co-articulation** (discussed in Chapter 1).

All of these aspects, i.e. stress, length, pitch, intonation, voice quality and co-articulation constitute the **suprasegmental** (i.e. above segmental level) or **prosodic** properties of speech. The term 'prosody' derives from the Greek verb meaning 'to sing with' or 'accompanying'. Prosodic aspects of speech, therefore, are those which accompany the segmental strings. While the prosodic aspects which we have mentioned above can, of course, relate to individual segments (a segment can be short or long as in [a] versus [aː], for example, and it can be uttered on a particular pitch), we tend to discuss prosodic aspects in relation to larger domains, i.e. the syllable, words and longer utterances.

The importance of prosodic aspects of speech

There is no doubt that prosodic aspects of speech are important. For example, we have stated above that a speaker's choice of pitch contour can help to indicate whether the utterance is a statement or a question and we have shown that stress location has a disambiguating role with relation to meaning. Perhaps even more crucially, in so-called **tone languages** such as Chinese, the pitch shape of a syllable performs a phonemic function. In tone languages, speakers must use particular pitch patterns in order to dif-ferentiate word meaning. For example, McCawley (1978, p.120) states that the syllable [ma] in Mandarin Chinese has four possible meanings, depend-ing on the tone which accompanies it, as follows:

[ma] high level pitch: 'mother'
[ma] high rising pitch: 'hemp'

[ma] low, or falling then rising pitch: 'horse'
[ma] falling pitch: 'cold'

So, it is clear that prosodic aspects of speech have communicative and linguistic relevance. It is also the case that prosody has **paralinguistic** importance. We may, for example, manage to judge speakers' attitudes or emotions based largely on the prosodic cues which exist in their speech. A narrower pitch range than usual, or lack of intonational variation, may, for instance, express a degree of negative emotion, or lack of interest on the part of the speaker.

We should also bear in mind that no utterance can be produced without prosodic aspects. Although speakers may manage, for example, to talk at length without producing a single glottal plosive, they cannot speak without voice quality, or pitch, or length, or loudness. For this reason, an analysis of speech output which ignores prosodic aspects will be incomplete.

We now move on to discuss prosodic aspects in detail. Throughout, we must remember that when we analyse prosodic aspects by ear, our analysis can only be subjective and relative rather than quantitative. For example, we can certainly suggest that male vocal pitch tends to be lower than female pitch, or that a given syllable is long in comparison with another one. However, it is only when we produce acoustic records of speech that can we provide proof for such statements, using precise measurements of length and pitch (*see* Chapter 9).

Stress

We define the term 'stress' here as syllable prominence. Prominence may, of course, derive from several phonetic factors such as increased length, loudness, pitch movement or a combination of these aspects. Later in this chapter, and in Chapter 9, we will see that it is sometimes important to specify exactly which kind of phonetic prominence is involved but, for the moment, we are not concerned with this level of specification. In transcription, it is important to indicate stress both within utterances and within words. Within an utterance, for instance, the location of the major stressed syllable can be responsible for changing the intended meaning, as illustrated in examples 1a and 1b, where the syllables which carry the major stress are capitalized:

1a I THOUGHT you would eat it (intended meaning: You have eaten it)
1b I thought you would EAT it (intended meaning: You have not eaten it)

With regard to indicating stress location within words, we are usually concerned with words consisting of two or more syllables, where the relative stress distribution needs to be specified. In such cases, it will normally be the case that one of the syllables is more stressed than the others, as in 'YESterday' and 'toMORRow'. Syllables which are not stressed are either secondarily stressed or unstressed. For example, in *complicATion*, it is likely that we will perceive some stress on the first syllable, as well as the major stress on the third. The IPA provides two symbols for marking stress, i.e. ['] for main stress and [ˌ] for secondary stress. So, for example, the following transcriptions capture the stress patterns of some English words:

'contradiction'	[ˌkɒntɹə'dɪkʃən]
'matrimonial'	[ˌmatɹɪ'monial]
'nevertheless'	[ˌnɛvəɹðə'lɛs]
'update'	['ʌpˌdɛit]

However, while the IPA marks may be adequate for capturing stress distribution in words consisting of two or three syllables, some phoneticians have suggested that further types of stress other than just primary and secondary need to be distinguished. For example, Gimson (1989, p. 224) points out that some pronunciations of 'examination' may allocate stress to each of the five syllables. He says that 'the syllables may be articulated with the following order of energy /neɪ/, /zæ/, /ɪg/, /mɪ/, /ʃn/', i.e. so that there is no single syllable that can be described as unstressed. For American English, Trager and Smith (1951) stated that four degrees of stress must be specified (i.e. primary, secondary, tertiary and weak), and their four stress marks (*see* Figure 6.1) are still in common use today in American studies where stress is discussed.

Within the context of generative phonology, i.e. the branch of study which attempts to account for possible phonological variation by means of a series of predictive rules, Chomsky and Halle (1968: 16), adopt a similar system consisting of four degrees of stress, indicated in Figure 6.2.

Even within individual types of stress, phoneticians have occasionally attempted to highlight distinct categories, particularly for the purpose of indicating stress distribution in long stretches of connected speech. In such contexts, we may wish to capture finer degrees of stress than needs to be recorded for individual words in citation form. For example, Gimson

primary	/ˈ/		primary	/¹/
secondary	/ˆ/		secondary	/²/
tertiary	/ˋ/		tertiary	/³/
weak	/˘/		quaternary/zero	/⁴/

Figure 6.1 Trager and Smith (1951) stress marks

Figure 6.2 Chomsky and Halle's (1968) stress marks

(1989) differentiated two versions of secondary stress, as does Wells (1990). For Gimson, the distinction is one of rhythmic stress versus non-rhythmic stress, where 'rhythmic stress' refers to a rhythmic beat which does not have primary stress. Taking the example of 'examination' again, the second syllable /zæ/ has a beat, but it is not the primary stressed syllable. Non-rhythmic stress, on the other hand, routinely occurs after the primary stressed syllable but, by definition, does not carry a rhythmic beat, as in 'Belfast' (i.e. [ˈbɛlˌfast]), where [fast] does not have a beat. Gimson's conventions for representing stress gradations within the category of secondary stress consist of a large filled dot for rhythmic stress and an unfilled dot of the same size to indicate non-rhythmic stress. He uses the large filled dot with an attached accent to indicate primary stress (which has potential pitch change) while the small dot indicates absence of stress, as the following examples illustrate:

eschatological . • . ˎ ..
previously   ˎ . .°

Wells (1990, p. 683) uses a similar system for distinguishing two types of secondary stress but, whereas Gimson (1989) used the term 'non-rhythmic stress', Wells (1990) refers to non-rhythmic secondary stress as 'tertiary'.

Although there is some variety in assigning levels of stress to syllables within words and utterance it is generally accepted that speakers and listeners routinely produce and respond to the two main varieties recommended by the IPA, i.e. primary and secondary stress.

Length

'Length' is generally a phonological term, whereas 'duration' is the term used in phonetics to describe the time parameter in speech. On the one hand, length may be seen as a segmental property, which enables us to convey phonemic distinctions of the kind described above for 'wood' and 'wooed'. However, as phonetic duration is frequently conditioned by surrounding segments (a vowel which is followed by a voiced consonant, for instance, will usually be perceived as longer than the same vowel followed by a voiceless consonant) we can classify it within the category of suprasegmentals since its effects extend over groups of segments. The IPA allows us to indicate phonetic duration or phonological length of individual segments by means of three diacritic symbols: [ː, ˈ, ˘] to indicate long, half-long and short, respectively. We can combine these diacritics so that, for instance, we can indicate segments which are excessively long (as in [jɛːːːːː] for an exaggerated pronunciation of 'yeah'.

It is often the case that length is not systematically indicated in transcription. One reason for this omission is the frequent assumption that there are some vowels which are, by definition, either short or long. For example, in English, it is usually stated that the set [ɪ, ɜ, ɑ, ɔ, u] constitute 'the long vowels', while [ɪ, e, æ, ʌ, ɒ, ʊ] are short by comparison. However, we wish to discourage the notion that particular vowels have inherent length characteristics associated with them, since the vowel length system is likely to differ considerably from accent to accent.

The term **gemination** is often applied to extra-long consonants. Long consonants may arise in languages due to morphological processes: for example, in English, where a long [nn] (or [nː]) occurs in 'unknown' [ʌnnoʊn]. This comes about due to the affixing of 'un' with its final [n] to 'known' with its initial [n]. However, geminate consonants may also be a part of the phonology of the language. An example of this is found in Italian where the words for 'ninth' and for 'grandfather' are contrasted solely by the length of the medial nasal segment: single in one example, geminate in the other: [nɔno] 'ninth', [nɔnno] 'grandfather'.

Pause

A further aspect of length which is frequently ignored in transcription is pause length. There are, however, good reasons for incorporating information on pause and pause length in phonetic transcription. First, the presence or absence of pauses can provide grammatical information which can help listeners decode meaning. For example, the following humorous example (contributed by Evelyn Abberton to an *Institute of Acoustics* bulletin) illustrates the point, where the success of the joke depends on the potential pause after 'eats' being omitted.

> A panda goes into a restaurant and has a meal. Just before he leaves he takes out a gun and fires it. The irate restaurant owner says 'Why did you do that'? The panda replies, 'I'm a panda. Look it up.' The restaurateur goes to his dictionary and under 'panda' finds: 'Black and white arboreal, bear-like creature; eats shoots and leaves'.

Second, the duration of a pause, combined with other information on overall speech rate and rhythm, may provide a useful index of a speaker's strategies in conversational turn-taking. Some speakers may, for example, allow too much time to elapse before they take their conversational turn, and such time lapses frequently suggest that the speaker has nothing more to say. On the other hand, speakers who intervene in the conversation too early, i.e. without leaving an appropriate pause may be perceived as impolite. In spite of the value of recording pause length in transcription, the IPA does not provide any guidance on how to do so. It is useful, therefore, to look to Crystal and Davy (1969) who suggest a method for transcribing four main types of pause, i.e. unit, double, treble and brief. They define a unit pause as 'the interval of an individual's rhythm cycle from one prominent syllable to the next, within a stable tempo' (Crystal and Davy, 1969, p. 171). Double and treble pauses imply multiples of this unit interval, whereas a brief pause refers to 'a silence perceivably shorter than (and usually approximately half as long as) unit length'. Each type of pause may be voiced or silent, and the suggested transcriptions are shown in Figure 6.3.

Pause	Silent	Voiced
unit	-	əː(m)
double	--	əːəː
treble	---	əːəːəː
brief	.	ə(m)

Figure 6.3 Crystal and Davy (1969) conventions for pause marking

The other means that exist for transcribing pause length are, arguably, more intuitive. For example, Brown (1990, p. 90) suggests the plus sign ([+]) to indicate a brief pause. For longer pauses she suggests [++] along with the specific time length measurements. So, her transcription looks as follows (capitalization is used by Brown to indicate the tonic syllable while underlining captures stress, whether lexical or contrastive):

> I *THINK* + the *pro*blem a*ris*es when *chil*dren *LEAVE school* ++
> they al*ready* have de*VEL*oped *some* po*TEN*tial + and they *don't*
> have the oppor*tun*ity THEN + to *go ON* with the *KIND* of +er
> + *SPORT* which *SHOULD last* them for the *next* ten YEARS.

Along similarly clear lines, although with the intention of transcribing pause length in disordered speech, Duckworth *et al.* (1990) offer the following system:

x(.)x short pause
x(. .)x medium-length pause
x(. . .)x long pause

Syllable juncture

We have said above that the basic domain for suprasegmental analysis is the syllable, rather than the segment. Given this information, it is obviously important that we can identify syllables and syllable boundaries or **junctures**. In many cases, the division of words into their component syllables is a relatively straightforward matter. In single syllable words, of course, we need only equate the whole word with the syllable ('zip' and 'pill', for example, constitute both the word and the syllable in each case). In words of more than one syllable, however, we may be less confident in locating syllable boundaries or syllable juncture. For example, in 'greenery', does the /n/ belong at the end of [gɹi] or at the beginning of [əɹ]? In practice, segments which could be attached to one of two syllables are known as **ambisyllabic**, but such potential ambiguity in syllable division does not, in English, interfere with the meaning of a word. In connected speech, however, there are cases in which the location of syllable juncture at one point rather than another completely alters the meaning of the phrase. Gimson (1989, pp. 304–6) cites some examples of this phenomenon:

piːstɔːks	(pea stalks/peace talks)
ə neɪm	(a name/an aim)
ðætstʌf	(that stuff/that's tough)
ðə weɪtəkʌtɪt	(the way to cut it/the waiter cut it)[1]
aɪskriːm	(I scream/ice-cream)
haʊstreɪnd	(how strained/housetrained)
waɪtʃuːz	(why choose/white shoes)

If we wish our transcriptions to be an accurate and unambiguous reflection of speech, we must record syllable juncture where necessary. The IPA offers the dot as a means of indicating syllable boundaries, as follows:

lightning	'laɪt.nɪŋ
lightening	'laɪt.n̩.ɪŋ (Ladefoged, 1982, p. 223)

Pitch

At the start of this chapter we stated that, in tone languages, the pitch shape of syllables differentiates the meaning of otherwise phonetically identical items. We also suggested that certain pitch patterns in speech might be responsible for differentiating statements from questions. As these two points illustrate, pitch is a suprasegmental quality which extends over individual segments and longer stretches of speech. In this section, we will concern ourselves with syllable pitch, and the pitch properties of longer utterances will be dealt with in Chapter 9. For the purposes of impressionistic phonetic analysis, we now suggest methods for describing and capturing syllable pitch variation in transcription, whereas Chapter 9 explains how to measure pitch characteristics by use of phonetic instrumentation.

---

[1] This example is relevant only for non-rhotic accents, i.e. where the /r/ in 'waiter' would not be pronounced.

When transcribing syllable pitch, we must first distinguish between level and moving pitch. Such syllables are commonly known as **static** and **kinetic**, respectively, although Pike (1948) used the terms **register** and **contour** to capture the same phenomena. Once we have identified level and moving syllables, we then must subdivide them according to the general area within the speaker's pitch range where they are produced. It is practice in phonetic study, especially within the American tradition, to identify five such areas, i.e. high, mid, low, mid-high, and mid-low. We might think of these, following Trager and Smith (1951) as a number of pitch 'levels' which are relatively constant for any given speaker. This notion of constancy means that a speaker will tend to gravitate round the five pitch levels with, perhaps, occasional excursions into extra-high and extra-low pitch ranges (known as **upstep** and **downstep**).

If the pitch is moving, we must specify the shape of the pitch movement and the degree of movement contained within the syllable. So, for instance, we might identify a rising pitch which covers a narrow range (say from low to mid-low), or a falling pitch which covers a wide range (say from low to high). Theoretically, any type of pitch movement can combine freely with any pitch height, although in practice speakers tend to adopt a fairly limited set of combinations for most of the time. So, for instance, while a low falling rising tone is certainly possible, it is rare. Figure 6.4 shows the syllable pitch types which are common in English, presented using the so-called 'tadpole' or inter-linear transcription method. Following this method,

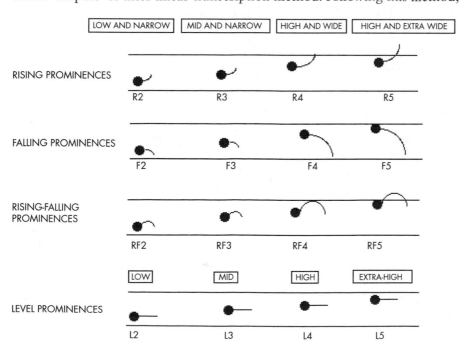

Figure 6.4 Common tone types in English

the upper and lower lines represent the top and bottom respectively of the speaker's pitch range. Within these lines, individual syllable shapes are shown iconically, by means of a filled dot from which a directional line emanates.

Phoneticians sometimes also use numerals to indicate pitch. So, for instance, a high followed by a low syllable indicated by one transcriber will capture the same pitch height as another's pitch levels 4 and 2 respectively. Information on pitch height might be represented as a configuration of numerals, or may be entered in an inter-linear transcription, as shown in Figure 6.5, in order to provide additional information to that provided in the interlinear version.

Within the context of generative phonology, investigators label pitch contours in terms of the binary features [+High/ –High] and [+Low/ –Low], where high and low level syllables correspond not to absolute pitch values, but to the relative pitch of a syllable or part of a syllable in comparison with what precedes it. Within high and low tones, there are three sub-divisions according to whether the tone is a pitch accent (marked H* or L*, for instance), a trailing tone, i.e. one following on from the pitch accent (marked H– or L–) or a boundary tone on the final syllable of the group (marked L% or H%). In Figure 6.6, for example, high and low tones are matched with their appropriate interlinear representation.

In fact, a wide range of possibilities exists for indicating syllable pitch in transcription. Figure 6.7, for instance, illustrates the systems developed by Chao and Yang (1947) for Mandarin Chinese, and by Westermann and Ward (1933) for Nigerian Igbo.

At this point, however, we wish to refer on the IPA suggestions for indicating syllable pitch. The IPA system is reproduced in Figure 6.8.

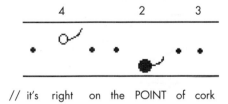

// it's right on the POINT of cork

Figure 6.5 Pitch level information entered on an inter-linear transcription

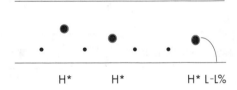

H*   H*   H* L-L%

Figure 6.6 High and Low tones marked on inter-linear transcription

Mandarin: ˥ = high level
˩ = mid to high rising
˧ = mid to low to mid high falling-rising
˨ = high to low falling

Igbo: isi [˙.]   smell
isi [˙ ˙]   head
isi [.\]   six

Figure 6.7 Conventions for representing syllable pitch in Mandarin Chinese and Nigerian Igbo

é̌	or	˥	Extra high	ě	or	ʌ	Rising
é		˦	High	ê		˅	Falling
ē		˧	Mid	é̌		˦	High rising
è		˨	Low	è̌		˩	Low rising
è̏		˩	Extra low	ē̌		˦˥	Rising-falling

Figure 6.8 IPA pitch marks

Up to this point in our discussion, we have discussed syllable pitch with-out regard to meaning, except in the case of tone languages. This is because the pitch characteristics of speech are frequently seen as raw acoustic fea-tures, which can be specified purely in terms of phonetic aspects, i.e. whether high or low, rising or falling, for instance and we shall see in Chap-ter 9 that it is also possible to provide measurements of raw pitch features using acoustic analysis. Using a segmental parallel, we have seen that it is possible to specify the phonetic aspects of individual speech sounds without any reference to meaning and that, once we start to investigate meaning, our discussion becomes phonological. When we view pitch characteristics as having particular meaning, or patterning in certain ways, we move into the area of **intonation**, and the notion of meaningful pitch patterns will be explained next. Although it is outside the scope of this book to offer detailed explanations of how intonation relates precisely to meaning, we suggest that, for useful illustrations of intonational functions, the reader should consult the 'Further reading' section at the end of this chapter.

Intonation

Most work on intonation can be classified into two broad categories, i.e. the **acoustic** and the **linguistic** approaches. The acoustic approach concen-trates on the physical and measurable side of intonation in terms of acoustic aspects of pitch, duration and intensity. The linguistic approach to intonation, on the other hand, examines correlations between pitch and linguistic features such as semantics, syntax and grammar. Linguistically oriented studies are usually impressionistically or auditorily based and have tended to be largely pedagogic in orientation, i.e. for the foreign learner (*see, for example*, Halliday, 1970; O'Connor and Arnold, 1973).

On the basis of the section above in which we discussed pitch, it is clear that the domain over which syllable pitch operates is easily identifiable, i.e. we need only to identify a syllable and assign a pitch height and pitch move-ment to that syllable. However, there is no such agreement concerning what constitutes relevant intonational domains in speech. The difficulty of estab-lishing intonational categories is described by Ainsworth and Lindsay (1986, p. 472):

One of the problems with research into intonation in English is that there is no general agreement as to the nature of the structure to be considered or of the realisation of the elements within that structure.

However, there is some consensus, at least, that we must look beyond the individual segments to longer stretches of speech in order to understand how pitch patterns convey meaning. These longer stretches of speech are commonly known as **tone-units** (Crystal, 1969), or **tone groups** (Halliday, 1967), although **phonemic clause** (Trager and Smith, 1951), **breath group** (Lieberman, 1967) and **intonation phrase** (Pierrehumbert, 1980; Ladd, 1986) refer to similar phenomena. Tone units have been defined by Halliday (1970, p. 3) as 'one unit of information'.

A variety of criteria, grammatical and phonological, have been advanced for the identification of tone units. Crystal (1969, pp. 205–206) suggests that there are particular boundary cues and internal structures which are involved in the identification of tone-units in RP, for example:

> each tone-unit will have one peak of prominence in the form of a nuclear pitch movement . . . then it is the case that after this nuclear tone there will be a perceivable pitch change, either stepping up or stepping down . . . there is always a pitch change following a nuclear tone, and this may be taken as diagnostic.

Within the tone-unit, it is usually recognized that there is one piece of new information which is highlighted by a single salient pitch change of the pitch contour known as the **nucleus** or **tonic**. Halliday (1970, p. 4), for instance, says:

> The tonic syllable is often longer, and may be louder, than the other salient syllables in the tone group . . . The tonic syllable carries the main burden of the pitch movement in the tone group.

Apart from the nucleus and tone-unit, the other relevant units of intonation, i.e. the **non-nuclear** aspects, are known as the **pre-head**, the **head** and the **tail**. The head consists of the stretch beginning with the first stressed syllable (also referred to as the **head onset**) of the utterance and extending up to the nucleus. Any unstressed syllables which precede the head constitute the pre-head. The tail refers to the unstressed syllable or syllables which occur after the nucleus, before the next tone-unit boundary. The nucleus is the only obligatory element of a tone-unit, i.e. while it is possible to have a tone-unit without a head or a tail, for instance, it is impossible for a tone-unit to exist without a nucleus.

We should bear in mind, however, that the intonational model described above, whose central elements are the tone unit and the nucleus, were established to deal with received pronunciation (RP), and a formal variety of RP at that. When we attempt to identify such elements in non-RP speech, however, we frequently encounter difficulties. For instance, whilst it is possible to identify units into which non-RP speakers divide their speech, it is often the case that such units are not differentiated in terms of a pitch change between the units. Second, where it is possible to identify one particularly prominent syllable within a unit, it may be that this syllable does not have the specific characteristics of a nucleus, so that, for example, a syllable which is produced on a level pitch may be perceived as prominent merely because it carries more amplitude than the other syllables within the unit. Furthermore, it may be impossible to identify just one prominent syllable in a given unit. In fact, numerous units may exist in which there are two or more syllables which are equally prominent in auditory and acoustic senses.

There are, therefore, differences between RP intonation and non-RP intonation at the level of phonetic correlates of intonation components, as well as the tonal shape of components. When we are concerned with analysing the intonation of regional varieties of English, therefore, the RP model may not be the best one to adopt, largely because elements such as the tone unit and the nucleus have been defined on strict grounds. In such cases, we suggest that it might be fruitful not to adopt the RP model wholesale. The components of the model suggested here and illustrated in Figure 6.9, i.e. the **tone sequence**, the **leading segment** (beginning with the leading syllable), the **prominence** and the **final sequence** correspond broadly to the tone-unit, head, nucleus and tail respectively as described by Crystal (1969), but the model allows the components to be identified on the basis of less strict phonetic criteria, described below.

The view taken here is that speakers divide their speech into relevant units which are characterized by external and internal features. The consistently reliable cue to unit boundaries is pause. Within each pause defined group, there is at least one particularly prominent syllable, but the phonetic

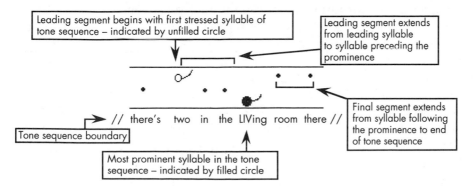

Figure 6.9 The tone sequence and its components

features which contribute to the perception of prominence intonation may be amplitude, or length as well as, or instead of merely pitch cues. As we have suggested above, it may also be possible to assign equal prominence to more than one syllable as illustrated in Figure 6.10.

Intonation transcription

Given what we have said so far concerning potential difficulties with intonation analysis, it will come as no surprise that there are also divergent approaches to intonation at the level of a notation system for representing the data in a visually meaningful way. Narrow and broad transcriptions described in Chapter 8 for segmental analysis have a parallel in intonation and are illustrated in the so-called 'tadpole' or inter-linear notation and tonetic stress marking respectively. Inter-linear notation allows a fairly detailed representation of all tones in a unit relative to one another. Tonetic stress marking, on the other hand, indicates the shape and height only of stressed elements within the tone group, using the IPA conventions shown in Figure 6.8. The choice of one notation system over relates to the amount of contrasts in the intonation which are considered to be important. For example, Halliday (1970) mostly uses tonetic stress marks; his model is strongly nucleus-centred because he believes that it constitutes the part which 'the speaker wants to show to be the most important in the message' (p. 4). O'Connor and Arnold (1973), on the other hand, transcribe all of the tone group in inter-linear fashion, because they consider all elements to be important in conveying a number of important attitudinal distinctions. Some investigators adopt rather idiosyncratic approaches to intonation transcription, such as Bolinger (1961, p. 87), who employs an iconic system as illustrated in Figure 6.11.

Voice quality

In its narrowest sense, the term 'voice' refers to presence of phonation (*see* Chapter 2). So, for instance, we can say that voice is produced on /a/ but not on /s/. In this sense, voice is a segmental linguistic feature since it is

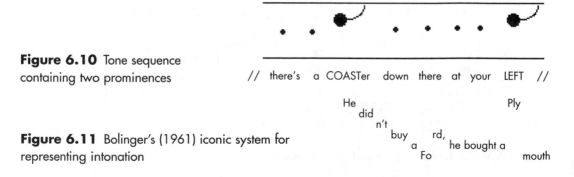

Figure 6.10 Tone sequence containing two prominences

// there's a COASTer down there at your LEFT //

Figure 6.11 Bolinger's (1961) iconic system for representing intonation

He did n't buy a Fo rd, he bought a Ply mouth

characterizes individual speech sounds and is responsible for conveying meaning distinctions, as in /fit/ versus /fid/, for instance. However, the notion of voice *quality* refers to longer term aspects of speech, such as over-all nasality, or breathiness, or creakiness, for example. As such, it is a suprasegmental feature which may have a paralinguistic function in so far as it can indicate the physical or emotional state of the speaker. The most influential model for analysing voice quality, i.e. that by Laver (1980) defines the term as the 'characteristic auditory colouring of a given speaker's voice'. The term was used earlier by Abercrombie (1967, p. 91), referring to 'those characteristics that are present more or less all the time that a person is talking; . . . a quasi-permanent quality running through all the sound that issues from his mouth'. Particular voice quality settings, therefore, may be responsible for identifying an individual, or a group of speakers.

Following Laver's (1980) model, it is possible to describe voice quality according to a number of so-called 'settings', where a setting refers to a particular kind of adjustment to the muscular apparatus which is respon-sible for producing speech. Voice quality settings are also known as 'artic-ulatory settings', and each setting is described according to the area of the vocal apparatus in which it is produced. Two main areas are distinguished – the **laryngeal** and **supralaryngeal**, also known as **glottal** and **supraglottal**.

Laryngeal/glottal settings

Laryngeal or glottal settings are those in which the muscular adjustments take place around the area of the larynx. Laryngeal settings are affected by the innate size and shape of the vocal cords, their speed of vibration dur-ing phonation and their relative proximity. Some examples of laryngeal/glottal settings are given in Table 6.1. It should be noted that modal voice is assumed to be the neutral or default setting, and it is defined as the quality which exists in the absence of falsettto, or whisper, for example.

Table 6.1 Laryngeal/glottal settings

Falsetto	High-frequency vocal fold vibration, resulting in overall high pitch
Whisper	Greater constriction in the vocal folds than for voiceless sounds
Creak	Low-frequency vocal fold vibration
Breathy voice	Incomplete glottal closure during normal voice production
Modal voice	The neutral laryngeal setting

The settings described above are known as **individual** settings, because they involve a single muscular adjustment. However, it is possible to combine settings with one another so that, for instance, high-frequency vocal fold vibration might combine with a high degree of constriction in the vocal cords to produce whispery falsetto. Such combinations are known as **compound** settings and other examples are whispery falsetto, harsh creaky voice, and harsh whispery falsetto.

Supralaryngeal/supraglottal settings

Supralaryngeal or supraglottal settings are those which involve adjustments in the area above the larynx. Supralaryngeal settings are usually subdivided into three types: **longitudinal, latitudinal** and **velopharyngeal** settings.

Longitudinal settings modify the area above the larynx lengthwise by means of raising or lowering the larynx to decrease or increase the length of the oral/nasal tract. As the larynx lowers, the tract becomes longer and the speech that is produced lowers in pitch. It is also possible to modify the length of the supralaryngeal area by pushing the lips outwards i.e. by means of **labial protrusion**. Finally, the supralaryngeal area can be modified by means of retracting the lower lip and bringing it up under the teeth, i.e. **labiodentalization**.

In latitudinal settings, voice quality is affected by modification of the area across its width or cross-sectional area. This modification takes place at specified places along the vocal tract such as at the **lips, tongue, pharynx** and **jaw**. Lip modifications result in **labial** settings, where the lips can expand or constrict the vocal tract. Tongue, or **lingual** settings involve particular movements of the tongue towards certain portions of the roof of the mouth. If it moves upwards and forward in the direction the hard palate area, **palatalized** voice is produced, while a backwards rising movement results in **velarized** voice. **Pharyngeal** settings refer to the constriction or expansion of the muscles in the pharynx walls. Finally, with regard to latitudinal modifications, jaw or **mandibular** settings result in **open jaw** and **close jaw** voice qualities, depending on the movement of the jaw during speech production. The relative tension or constriction which exists in pharyngeal and mandibular settings results in overall **tense** and **lax** voice qualities.

The third major category of supralaryngeal modifications, i.e. velopharyngeal settings derives from the relationship between velum and pharynx and result in **nasal** and **hypernasal** voice, for example. Clearly, following on from the explanation of nasal sounds in Chapter 5, the more the velum is lowered, then the greater will be the amount of nasal resonance that exists. Figure 6.12 summarizes in diagrammatic form the major categories of voice quality settings, according to the area in which they are produced.

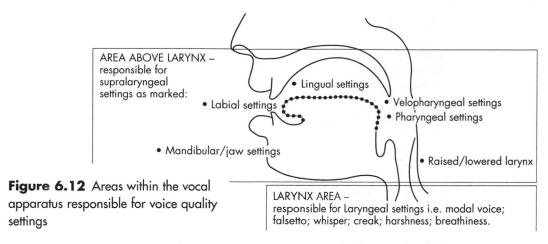

Figure 6.12 Areas within the vocal apparatus responsible for voice quality settings

We have said above that voice quality may operate as a paralinguistic system, i.e. as a means for signalling emotional state, for example. Clearly, there are certain aspects of voice quality that are outside the control of speakers because of physical make-up or medical conditions such as laryngeal cancer. However, speakers are frequently able to manipulate their voice quality. We might think of breathy voice quality as having sexual overtones, or palatalized voice as conveying a patronizing attitude of the sort that adults sometimes use when talking to babies. In some cultures, particular voice qualities function as markers of social deference. In Bolivia, for example, females frequently adopt breathy voice quality as a sign of respect when speaking to males. However, it is also the case that voice quality functions phonemically in some languages. For example, breathy voice is responsible for distinguishing one set of vowels from another in Dinka, a Sudanese language, as is creaky voice in some Indian languages.

As well as being able to describe voice quality settings with reference to the areas of the vocal tract from which they emanate, we may also wish to transcribe them. While the IPA offers a number of diacritics for transcribing segmental quality (e.g. nasalization diacritic), it is less useful for indicating the quality of longer stretches of speech. For this purpose, we recommend Laver's (1994, p. 197) suggestion for transcribing creaky voice, i.e. whereby a simple 'C' (to indicate creaky) is placed outside the phonetic brackets. We also wish to supplement Laver's suggestions with the VoQs conventions for transcribing voice quality, reproduced in Appendix 1.

Rhythm

When we are listening to music, we are frequently aware of a clear rhythmic beat, i.e. a pulse that recurs at more or less equal intervals of time.

(i) Variations in tempo:

allegro	{alleg}
allegrissimo	{allegriss}
lento	{lento}
lentissimo	{lentiss}
accelerando	{accel}
rallentando	{rall}

(ii) Variations in volume:

forte	{f}
fortissimo	{ff}
piano	{p}
pianissimo	{pp}
crescendo	{cresc}
diminuendo	{dimin}

(iii) Variations in rhythmicality:

rhythmic	{rhythm}
arhythmic	{arythm}
staccato	{stac}
legato	{leg}

(iv) Various vocal effects, simultaneous with speech, which inevitably have an effect on the overall quality of speech. These would be simply labelled within the braces, e.g.
    {sobbing}
    {tremulousness}.

Figure 6.13 Crystal and Davy's (1969) system for representing vocal effects in conversation

When we listen to speech, it is unlikely that we are able to identify such a regular pulse unless, of course, the speech in question is a stylized form of poetry reading where the rhythm is being somewhat exaggerated. Nevertheless, it is usually thought that there is some sort of rhythmic structure which underpins speech production and perception. With particular reference to speech, we can interpret the term 'rhythmic structure' as referring to combinations of stressed and unstressed syllables. It is common practice to classify languages depending on whether they are **stress-timed** or **syllable-timed**. Stress timed languages include English and Russian, whereas syllable timed languages include French, Spanish and Italian. In stress-timed languages, it is assumed that the stressed syllables occur at regular time intervals and that the speed of the intervening unstressed syllables is adjusted to fit in with the rhythmic structure established by the stressed syllables. In syllable-timed languages, on the other hand, it is thought that the syllables occur at regular time intervals. Both the notion of stress-timed and syllable-timed languages have been questioned in the literature and it seems that they are so ineffectual in dealing with real speech, that they represent far from useful descriptive categories.

Various theories exist for analysing the rhythmic structure of speech. For example, Abercrombie (1967) suggests a model based around stressed syllables. He identifies a rhythm unit called the **foot**, which must begin with a stressed syllable. Any unstressed syllable which follows belongs within the same foot. If an utterance begins with an unstressed syllable, then that syllable is effectively ignored (it therefore fulfils a role rather like that of an upbeat in music), and the first stressed syllable is located. O'Connor and Arnold (1973) offer a model which is similar to Abercrombie's insofar as it focuses on stressed syllables around which, it is suggested, all other syllables are organized.

This theory, however, is somewhat problematic since, if presented with an unstressed syllable, it may be difficult to decide whether that syllable belongs with the preceding or the following stressed syllable. According to O'Connor, (1980 p. 198) 'unstressed syllables which precede the stress are said particularly quickly'. The implication here is that we can judge the relative speed at which syllables are uttered and, on the basis of whether they are relatively fast or relatively slow, we can confidently group them with the following or the preceding stress respectively. O'Connor (1980, p. 97) exemplifies his point as follows:

> In the group | | ɪt wəz betə | | there are two unstressed syllables before the stress and one after it. The first two are said quickly, the last one not so quickly, taking the same amount of time as /be-/

Pike's (1962) attempt is largely similar insofar as it attempts to define rhythmic units around stressed syllables, but he offers more explanatory detail than O'Connor. Other theories for identifying rhythmic structures consist of assigning units simply according to the location of stressed syllables (*see* Halliday, 1967). It may be that particular types of rhythm analysis are better suited to one language rather than another. For example, O'Connor's (1980) approach (whereby rhythmic units are identified on at least an impressionistic phonetic basis) seems useful for a stress-timed language such as English, whereas Halliday's (1967) stressed syllable method is more applicable to Italian, for example.

For the purpose of indicating in transcription where rhythmic unit boundaries occur, there are several options. Abercrombie (1967), for instance, used a vertical bar [|], Halliday (1967) the slash [/]. Pike (1962) suggested a low reverse slash [\] and O'Connor (1980) uses a word space [ ].

In addition to the aspects we have mentioned above, it is frequently useful to mark variations in tempo, volume, rhythmicality and a range of vocal effects in transcription, particularly where such variations have interactive importance (in conversation management, for example). For indicating these aspects in transcription, we recommend the system offered by Crystal and Davy (1969), presented in Figure 6.13.

Summary

In this chapter, we have explained the main suprasegmental aspects of speech and we have indicated how they might be described and transcribed. We have also stated that a phonetic description which does not include suprasegmental information is severely limited. It is recommended that suprasegmentals should be systematically recorded in transcription. The value of detailed transcription is discussed in more detail in Chapter 8.

Further reading

For the most detailed and wide-ranging review of suprasegmental features of speech, Couper-Kuhlen (1986) is recommended. With specific regard to intonation, Cruttenden (1997) provides an updated account of approaches to intonation analysis, and also offers useful insights to functional and comparative accounts of intonation. Tench (1996) is a valuable source of information on historical and transcriptional aspects of intonation study.

Short questions

1 What is a tone language?
2 Summarize the main elements of the tone-unit based approach to intonation analysis.
3 What is the difference between pitch and intonation?
4 What options exist for the transcription of intonation?
5 Explain the relevance of the terms 'glottal' and 'supraglottal' with reference to voice quality.

Essay questions

1 Explain the tone-unit based approach to analysing intonation and assess its value with reference to one accent with which you are familiar.
2 Assess the contribution which suprasegmental aspects of speech make to communication.
3 'It is part of the general human experience of speech that listeners confidently identify their friends and acquaintances through the familiar consistency of their voices' (Laver, 1994, p. 398). Discuss the 'familiar consistency' of voices in terms of voice quality settings.

7

Multiple articulations, co-articulation and the parameters of speech

Introduction	Co-articulation
Double articulations	Parametric phonetics
Secondary articulations	

Introduction

In previous chapters we have examined the production of segmental and suprasegmental aspects of speech. This suggests that we can easily classify all phonetic manifestations into one or other of these categories. However, it becomes clear when we investigate more closely that segments exist of varying degrees of complexity, and phonetic features do not all have identical boundaries. This means we need to look at segments with multiple, co-occurring aspects of articulation, and we need to examine whether segments have clearly identifiable boundaries at all.

This first aspect is classified into segments having **double articulations** and those having a **primary** and a **secondary articulation**: this distinction is explained below. The second aspect leads us to examine the status of segments themselves, and then the intersegmental co-ordination of different phonetic features. We conclude this chapter with an examination of parametric phonetics: an approach to phonetic description that seeks to go beyond the segment and concentrate on phonetic features and their relative timings.

Double articulations

It is possible to produce segments with two simultaneous and equal articulations, and these are called **double articulations** or 'doubly articulated' sounds. In this description, the term 'simultaneous' is self-explanatory (although in double articulations there may be very slight overlap between the two strictures), but what do we mean by two 'equal' articulations? As noted in Chapter 3, there is a hierarchy of segment types, from the 'strongest' manner of articulation (stops), through progressively weaker ones (fricatives, approximants) to vowels, the 'weakest'. A double articulation must have both articulations in the same strength category, i.e. two stops, two fricatives, two approximants.

Two simultaneous articulations are possible because the active articulators in sound segment production can be decoupled from each other. In other words, the lips can operate independently from the tongue, and even with the tongue, the tip and blade can operate independently from the back of the tongue. This means that combinations such as bilabial with velar, bilabial with alveolar, and alveolar with velar are perfectly possible. Not all possibilities for each manner of articulation are exploited, however, and we will note only the more commonly occurring combinations.

For plosives, voiceless and voiced **labio-velars** are quite common in many West African languages (*see* Figure 7.1). They are transcribed as [k͡p, g͡b] conventionally, although there is no reason why the symbols should not be the other way round (which would, in fact, reflect the way the sounds are normally described). The tie-bar, which we encountered before as a way of showing affricates, is used here to denote simultaneous articulation. The two usages should not be confused for, if the symbols are the same manner of articulation, they must be a double articulation whereas, if the first is a stop and the second a fricative, then they must represent an affricate. **Labio-alveolar** stops also occur, and are usually transcribed [p͡t, b͡d]. Stops at any place of articulation may be subject to glottal reinforcement (this is quite common in English). Here, we have a simultaneous glottal stop and oral stop, although the glottal stop may, in fact, just precede the oral one. In English, glottal reinforcement occurs in some varieties before word-final voiceless stops, e.g. [ʔ͡p] in 'map'.

Double fricatives also occur at a variety of places of articulation. For example, they have been reported as occurring with a labio-velar combination [x͡ɸ, ɣ͡β], labio-alveolar [ɸ͡s, β͡z], uvular-pharyngeal [χ͡ħ], and post-alveolar-velar [ʃ͡x] (*see* Figure 7.1). This last is used in some accents of Swedish, and can also be transcribed as [ɧ]. Labio-velar [ʍ] (as in Scottish English 'when') is generally deemed a voiceless fricative.

Approximants, as noted previously, can be classed as double articulations when there is an approximation at both the labial position, and elsewhere. We noted in Chapter 5 that [w] and [ɥ] were labio-velar and labio-palatal approximants, respectively, even though there is only a single symbol used to transcribe each sound. The names of these sounds suggest that there is a double articulation involved, but we must be careful of double-sounding names. The *labiodental* approximant is a single articulation; here the name of the place of articulation points out the two articulators involved.

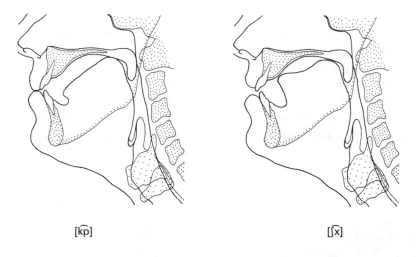

[k͡p]   [ʃ͡x]

Figure 7.1
Double
articulations:
[k͡p], [ʃ͡x]

Finally, we can consider vowels. It has been suggested by some authorities that, as vowels have a tongue position and a lip position (i.e. rounded or unrounded), they are, in effect, double articulations in any case. However, we will consider here whether a further vowel-like articulation can be added to the basic vowel. In many languages post-vocalic rhoticity (i.e. 'r-ness') is realized, at least some of the time, not by adding a full approximant segment after the vowel, but pronouncing part or all of the vowel with tongue tip raising and maybe also retroflexion. These 'r-coloured' vowels can be thought of, then, as being double articulations between the tongue body (assuming the position for the vowel in question), and the tip (undergoing raising and retroflexion). The IPA suggests that such vowels can be transcribed with an added diacritic, as [ɚ] or [ɝ], etc.

Table 7.1 illustrates some of these double articulations in a range of languages.[1]

Secondary articulations

When we specify the place and manner of articulation of a consonant, we do not necessarily describe every articulatory gesture being made at that time: we normally only describe the most important one. For example, if we make [m] (a bilabial nasal) we do not specify the position of the tongue. This may be in the front of the mouth (perhaps preparing for a following front vowel) or the back of the mouth (if the following vowel is a back one). Similarly, with [t] (an alveolar plosive) we do not normally describe the lip shape. This may be rounded if the [t] is followed by a rounded vowel, or

---

[1] The approximants were also dealt with in Chapter 5, but are repeated here for the sake of completeness.

Table 7.1 Double articulations

	Labio-velar	**Labio-alveolar**	
Plosives	Efik [ak͡pa] 'river' Yoruba [g͡be] 'to carry'	Bura [p͡ta] 'hare' Yeletnye [p͡tənə] 'lung'	

	Labio-velar	**Labio-alveolar**	**Post-alveolar-velar**	**Uvular-pharyngeal**
Fricatives	Urhobo [oxɸʷo] 'person'	Shona [ßzose] 'all'	Swedish [ɧal] 'scarf'	Abkhaz [ax͡ħə] 'head'

	Labio-palatal	**Labio-velar**
Approximants	French [ɥit̪] 'eight' Tikar [bùkɥê] 'mats'	French [wi] 'yes' Welsh [wɪwɛr] 'squirrel'

spread if the next vowel is a spread one. These **secondary articulations** are often ignored, because they are usually predictable co-articulatory effects, that is to say effects caused by the neighbouring sound segments. However, we will see that secondary articulations can be described, either because we wish to give as complete a description of the varieties (or allophones) of a phoneme, or because they can be contrastive in some languages.

First, we need to be certain what the difference between double and secondary articulations is. Double articulations have two strictures of equivalent strength on the segment hierarchy, as noted in the previous section. A secondary articulation is always of a weaker type than the primary. In reality, secondary articulations are always of an open approximation type, and so are considered to be weaker than stops, fricatives and so on. They are also considered to be weaker than lateral approximants, though if they occur with central approximants (as [w] described above), these count as double articulations. The reason for this is that lateral approximants do maintain a complete closure in the oral cavity (with lateral airflow), whereas central approximants do not.

There are four commonly occurring secondary articulations (though others do exist, as described in Laver, 1994, for example).[2] **Labialization** is a secondary bilabial approximation coinciding with another sound. It is a common allophonic characteristic, and is found in English consonants

---

[2] Long-term articulatory settings may also be considered to be secondary articulations. A range of these were dealt with in Chapter 6.

preceding rounded vowels, e.g. [tʷ] in 'two'. The use of these secondary features contrastively is illustrated in Table 7.2 below.

Palatalization is a secondary approximation of the front of the tongue towards the hard palate. This can co-occur with labials, but due to the flexibility of the tongue, it can also be found with apical sounds. This type of secondary articulation is often heard as a [j] type glide following the consonant concerned; this is because the secondary articulation may be released slightly after the primary. In many accents of English, a palatalized [l] may be used before vowels, e.g. [lʲ] in 'leaf', and this type of pronunciation has been termed a 'clear-l', due to the higher pitch of the voice found in palatal and palatalized consonants. While languages may use palatalization as a co-articulatory effect in front of high front vowels, it also appears contrastively in quite a few instances (e.g. in Russian and Irish). Contrastive usage is illustrated in Table 7.2, and a palatalized alveolar stop is shown in Figure 7.2.

Velarization is a secondary approximation of the back of the tongue towards the soft palate (velum). As with palatalization, this feature can co-occur with labials and apicals. In English, many varieties use a velarized [l] following vowels, e.g. [lˠ] in 'feel', and this type of pronunciation has been termed a 'dark-l', due to the lower pitch found in velar and velarized consonants. One commonly finds dark-l transcribed [ɫ], that is to say with a 'tilde' diacritic going through the centre of the symbol. The IPA allows this diacritic to be used as a cover for both velarization and pharyngealization, as in many languages these two secondary articulation types appear to be interchangeable and may depend on speaker preference. A velarized alveolar stop is shown in Figure 7.2.

Pharyngealization involves a secondary approximation of the back and root of the tongue into the pharynx. This secondary feature can co-occur with a range of labial, tip and blade consonants, though not with dorsal sounds as the retraction of the tongue root also affects the tongue body. This secondary articulation does not occur in most varieties of English (though in some regional accents such as Merseyside it may occur), it is however contrastive in Arabic, and the term 'emphatic' is applied to pharyngealized consonants in Arabic linguistics. An example of a voiced

Table 7.2 Secondary articulations

Labialization	Palatalization	Velarization	Pharyngealization
Tabassaran [naqʼ] 'yesterday' [naqʷ] 'grave'	*Irish* [bo] 'cow' [bʲo] 'alive'	*Marshallese* [le] 'Ms, Madam' [lˠe] 'Mr, Sir'	*Tamazight Berber* [izi] 'gall-bladder' [izˤi] 'a fly'

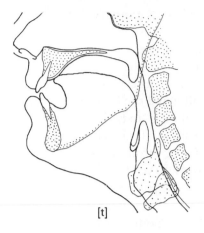

[t]

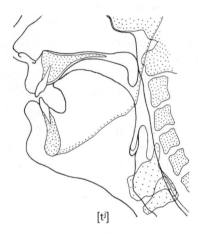

[tʲ]

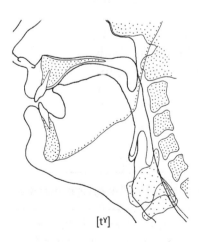

[tˠ]

Figure 7.2 Secondary articulations: [t] , [tʲ], [tˠ]

pharyngealized apical plosive in transcription is [dˤ], although (as noted above) the medial tilde is still frequently found: [ɗ].

Laver (1994) includes 'laryngealization' as a secondary articulation. This refers to glottal constriction of varying types accompanying a sound. This normally manifests itself as creak or creaky voice (*see* Chapter 2) and/or accompanying glottal stop. We treat this range of features as either phonatory, or glottal reinforcement of other sounds, rather than secondary articulation.

Co-articulation

Co-articulation and the status of the segment

The use of the term 'segmental' in phonetics assumes that such things as segments actually exist; however, detailed knowledge of speech production (gained from acoustic instrumentation to be described in Chapter 9 and articulatory instrumentation to be described in Chapter 12) suggests that this may not be the case if we define segments strictly. So, if our definition of a segment is an entity with discrete boundaries separate from neighbouring segments then such a definition is incompatible with the phonetic facts.

Nevertheless, there are certainly phonetic entities that are perceived by listeners as segments (i.e. consonants and vowels), and other entities that are not so perceived (e.g. intonation, voice quality). The problem arises because the various phonetic features described in earlier chapters that go to make up segments (e.g. phonation, nasality, articulatory stricture) do not always have co-terminous boundaries. By this we mean that, for example, voicing may change to voicelessness before the articulatory release in a plosive; or the soft palate may lower before the articulatory posture for a nasal stop is put into place; or lip rounding for a rounded vowel may be commenced during a preceding consonant that would not otherwise have such rounding. In phonetics, therefore, we have to assume a looser definition of segment if we wish to retain this term, and we have to investigate the various boundary effects between segments that occur: which we term **co-articulation**.

Types of co-articulation

This term stands for more than just the fact that different parameters of phonetics may not have co-terminous boundaries: it is an area of phonetics that seeks to explain why such differences may occur. In fact, 'co-articulation' literally means two (or more) features or sounds being articulated simultaneously, and some phoneticians (e.g. Catford, 1988) have used the term to stand for double and secondary articulations. However, its normal current usage has moved away somewhat from its original meaning, as we noted above, though alternative terms such as **intersegmental co-ordination** also exist. In this section, we will look at some of the main types of co-articulation, and illustrate them with examples. These will mainly be from English, but it should be stressed that co-articulation has been found in all languages investigated, though some of the patterns are language-specific. It should also be noted that co-articulatory effects between segments need not be limited by word boundaries; especially in rapid speech, effects across word boundaries are common.

There are various ways in which we can classify co-articulation: the direction of influence between segments; the parameters of articulation that are affected; and the extent to which co-articulation actually changes neighbouring sounds (what we might term the 'functional aspect'). We will look at each of these topics in turn. In terms of direction of influence, we can imagine a sequence of segments X,Y; if aspects of the pronunciation of X overlap with or influence the pronunciation of Y then the influence is moving forward. This direction of influence is termed **perseverative** (or 'progressive' or 'left-to-right'). Alternatively, if aspects of the pronunciation of Y overlap with or influence X then the influence is moving backwards. This direction of influence is termed **anticipatory** (or 'regressive' or 'right-to-left'). In English certainly, and probably in the majority of languages, anticipatory co-articulation is more common than perseverative. We will illustrate the two directions below, when we discuss the main functional categories of co-articulation.

A second division of this area concerns the aspects of articulation affected by co-articulation. Farnetani (1997) notes that there are four main vocal organs involved: lips, tongue, velum and larynx. This, of course, suggests that there are only four articulatory aspects, but this would be an over-simplification. The tongue, for example, is in effect a complex articulator, as tip and blade action is to a large extent independent of dorsum activity; the velum in Farnetani's classification covers the three-way distinction between oral, nasal and nasalized; and the larynx is Farnetani's cover term for all types of phonatory activity and how this is timed in respect to articulatory activity (e.g. stop release).

Our final division of co-articulation is the functional one. By this we mean that intersegmental co-ordination can have a variety of consequences in the phonology of the language. (This categorization, therefore, is phonological rather than purely phonetic.) If a segment slightly alters one of its phonetic features due to the influence of a neighbouring sound, and the resulting altered segment is still perceived by speakers of the language concerned as nothing more than a variant (or 'allophone') of the basic segment type, then we term this type of co-articulation **allophonic similitude**. On the other hand, if the number of features affected, or the amount of change undergone, is such that the altered segment is perceived to be a different segment type altogether (or different 'phoneme'), then we term this type of co-articulation **phonemic assimilation**. Assimilation can be partial, in that the changed segment is closer to, but not identical with the source of the influence; or total when the changed segment and the source segment become identical. Finally, we have to account for the fact that accommodation processes found in co-articulation need not be restricted to influence between neighbouring segments. We can find that a particular phonetic feature can spread across a series of segments, even a whole word or string of words.[3] If this results in the segments concerned altering only allophonically, we term this **allophonic feature spread**; on the other hand, if the result is a series of changed phonemes, this falls into the category normally termed **consonant** or **vowel harmony**. Naturally, this long range influence may result in mixed allophonic and phonemic changes.

The easiest way to illustrate this complex set of categories is to use examples from English, where possible. We show these in the following tables in terms functional category first, followed by articulator location, and then direction of influence.

In Table 7.3, the articulator places are those of the changed segment. Because these coarticulatory changes are normally phonetically greater than in similitudes, most articulator changes involve moving from one of the categories to another.

The Scots Gaelic example in Table 7.4 is slightly anomalous, in that this change does not occur after all word-final nasals, but is restricted to a small subset of these (i.e. a lexically conditioned change). This table does not include **coalescence**, which is the term used when two neighbouring segments are merged into a new and different segment (normally another phoneme of the language). An example from rapid colloquial speech in

---

[3] To some extent, this area overlaps with articulatory settings in supralaryngeal aspects of voice quality discussed in Chapter 6. However, here we are concerned only with features that spread due to their occurring in a segment within the utterance concerned.

Table 7.3 Allophonic similtudes

Anticipatory	Perseverative
Lips Lip rounding through consonants when followed by rounded vowel [tʷu] 'two'	Lip rounding during preliminary part of consonant following rounded vowel [ɔtʷ] 'ought'
Tongue tip/blade Dental articulation of [t] when preceding dental fricative [eɪt̪θ] 'eighth'	Post-alveolar articulation of [t] when following [ɹ] in rhotic accents of English [kɔɹt̠] 'court'
Tongue dorsum Fronted velar articulation of [k] before a front vowel [k̟i] 'key'	Fronted velar articulation of [ŋ] after a front vowel [sɪŋ̟] 'sing'
State of the velum Nasalization of vowel before nasal consonant [ō̃ʊn] 'own'	Nasalization during preliminary part of vowel following nasal consonant [nō̃ʊ] 'no'
Phonation Voicing of [h] word medially following a vowel [bəɦeɪv] 'behave'	Devoicing of nasals following voiceless consonants [sm̥oʊk] 'smoke'

Table 7.4 Phonemic assimilations

Anticipatory	Perseverative
Lips Alveolar to bilabial before bilabials [tem men] 'ten men'	[n] to [m] after bilabial plosive [hæpm̩] 'happen'
Tongue tip/blade Alveolar to post-alveolar before post-alveolars [ðiʒ ʃuz] 'these shoes'	Alveolar to post-alveolar after post-alveolars in some accents [kɔɹʃ] 'course'
Tongue dorsum Alveolar to velar before velars [teŋ kʌps] 'ten cups'	[n] to [ŋ] after velar plosive [beɪkŋ̩] 'bacon'
State of the velum Nasalization of alveolar stops/fricatives before [n] in rapid speech [dʌnn noʊ] 'doesn't know'	Scots Gaelic initial oral to nasal stops after certain words ending in nasal [nən] + [kat] > [nə ŋhat] 'of the cats'
Phonation Devoicing of fricatives before voiceless stops in certain phrases [hæf tu] 'have to'	[z] in 'is', 'has', etc. devoices in abbreviated form after voiceless stops [ðə kæts] 'the cat's . . . '

English would be 'hit you' being pronounced as [hɪt͡ʃu] instead of the more careful [hɪt ju].

In our final table (Table 7.5), we will include only one or two examples of feature spreading and segment harmony for illustrative purposes.

Theories of co-articulation

Farnetani (1997) discusses various theoretical approaches to speech production that would account for co-articulation. These are competing accounts, and as yet there is no one overall agreed model of co-articulation that would seem to support the facts from a large range of languages studied by phoneticians.

One approach views co-articulation as **speech economy**. This means that co-articulatory effects are viewed in the main as being strategies adopted by speakers to make the transition from one sound to another easier to manage. In this case, 'easier' might mean requiring fewer neuromuscular actions, or requiring fewer simultaneous neuromuscular actions. For example, a co-articulation that changes an alveolar to a dental stop before a dental fricative (as in Table 7.3), results in only one set of neuromuscular actions for the tongue tip, instead of two. Also, a co-articulation

Table 7.5 Feature spreading and segment harmony*

Feature spreading

Post-alveolar spreading in modern colloquial English; anticipatory	Across three segments, e.g. [ʃt̯ʲit] 'street'
Nasalization spread over vowels and approximants; anticipatory and perseverative	Across four segments, e.g. [ũĩnã] 'ulna'

Segment harmony

Vowel harmony in Turkish: vowels agree in frontness/backness and rounding; perseverative	Vowel in suffixes must harmonize with vowels in root:
	    [gøzym] eye + my 'my eye'
	    [evim] 'my house'
	    [kolum] 'my arm'
	    [adamɨm] 'my man'

Consonant harmony in Etsako: tense consonants can only occur with tense or neutral; lax consonants can only occur with lax or neutral	Lax consonants shown with added [h]:
	    [àgógô] 'bell'
	    [àghòghò] 'brains'

*More details on both harmony cases are given in Laver (1994).

that sees the velum lowering during a vowel preceding a nasal consonant means that this gesture does not have to be co-programmed with the tongue movement commands needed to move from vowel to nasal stop, thus easing possible overload on the neuromuscular system.

Speech economy can also be seen in the 'undershoot' found in rapid speech in areas such as vowel production (especially with diphthongs). In such cases, the 'canonical' realization of a vowel might not be reached, or the full glide of the diphthong may be curtailed. However, speech economy must also be balanced with the need to maintain contrastivity for the listener. So theorists have stressed the importance of acoustic and perceptual factors in deciding just how much variability can be allowed during co-articulation. For example, the exact articulation of Spanish /s/ seems to vary in different contexts much more than English /s/. This may well be because while English also has /ʃ/ (so /s/ cannot become too similar to that sound without risk of confusion), Spanish does not. This means that Spanish /s/ can become quite [ʃ]-like without risk of misinterpretation.

Other approaches to co-articulation have stressed the idea of **co-production**. Researchers holding this view see speech production as consisting of a series of articulatory gestures, which – rather than being produced sequentially and separately – are more likely to overlap. In this model, anticipatory co-articulation derives from the effects of a second gesture overlapping a previous one, whereas perseverative co-articulation derives from the carry-over of one gesture on to the gesture following it. Such views sit well with some recent models of phonology (for example, gestural phonology, *see* Kent, 1997a), and there is debate within phonetics as to the extent that co-articulation is rule-governed by the phonology of the language, or quasi-automatic responses to physical limitations of the vocal system.

Parametric phonetics[4]

Speech is a dynamic process, but phonetic symbolization treats it as if it were static. An alternative method of describing speech on paper that avoids the bias of traditional phonetic symbolization might well be useful, therefore. Parametric phonetic description attempts to augment IPA-like transcriptions, and to demonstrate how the range of phonetic features (or parameters) actually interact with each other in time in the course of a particular utterance. Such an approach will clearly allow us to illustrate the co-articulatory effects described earlier in the chapter.

We will explore first what phonetic parameters we might chose for such an approach, and then how they might be shown in diagrammatic form. We

---

[4] Much of this section is based on Ball (1993).

will conclude with examples of speech plotted onto parametric phonetic diagrams. Information on the pitch movements of intonation and other suprasegmental features, while possible to add, is not dealt with here. The resultant diagrams would be too cluttered to read with ease.

As noted in Chapter 3, both consonants and vowels have been described by three-term labels. However, this is the basic information required to tell one sound apart from another. The full range of phonetic parameters that can be exploited during periods of consonant-type articulations might include the following (slightly expanded from the set we presented in Chapter 3):

1 Air-stream mechanism: a) type, b) direction
2 Phonation/voice quality type
3 Manner of articulation
4 Place of articulation
5 Location of release a) median release, b) lateral release
6 Type of release (plosives): a) nasal, b) lateral, c) aspirated/unaspirated, d) affricated
7 Secondary articulations
8 State of the velum: a) oral, b) nasal, c) nasalized
9 Amount of air pressure (fortis/lenis)
10 Duration of segment.

For vowel-like articulations, a similar list might be drawn up:

1 Air-stream mechanism: a) type, b) direction
2 Phonation/voice quality type
3 Tongue height
4 Tongue position anterior–posterior
5 Lip-shape
6 Secondary articulations
7 State of the velum: a) oral, b) nasalized
8 Amount of tongue tension (tense/lax)
9 Duration of segment.

Even in a parametric account, some of this information can be treated as redundant: that is to say can be omitted unless marked as exceptional. For instance, we do not need to specify a pulmonic egressive air-stream unless another one is being used. Further, the fortis–lenis distinction usually co-occurs with voiceless–voiced, and the tense–lax with peripheral–non-peripheral. Finally, secondary articulations need only be marked if they are present, and if they contribute noticeably to the specific sound quality, and consonantal release can be considered central unless specified as lateral.

We are left then with some half-a-dozen parameters that need to be mapped for any utterance in a parametric transcription, and we can do this

via a **parametric phonetic diagram**. The basic format for a parametric phonetic diagram is agreed upon by most researchers in this area. We have
already seen basic diagrams of this type in Chapter 4 when we examined
various release types for plosives. The utterance in question is written
across the top (usually in IPA transcription), and below are several 'levels'
reserved for specific parameters (e.g. phonation, velic action etc.).

Disagreements arise as to how to characterize the states of the various
parameters. Basically, one approach has lines that move (for example)
upwards to show a raised velum, and downwards to show a lowered velum
(*see* Brosnahan and Malmberg, 1970), while the other would use a straight
line throughout but alter its form (e.g. dots or dashes) to show the change
in the velum. To some extent, of course, this is just a representational difference; but the use of a moving line in this instance does allow us to explic-
itly note the fact that different degrees of velic lowering occur at different
points in time, resulting in different degrees of nasality. Figure 7.3 illustrates these different approaches for just the velic parameter with the word
'sunny'.

Another, more intractable problem, concerns how to characterize place
and manner of articulation for consonants, and tongue height and position
for vowels. For place of articulation, the decision has to made whether the
active articulator, the passive articulator, or both will be represented. For
manner of articulation, on the other hand, we need to decide whether
differences between, for example, stop and fricative are shown simply by
different types of line, or whether we attempt to show these iconically by
illustrating different degrees of channel size through distances between a pair
of lines. Similarly for vowels: do we show tongue height and position simply
through the use of different line types, or do we use an iconic approach?

It is clearly easier to utilize the vertical space of parametric diagrams
than the horizontal (as that represents the time the utterance takes). One
solution, therefore, is to use the vertical space to show tongue height for both
consonants and vowels (i.e. manner of articulation for consonants), but to
represent place for consonants and position
for vowels by different line types. The problem
with this approach is the need for a large vertical space to be set aside for different degrees
of height. To simplify things, therefore, we
include a level for 'manner' to distinguish the
main articulation types. For consonants also,
we retain a different level for the division of
the tongue involved (also for side of the tongue
to show lateral release), and for the divisions
of the hard palate: this allows us to specify
things like retroflex articulation.

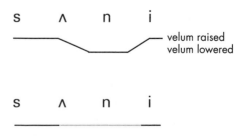

Figure 7.3 Velum diagram 'sunny'

The set of parameters, and their representation is shown below.

1 Phonation:
    Voiced: ᴧᴧᴧᴧᴧᴧᴧᴧᴧᴧ
    Voiceless: ————————

2 Velum (drawn high for raised, low for lowered):

    ⅢⅢⅢⅢⅢⅢⅢⅢⅢⅢⅢ

3 Manner of articulation:
    Stop: ⴽⴽⴽⴽⴽⴽⴽ
    Fricative: σσσσσσσσ
    Approximant: AAAAAAAA
    Vowel: ΩΩΩΩΩΩΩΩ

4 Division of tongue:
    Tip: ....
    Blade: ///////////////////////////
    Front: ----------------
    Back: \\\\\\\\\\\\\\\\\\\\\\\\\\\\\
    Side rims: ᵛᵛᵛᵛᵛᵛᵛᵛᵛᵛᵛᵛ

5 Division of the palate:
    Dental: ⊓⊓⊓⊓⊓⊓⊓⊓⊓⊓⊓
    Alveolar: ⊔⊔⊔⊔⊔⊔⊔⊔⊔⊔
    Palatal: ᵗᵗᵗᵗᵗᵗᵗᵗᵗᵗᵗᵗᵗ
    Velar: ⊂⊂⊂⊂⊂⊂⊂⊂⊂⊂⊂⊂⊂
    Uvular: ʁʁʁʁʁʁʁʁʁʁ
    Glottal: ʔʔʔʔʔʔʔʔʔʔʔʔʔ

6 Vowels:
    High: ⊥⊥⊥⊥⊥⊥⊥⊥⊥⊥⊥⊥
    Mid: ~~~~~~~~~~~~
    Low: ⊤⊤⊤⊤⊤⊤⊤⊤⊤⊤⊤⊤
    Front: ++++++++++++
    Back: ⊦⊦⊦⊦⊦⊦⊦⊦⊦⊦⊦⊦

7 Lips:
    Bilabial articulation: ∘∘∘∘∘∘∘∘∘∘∘∘∘∘∘∘
    Rounded: ∘∘∘∘∘∘∘∘∘∘∘∘∘∘
    Unrounded: ═══════

These diagrams run the risk of becoming too complicated if we attempt to integrate further information (for example, on secondary articulations and other places of articulation), but in principle there is, of course, no reason why they could not be further extended. In practice, we may well simplify our diagrams by using only those parameters that illustrate a particular point.

We will now show how the full set of parameters can be used to illustrate an utterance. The phrase is 'the topmost spire': [ðə ˈtʰɑpⁿmõ̃ũstʰ ˈsp⁼aɹɹ]

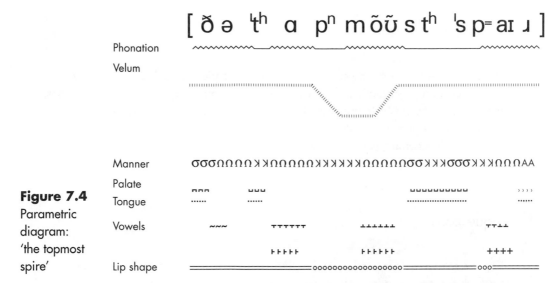

Figure 7.4
Parametric
diagram:
'the topmost
spire'

(General American pronunciation). This allows us to investigate various features, including aspirated versus unaspirated stops and voice onset time, nasal release, nasalization of vowels, diphthongs, and retroflexion. Figure 7.4 shows a full parametric diagram of this phrase, and you should study this to identify the features just mentioned. Note how the aspirated stops are followed by a period of voicelessness (shown at the vocal fold level) whereas the unaspirated one is not. Note also how the articulators do not move after the first [p], but remain where they are while the velum level shows the lowering of the soft palate; the raising of the soft palate shows how nasalization spreads into the following diphthong. Finally, the tongue tip line interacting with the palatal line shows the retroflexion at the end of the phrase.

Further reading

The main phonetics texts referred to in earlier chapters deal with double and secondary articulation. Laver (1994) can be recommended for detailed treatment. Co-articulation is not always dealt with in introductory texts. However, Laver (1994) discusses it and Farnetani (1997) deals with the theoretical issues in detail. Farnetani also has references to the classic early studies in co-articulation.

Little has been written on parametric phonetics and feature diagrams. An important reference, apart from Brosnahan and Malmberg (1970), is Tench (1978), who uses line movements rather than line types to show the interaction of parameters. Line types have been used in America, devised by R and J McCall (*see* Barton Payne, 1990). More example diagrams are found in Ball (1993).

Short questions

1 How are double articulations defined? Give some examples of double articulations.
2 How are secondary articulations defined? Give some examples of secondary articulations.
3 What are the problems with use of the term 'segment' in phonetic description?
4 List the directions of co-articulation, and the vocal organs involved.
5 List the main functional types of co-articulation.

Essay questions

1 Using the references provided, compare and contrast some of the theoretical models of co-articulation proposed in the literature.
2 Using any word or phrase of at least four syllables, undertake a parametric analysis and draw a parametric diagram, including all the main parameters described in the chapter.
3 Use parametric analysis and diagrams to describe the production of two double articulated consonants, and two consonants with secondary articulation from any language.

8   Principles and methods of phonetic transcription

Introduction

When we undertake the study of speech, it is inevitable that we will need to provide transcriptions of a range of segmental and suprasegmental aspects. Transcriptions are usually produced as a result of auditory analysis, where the transcriber listens to data and matches each sound with its nearest appropriate IPA target. It is this type of auditory impressionistic transcription which is discussed in the present chapter. Of course, it is possible to subject the auditory transcription to instrumental verification, and methods of acoustic investigation and quantification are discussed in Chapter 9. Here, we discuss the role of auditory phonetic transcription in the study of speech, explore differences between general and more detailed transcriptions, and offer guidance for carrying out transcriptions.

A note on phonetic ability

In our experience, there is a wide variety of ability among phonetics students, just as is the case for other academic disciplines. For students themselves, an initial difficulty with perceiving, producing and transcribing sounds is frequently a cause for concern. Shriberg *et al.* (1987, p. 91) for example, sum up variations in phonetic ability as follows:

> Every phonetician must have had the experience, at some time or other of meeting a person to whom the imitation of the most exotic sounds at first hearing presented no difficulty at all. At the other extreme are a more numerous minority . . . for whom any deviation from the native sound system is apparently impossible.

However, there is no reason for students who encounter such difficulty to despair, since sustained practice and hard work, combined with appropriate input from instructors will allow even those students who possess - less-than-ideal auditory skills to reach an acceptable standard (*see* Rosenthal, 1989; Strevens, 1978).

The role of auditory transcription in phonetics

At its most basic level, a phonetic transcription is an economical means for capturing speech sounds on paper, using largely the IPA as the central tool. (We have seen in this book, however, that we sometimes need to adopt symbolizations from sources other than the IPA, i.e. extIPA and VoQS.) A transcription provides a record of speakers' pronunciation across a variety of speech sounds and the information which is derived from a transcription might then be used, for example, as a description of one style of speaking or one accent versus another, or of normal versus disordered speech. In addition, a transcription can also help to highlight patterns of pronunciation which would be difficult to pinpoint just by listening alone. We may, for instance, notice auditorily that a speaker produces occasionally friction on a target /t/, so that the resulting sound is a so-called 'slit /t/', transcribed as [θ̲]. However, it may perhaps only be when we examine a transcription of a stretch of speech that we can confirm whether the process occurs randomly, or only in particular phonetic contexts, such as word-final or syllable-initial, for example. A phonetic transcription, therefore, provides an easily accessible tool for examining articulatory aspects of speech sounds. Later on in this chapter, we will outline the types of transcription that exist and suggest guidance for carrying out each type. Before this, however, we will clarify a number of terms which proliferate in the literature relating to phonetic transcription.

Terminology relating to transcription

At the outset, the student may encounter a potentially bewildering array of terms relating to the study of speech, such as **phone**, **allophone**, **phonetics**, **phonemics** and **phonology**. Admittedly, the phonetics literature has frequently been responsible for causing the confusion, so, given the lack of clarity concerning aspects of terminology, we will elucidate the relevant terms here. It is crucial that that students make every effort to understand them as a prerequisite to transcription.

The use of the term 'phonetic' is frequently wide-ranging and taken to mean simply 'anything to do with speech'. So, for instance, aspects such as the physiology of speech production, along with articulatory differences between vowels and consonants as well as smaller pronunciation details of individual sounds are considered to be 'phonetic'. Within this broad area, phonetics, we can identify three main areas which tend to attract academic interest, i.e. 'auditory phonetics', 'articulatory phonetics', and 'acoustic phonetics'. Auditory phonetics refers to the method of listening to and recognizing and differentiating sounds. Articulatory phonetics consists of the system of classifying sounds according to their articulatory categories. Finally, acoustic or instrumental phonetics deals with the measurement of speech, in terms of its physical properties of intensity, duration and frequency (*see* Chapter 9), or in terms of its dynamic articulatory properties. Whereas auditory and articulatory phonetics are subjective and impressionistic, acoustic phonetics provides quantitative evidence for the presence of absence of certain features.

Of course, we agree that all of the above aspects do indeed constitute the full range of phonetic study but, when we are dealing with transcriptional aspects, we need to have a more focused definition of the term. In this chapter, we will reserve the term 'phonetic' to refer to small articulatory differences between sounds so that /ɛ/ and /a/, for example, are distinguished on the grounds of vowel height.

A phonetic approach to speech, therefore, analyses the precise articulatory features of given sounds. A phonemic approach on the other hand, categorizes speech in terms of a number of general sound types, e.g. fricative versus plosive. The term 'phoneme', by implication, refers to general classes of sound, so that we can refer to all of the sounds on the consonant grid and vowel trapezium of the IPA as phonemes. Consonant phonemes are specifiable in terms of their mode of phonation, place and manner of articulation while vowel phonemes are classified according to tongue height, tongue advancement and lip-rounding features. Although it is certainly the case that substituting one of these phonemes for another may change the meaning of the word that is produced, we do not, at this stage, wish to invoke the notion of meaning differences as forming part of our definition. It is sufficient at this point to state that all sounds are *potentially* contrastive, i.e. it is possible that substituting one for another will result in a change of meaning.

Phonemic and phonetic transcription

As we have stated above, transcription seeks to capture speech sounds on paper. Before we undertake a transcription, however, we must decide how detailed we wish it to be. Our recommendation is that we always seek to transcribe as accurately as possible, i.e. by recording all the articulatory detail that exists in the speech sample. So, for instance, we might need to indicate that the /m/ sound in 'home' is idiosyncratically realized as[m̥], i.e. as a voiceless bilabial nasal. When we have produced such an analysis, we can, if necessary, exclude from the transcription any detail which we deem to be unimportant for the next stage of our investigation. For instance, we may decide that we wish to pursue an analysis of voicing characteristics of consonants, i.e. whether fully voiced or voiceless, or having an intermediate voicing characteristic. On the other hand, if our transcription is made only with reference to general phoneme categories then it will be impossible to infer articulatory details from that transcription at a later stage of analysis. We therefore would assume that all target alveolar nasals are, in fact, voiced. A phonemic transcription, therefore, has the potential to be misleading.

It is as well to point out at this stage, however, that the perfect or ideal phonetic transcription probably does not exist, given that transcribers are likely to differ in at least a small way in their transcription of various sounds. Indeed, it may be the case that an individual transcriber produces somewhat different transcriptions of the same data sample at different time intervals. These phenomena are known as **inter-transcriber** and **intra-transcriber** variability, respectively. Nevertheless, it is important that we aim for a high level of accuracy when we transcribe, and it is also important that our transcriptions can be subject to reliability checks either from our peers or teachers. Edwards (1986) provides targets of accuracy to aim for in transcription. She suggests that a score of 95 per cent success in transcribing real words and 90 per cent for nonsense words should be achieved in each exercise before students proceed to the next one. These targets are effective means of monitoring progress in transcription, both for teachers and for the students. The targets are also effective in reminding us of the need for accuracy in transcription.

Types of information recorded in phonetic transcriptions

As has been indicated above, transcription offers us the option of indicating either general or detailed contrasts between sounds. A general transcription may be referred to as **phonemic** or **broad**, because it attempts to capture broad differences. A more detailed or phonetic transcription is also known as **narrow**, since it captures the exact articulatory details of each sound. On the one hand, the consonant grid and the vowel trapezium provided by the IPA identify only general categories of sounds. As we have said above, each one of these sounds may be thought of as a phoneme, in the sense that each has the potential to function contrastively. So, for instance, we might use the resources of the consonant chart and the vowel chart to transcribe an utterance in the following way:

Does she even need to ask for permission?
[dʌz ʃi ivən nid tu ask fɔ pəmɪʃən]

Inherent in this transcription is the assumption that each of the written symbols is an accurate representation of the spoken sample. The first consonant in the example, for instance, suggests a sound which is voiced and alveolar. With regard to the third and the fourth sound, the implication is that the speaker produces a voiced alveolar fricative, then moves the lingual obstruction to the post-alveolar place of articulation while simultaneously stopping the vocal folds from vibrating. In the case of vowels, the [i] suggests that the speaker is pronouncing a fully front, fully close vowel, i.e. Cardinal Vowel 1. It may well be that, in a hyper-formal citation type of realization, a speaker does pronounce the given sentence in this way. However, there may well be cases in which we would want to indicate that a speaker produces the /d/ with the tongue behind the upper teeth, hence [d̪] or that the articulation of two potential consonant sounds is collapsed into a single one, hence /z/ and /ʃ/ become merely [ʃ]. With regard to vowels, we might need to specify that realizations are lower, for example, than the Cardinal vowel transcription suggests. Given that we wish to indicate this level of phonetic or articulatory detail in transcription, we will need to use a narrow or phonetic transcription.

The IPA offers a set of so-called **diacritics**, whose purpose it is to indicate narrowing, or articulatory detail. These diacritics provide us with the capability of indicating, for example, that a particular vowel in a given speaker's accent is produced further forward than the nearest Cardinal vowel equivalent, or with more lip-rounding. The full range of IPA diacritics is given in Figure 8.1 whilst Figure 8.2 demonstrates how they relate to vowel categories.

Learning transcriptional skills: the contribution of auditory and articulatory phonetics and phonology

The process of learning phonetic transcription is rather like learning a second language. In language learning, it is crucial that we acquire a set of tools, such as how to pronounce the sounds of the new language, what the words mean and how words go together to make sentences. Similarly, in learning transcriptional skills, we have to become proficient in recognizing, producing and capturing the symbol which corresponds to particular sound types. However, we wish to point out forcefully that transcription is not merely a memory test in which listeners match a perceived sound up with a symbol which is stored in a listener's mental dictionary. Such sound–symbol

DIACRITICS   Diacritics may be place above a symbol with a descender, e.g. ŋ̊

◌̥	Voiceless	n̥ d̥	◌̈	Breathy voiced	b̤ a̤	◌̩	Dental	t̪ d̪
◌̌	Voiced	s̬ t̬	◌̰	Creaky voiced	b̰ a̰	◌̺	Apical	t̺ d̺
◌ʰ	Aspirated	tʰ dʰ	◌̼	Linguolabial	tA d̼	◌̻	Laminal	t̻ d̻
◌̜	More rounded	ɔ̹	◌ʷ	Labialised	tʷ dʷ	◌̃	Nasalised	ẽ
◌̜	Less rounded	ɔ̜	◌ʲ	Palatalised	tʲ dʲ	◌ⁿ	Nasal realease	d
◌̟	Advanced	u̟	◌ˠ	Velarised	tˠ dˠ	◌ˡ	Lateral release	d
◌̠	Retracted	e̠	◌ˤ	Pharyngealised	tˤ dˤ	◌̚	No audible release	d
◌̈	Centralised	ë	◌̴	Velarised or pharyngealised	ʱ			
◌̽	Mid-centralised	e̽	◌̝	Raised	e̝	(ɹ̝ = a voiced alveolar fricative)		
◌̩	Syllabic	n̩	◌̞	Lowered	e̞	(β̞ = voiced bilabial approximant)		
◌̯	Non-syllabic	e̯	◌̘	Advanced tongue root	e̘			
◌˞	Rhoticity	ɚ ɚ	◌̙	Retracted tongue root	e̙			

Figure 8.1 IPA diacritics

matching is no more than the first step and, if we were to progress no further than this, we would manage to produce nothing better than a broad phonemic transcription of speech, the inadequacies of which we have already explained.

When we are attempting to acquire transcriptional skills, it is also crucial that we equip ourselves with abilities in auditory and articulatory phonetics. Auditory phonetics, i.e. the sub-field within phonetics which trains listeners to focus on individual speech sounds, enables us to identify sounds that we hear and to recognize contrasts between one sound and another. Articulatory phonetics allows us to classify sounds according to their articulatory make-up and provides a set of target points within the vocal apparatus for us to follow. So, for instance, if we hear a vowel which differs from its nearest Cardinal equivalent, we need to be able to reproduce the sound and relate the auditory difference to the activity of the articulators in the vocal cavity.

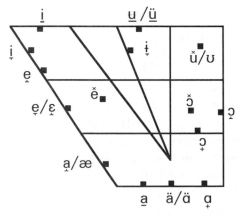

Figure 8.2 Diacritic usage with vowels

Indicating phonological aspects of speech in transcription

As stated above, skills in auditory and articulatory phonetics provide important contexts for carrying out phonetic transcription. In addition, a knowledge of the phonology of speech is also helpful. For our present purposes, we will define phonology as aspects of connected speech which derive from the transition of one sound to another. We might also refer to such aspects of connected speech as **co-articulation** or **phonological processes**. For example, students will frequently assume that 'strength' is produced as [stɹɛŋθ] and, while this may be a possible pronunciation, it is more likely that [stɹɛŋkθ] represents an naturalistic pronunciation. Using this example, we can state that, in naturalistic speech, a phonological process of **insertion** has operated, whereby the inserted velar plosive provides an anchor point for the back of the tongue, as it moves from a velar to a dental place of articulation. Although listeners may not have been aware of this process on initial listening, the new knowledge that such processes may occur helps train their ears to listen for similar phenomena elsewhere. We can best view the phonological organization of speech as a set of processes (*see* Grunwell, 1987; Hodson, 1980; Ingram, 1981; Shriberg and Kwiatowski, 1980; Weiner, 1979).These processes fall into two general categories, i.e. **substitutions** (where the target phoneme is realized by a sound which differs in some phonetic respect from the target) and **omissions** (where a target sound is completely left out). Within the category of substitutions, we can envisage examples of assimilation and dissimilation.

Since these processes do not occur for all speakers, so we can refer to them as being **optional**. There are also several **obligatory** phonological processes which operate in English, i.e. processes which are thought to be physiologically dictated and therefore outside the control of the speaker, such as vowel nasalization in the environment of a nasal consonant, or aspiration of a voiceless plosive where the plosive occurs in stressed word-initial, syllable-initial position. It might be argued that, if these processes are obligatory and predictable, there is no need to indicate them in transcription. However, we wish to argue here that obligatory processes should be recorded, since the ideas of compulsory and predictable may vary according to the particular variety of speech which is produced, and it will also differ between normal and disordered speech. In the section which follows, we will suggest some tools which you might use for training yourselves to arrive at a realistic transcription.

The phoneme and phonemic analysis

Above, we have defined a phoneme as a general sound category. Using this definition, all the sounds represented on the IPA consonant and vowel charts constitute phonemes. Traditionally, however, the term 'phoneme' has been reserved for a speech sound that, when substituted for another, brings about a change in meaning. For example, in the English word 'flint', there are five separate speech sounds or phonemes, that is /f, l, ɪ, n, t/. In a further English word glint, there are also five speech sounds, /g, l, ɪ, n, t/. The only difference between 'flint' and 'glint' is the initial sound in each word and the meaning of the words. When we substitute /g/ for /f/ in this way and bring about a change in meaning, we say that the sounds in question are phonemes and that there is a phonemic distinction between them. A pair of phonemes is also known as a **minimal pair**.

Phonemic distinctions can occur in any position within a word. We could also identify, for example, a word-medial phonemic distinction, where the /d/ and /l/ in 'bidding' and 'billing' constitute separate phonemes, as well as word-final phonemes such as the /s/ and /g/ in *place* and *plague*. It is important to note that when we are attempting to identify phonemes we must do so on the basis of sounds which occur in identical positions in otherwise identical items (i.e. in **parallel distribution**).

We can also identify phonemic contrasts on the basis of units somewhat smaller than the traditional segment. In some varieties of English, for example, differences in vowel length may be responsible for a phonemic difference, 'heed' [hid] versus 'he'd' [hiːd] and 'road' [rod] versus 'rowed' [roːd]. The concept of sound change resulting in meaning change or contrastivity is therefore central to the definition of phoneme.

If the substitution of one feature for another does *not* result in a change in meaning, then we say that the sounds or features in question are in **free variation**. For example, in some varieties of English, we have the glottal stop frequently substituted for a /t/. These substitutions are merely alternative phonetic realizations of the target sound, they do not result in a change of meaning.

When we undertake an analysis of a speaker's output, it is likely that we will want to uncover the full range of phonemic contrasts that the speaker can produce, as well as their articulatory capabilities. This will be relevant, for example, in determining the phonological stage that a child has reached. The phonemic system of normal adult English speakers contains approximately 40 sounds, i.e. 40 sounds which are potentially contrastive. Of these 40, 24 are vowels and 16 are vowels (for a discussion of the phonemic inventories in a range of languages, *see* Laver, 1994, p. 573). The consonant phonemes are given in Figure 8.3. The task of establishing the core vowel phonemes of English, however, is less straightforward, because enormous variation exists in vowel realization for most accents. For RP and GenAm, though, see Wells's (1990) list of vowel phonemes which he categorizes in terms of short vowels, long vowels and diphthongs.

```
   m              n         ŋ
p     b        t  d  tʃ  dʒ  k  g
f  v  θ  ð  s  z  ʃ     ʒ
   w              l r     j     h
```

Figure 8.3 Inventory of consonant phonemes

Whereas the notion of phonemic contrasts underpins much of successful communication (it is, for example, important that speakers master the /p, f/ contrast if they are able to make the distinction between 'pair' and 'fair'), we might envisage situations where the normal system of phonemic contrasts has broken down either temporarily, or more permanently. For example, speakers with dental appliances may have difficulty with dental sounds, so that the required /s, θ/ contrast for 'mouse' and 'mouth' is not made. In cases such as this, listeners are reliant on the context in order to interpret the utterance. Without the aid of context, such phonemic collapses would have a significant effect on intelligibility and communication.

From what we have said in this section, it will be clear that a phonetic analysis combined with a phonological description of speech offers a usefully detailed account. One type of analysis without the other runs the risk of being somewhat limited. For example, if we perform a solely phonemic transcription, the underlying assumption is that phonetic variation is either non-existent or unimportant.

Do we store sounds as phonemes or allophones?

The aspects of phonetic and phonemic analysis and transcription, along with insights from phonological organization which we have been discussing so far in this chapter obviously provide us with a useful means of understanding important strands in the study of speech. However, they also offer us a framework for understanding some of the mental processes which operate when we produce speech. For example, while we know that we can transcribe sounds depending on whether they are targets or allophonic variants, it may be interesting to ask how we actually store these sounds in the brain. Do all speakers of English, for example, store a set of target phonemes in their mental lexicon and just add the appropriate articulatory variation at will? Or is it the fact that we store sounds in their allophonic form? This aspect of phonetic study, i.e. in which we attempt to explain how listeners and speakers organize and perceive speech is known as **psycholinguistics**.

Within the discipline of psycholinguistics, it is suggested that speech production and perception can be described in two possible ways, i.e. using either a **phonological** or a **physiological** model. The phonological model suggests that we store sounds as discrete phonemes and that narrow phonetic details are not important. So, for instance, we store /z/ rather than [z̥], i.e. a devoiced variety of /z/. According to phonological models, when we need to produce speech, the required sounds are transmitted in the form of a series of neural impulses. In the case of /s/ followed by /l/, for example, various nerves control voicelessness, frication and alveolar place of articulation. They then return to rest and regroup themselves in order to produce voice, lateral stricture and a second alveolar place of articulation. Physiological models of speech production, on the other hand, state that such a rigid phonemic ordering of sounds would be physically difficult, if not impossible to achieve. They suggest, by contrast, that sounds may be produced simultaneously and overlap with one another. This notion of inter-relationships among sounds, i.e. whereby one sound affects another, is part of what we have been referring to in this book as 'phonology', and has also been described as 'parametric phonetics' (*see* Ball, 1993; Laver, 1994).

It is interesting to question whether listeners perceive speech either on a phonemic level or a phonetic level. Once more, phonological models tend to suggest that we understand speech by processing it on a broad phonemic level. So, when we hear a word such as [bʌtəɹ] the particular allophonic detail of the /t/ (which may indicate the speaker's regional background, for instance) is a level of message-decoding that comes after the basic interpretation of the semantic meaning. The physiological studies, however, suggest that the allophonic decoding is part and parcel of the overall perception of the speech signal.

What do we need to transcribe?

Since we have established that we wish our transcriptions to be accurate reflections of a speaker's output, it is clearly important that we sample a range of speech styles, i.e. formal and informal. Many existing textbooks in phonetics pay rather little attention to the kind of detailed articulatory aspects of sounds we have mentioned above. Instead, they tend to focus on a largely phonemic approach to transcription. The implication of using phonemically oriented textbooks is that students may well become adept at phonemic transcription without having any idea how to approach tasks where more detailed analysis is required. In this book, our aim is to target detailed phonetic listening, using data from a range of accent and style-varied contexts. Even though formalized data, such as nonsense words and citation forms, offer an important means of training listeners to achieve auditory competence, we must aim towards a detailed transcription of realistic, casual speech forms. In the next section, we look at methods for acquiring the skills which are necessary for producing a detailed phonetic transcription.

Materials for learning phonetic transcription

Here, we suggest a number of tools for equipping students with the skills which are necessary for phonetic transcription, and it is hoped that many of the methods we discuss will also be relevant to the more advanced student. In particular, we examine the role of computer programs, books, audiotapes and videotapes. While not all of these materials are overtly designed to help with transcription, they do, however, highlight a number of auditory and articulatory skills which, as we have seen, are a crucial prerequisite to transcription.

Books

It is probably true to say that most students learn their introductory phonetics largely from a textbook. However, whilst a textbook can offer a solid grounding in the explanation of phonetic terms and concepts, it can never offer the auditory stimulation which is a crucial element of phonetics learning. Furthermore, as we have stated, existing textbooks tend to concentrate on only a broad phonemic approach to transcription. One of the few exceptions is Laver's (1994) *Principles of Phonetics* which contains a detailed section on principles of transcription, with particular focus on the phonemic/phonetic distinction. We might therefore envisage a situation, for instance, where students could acquire detailed competence in describing all the IPA phonemes without actually recognizing them when they occur in their own speech. Clearly, it would be highly dubious to refer to such a skill as a truly phonetic ability. So, it is important to *hear* each one as it is introduced and it is crucial to be able to reproduce each one, for the purpose of identifying articulatory activity. In fact, when it comes to identifying and transcribing allophonic detail in speech, transcribers can do so only on the basis of identifying and reproducing the original sound.

Audio recordings

Given that auditory skill is an requirement for transcription, it is obviously crucial that students are exposed to a range of speech samples in order to enhance their perceptive abilities. While many samples may, of course, be provided live in the classroom context, it is important that additional audio-taped material is also used, for use outside class. Such tapes may be provided by the teacher, as an accompaniment to the phonetics course, or they may be available on a commercial basis. In all cases, taped material should be used to reinforce particular aspects of phonetics. Classes on accent variation, for example, might link up with taped sections where students are asked to transcribe target vowels in a range of accents.

Video recordings

In this section, we wish to highlight two main types of video-taped materials which are likely to be of use in acquiring transcriptional skills. First, there are those which provide visual imaging of the activity of the vocal organs and the articulators during speech production. For example, it may well be the case that a student who has difficulty with relating vowel theory to lingual activity might be aided by an X-ray video of the tongue. It will also be possible to gain a greater understanding of lingual activity and dynamism during speech production by means of videos which were developed to explain certain investigative phonetic techniques, such as electropalatography (EPG). Of course, the ideal situation would be for students to perform EPG investigation themselves, i.e. by use of a pseudopalate interfaced with appropriate computer software. However, where such facilities are unavailable, video extracts have the potential to illustrate basic points. Figure 8.4, for example, shows a sample video screen of normal and abnormal productions of a target sound.

The second category of video material has, perhaps, a more obvious application to transcription skills, insofar as it demonstrates a range of speech sounds produced by live speakers. By hearing and watching the speakers, it is possible to acquire prowess in auditory training and in recognizing the visual cues which enable the identification of speech sounds.

Computer software

In recent years, the use of computerized phonetics learning packages has become widespread. Most packages contain similar components and target general phoneme identification skills. They allow students to perform two main tasks, i.e. to hear individual IPA sounds by clicking on an appropriate symbol, and to identify IPA sounds which the computer generates randomly, in the format of a quiz. Figure 8.5, for instance, shows the screen from the vowel section of phonetic symbolic guide, while Figure 8.6 shows the consonant screen.

Some programs, however, are rather more ambitious than those mentioned above. For example, as well as containing symbols and digitized sounds corresponding to each symbol, *Phonetics Training Tools* shows vocal tract configurations for every sound. Such a means of presentation allows users to view articulatory activity in a way which has only previously been available to those engaged in phonetics research. (We should note, however, that as many of these programs were prepared pre-1986, they do not incorporate the 1989 revisions to particular IPA symbols.)

The software packages mentioned above play an important role in acquiring the skills which are needed for phonetic transcription, but there are also packages available which target transcriptional skills directly. Without doubt, the most valuable of these is the IPA

Figure 8.4 An electropalatographic trace

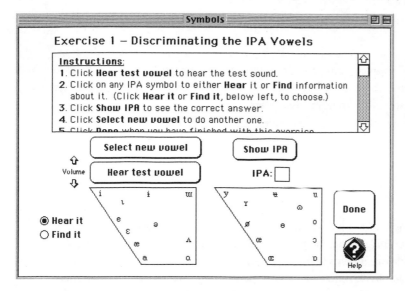

Figure 8.5 Vowel screen from 'Phonetic Symbol Guide–Electronic Edition'

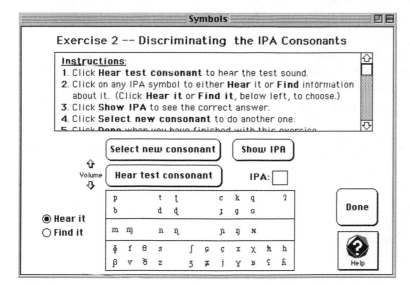

Figure 8.6 Consonant screen from 'Phonetic Symbol Guide–Electronic Edition'

Transcription Tutorial Model 4335 program running on the Kay Computerized Speech Lab™ (CSL). Although this allows us to perform the tasks which are covered in more basic programs (i.e. sound–symbol correspondences), it also enables students to assign symbols to their own data. For example, if users have difficulty in choosing a symbol to represent particular pronunciations, they can view stored samples of similar sounds along with their spectrographic and palatographic versions. They can, therefore, decide which sound corresponds most closely to the one they are investigating.

Summary

In this chapter, we have covered a range of topics which are important for successful auditory transcription, where 'successful' means that the transcription has captured detailed articulatory aspects of the original sample. We have also offered some guidance for training oneself to acquire the skills which are necessary prerequisites to the transcription process.

Further reading

With respect to transcription, the best work that can be done is to engage in the task itself as often as possible. For this reason, the tasks given in the questions below are of a practical nature. In addition, it helps to train oneself in auditory skills, using the techniques mentioned in this chapter. With regard to video-taped material which helps to enhance perceptual phonetics, those produced by the University of Edinburgh, UK, are particularly valuable. The videotape illustrating the technique of electropalatography is available from the Department of Linguistic Science at the University of Reading, UK. The 'Phonetic Symbol Guide–Electronic Edition' (PSG) is a HyperCard-based version of Pullum and Ladusaw's (1986) book *Phonetic Symbol Guide*, whereas the Kay software referred to is *IPA Transcription Tutorial Model 4335* program running on the Kay Computerized Speech Lab™ (CSL). *Phonetics Training Tools* is available from the Department of Linguistics, University of Michigan.

Short questions

1   Give the phonetic symbols for the consonants in the following words:

rough	[	]
hymn	[	]
cough	[	]
catch	[	]

2   Produce the following consonant sounds (followed by a vowel sound):

[w]	[s]
[ʃ]	[x]
[dʒ]	[ŋ]
[ʍ]	[ð]
[θ]	[j]

3 Give the phonetic symbol which corresponds to each of the following descriptions. Then produce each of the sounds.

voiced, bilabial, plosive	[ ]
voiceless, bilabial, plosive	[ ]
voiced, velar, nasal	[ ]
voiceless, labio-dental, fricative	[ ]
voiced, velar, plosive	[ ]
voiceless, velar, fricative	[ ]
voiced, alveolar, approximant	[ ]
voiced, palatal, approximant	[ ]
voiced, alveolar, tap or flap	[ ]
voiceless, post-alveolar, fricative	[ ]

4 State whether the following descriptions are possible articulations.

voiced, bilabial, nasal
voiced, alveolar, ejective
voiceless, glottal, fricative
voiced, bilabial, implosive
voiced, palatal, fricative.

5 State whether the following descriptions constitute possible vowel articulations or not. If the articulation is possible, give the appropriate IPA symbol for the sound.

front, close, unrounded
front, open-mid, close, rounded
back, central, close, rounded
back, centralized, close, rounded
back, open, rounded.

Essay questions

1 What role does phonetic transcription play in accounts of speech production characteristics of individuals?
2 How have psycholinguists attempted to explain how language is stored in the brain and transmitted to the appropriate vocal organs?
3 Explain the notion of 'contrastive function' with regard to English, or one other language with which you are familiar.

9   Acoustic characteristics of speech

Introduction

For most of this book, we have been discussing ear-based approaches to phonetic study. Such approaches have an important place in phonetics, since not even the most basic of analyses could be performed without reasonable auditory skills. Nevertheless, there are, inevitably, cases where solely ear-based approaches are inadequate. For example, when our transcription indicates that particular sounds have certain articulatory features, we may wish to confirm that these articulatory characteristics are, in fact, present acoustically. As well as satisfying our own aims towards accuracy, we may also need to prove to others that our descriptions or transcriptions are correct, and acoustic analysis offers a useful tool in this process.

Furthermore, in legal trials, for instance, phoneticians are increasingly being called upon as expert witnesses. They may, for example, be asked to comment on whether the voice on a tape-recorded phone call is likely to be that of a given suspect. In such cases, it is obviously important for phoneticians to offer some acoustic, quantifiable data to back up their opinions.

Finally, there are other situations where *only* acoustic measurements have any real validity. For instance, if we wish to focus on the pitch of a speaker's voice then auditory analysis will merely allow us to state that one speaker is relatively high or low in comparison to another speaker, or that that speaker has a comparatively wider or narrower pitch range. However, we can only offer quantifiable evidence for such impressions when we carry out acoustic analysis. Indeed, we imagine that the future of phonetic study may move in the direction of largely acoustic accounts, and away from the traditional impressionistic and auditory bias.

In this chapter, we will introduce aspects of the acoustics of speech transmission, with particular focus on pitch and intensity. We will then explain methods for measuring these features and we will suggest some contexts in which the results might provide interesting insights to various aspects of phonetic study.

The acoustics of speech transmission

When we hear the speech of people we know well, we are aware of a number of aspects which characterize those speakers in particular and distinguish them from others. For instance, males will usually speak at a lower pitch level than females, and members of a given speech community may tend to produce vowels and consonants somewhat differently to those outside the community, even though they share the same overall inventory of sounds. As well as recognizing these relatively permanent traits in speech output, we may also notice when individuals speak, for example, more loudly than usual, or at a higher pitch than is normal, or with a rather nasal voice. These temporary modifications to the speech may lead us to infer that the speaker is angry, or nervous, or suffering from the cold. All of these features, i.e. loudness and pitch and nasal resonance, are aspects of the acoustic make-up of the speech. Despite the fact that listeners tend to be intuitively aware of such aspects of the speech signal, and routinely use them to identify speakers and to decode mood, we are rarely informed as to how the full range of acoustic properties of speech contributes to the overall message. In this section, we will explain the acoustic properties of speech, and demonstrate how modifications to each of these acoustic aspects affects the speech signal.

Aspects of sound transmission

Every sound, whether speech or non-speech, begins with a body of air which is set in vibration. As we will explain in Chapter 10, it is this vibrating body of air which stimulates the nerves of the auditory system, thus transmitting sound waves to the inner ear. The particular type of sound which is produced will vary according to two main factors. The first of these concerns the size and the shape of the body of air in question. A short and narrow body of air in vibration will produce a higher pitched sound than will a longer and wider body or air (a piccolo, for instance, will sound an octave higher than a flute, because of the piccolo's smaller size). Second, the sound will vary depending on how forcefully it is produced. As a general rule, a forceful initiation will result in a relatively loud sound while a comparatively weak initiation will produce a quieter sound.

We can illustrate the process of sound transmission in more detail using the simple example of a pendulum in motion. The process of setting a pendulum in motion consists of three main stages which are schematized in Figure 9.1.

First, the pendulum begins at a position of rest (C). Second, it is hit so that it moves away from the rest position. The more forcefully the pendulum is hit, the greater the disturbance to the surrounding air will be, and the further it will move away from the rest position. Once it has reached the furthest point beyond the rest position (B) its action reverses and it attempts to return to rest. However, the movement has, by this stage, built up momentum and the effect of this momentum is that the pendulum is pushed beyond the rest position. As a result, it overshoots the rest position, and arrives at position (A). The movement of the pendulum will continue until it loses momentum, either gradually, or by being physically damped.

We can translate the simple movement of the pendulum into an acoustic representation known as a **waveform**. In Figure 9.2, the waveform illustrates a movement from rest to positions above and below the rest line. We can describe the movement from rest to position 2, through position 3 and back to rest again as a **cycle**, whereas the distance from rest to the peak of the wave is known as **displacement**.

Simple and complex waveforms

We have shown in Figures 9.1 and 9.2 that certain sounds produce visually regular waveforms. In each case, the rather neat rising and falling contours

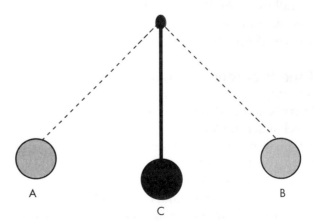

Figure 9.1 A pendulum in motion

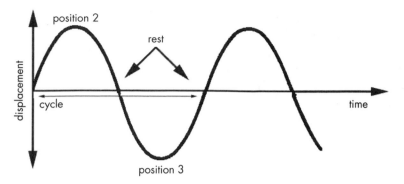

Figure 9. 2 A sound waveform in diagrammatic form

of the waveform reflect the backwards and forwards movement of body of air in vibration. This kind of regular waveform is known as a **simple** or **periodic** wave form. Other simple waveforms would be produced by a tuning fork being hit off a hard surface, or a drum consistently being hit in the same place. In all of these cases, the sound produces regular vibrations in the inner ear of the listener (the role of the ear in receiving sound vibration will be discussed further in Chapter 10). However, not all waveforms are simple. In speech, for instance, there will be waveforms of the type shown in Figure 9.2 but, within each cycle (e.g. from A to B), it is likely that further components, or cycles, will be present, in the form of a **complex** or **aperiodic** wave, as illustrated in Figure 9.3.

In speech, it is likely that we will have a combination of relatively simple and complex wave forms, as Figure 9.4 illustrates for a short stretch of speech.

This variation between simple and complex waveforms comes about because, as we have seen, speech production is the result of a number of interacting aspects. The basic frequency, or **fundamental frequency** (F_0) of speech derives from the rate of vibration of the vocal folds, and this particular wave is known as the **source** wave. The other frequencies, i.e. those which are above the basic frequency, are known as **filters** or **harmonics** and are multiples of the fundamental. If the vocal folds, for instance, vibrate at 150 Hz per second, then the second harmonic will be at approximately 300 Hz, the third will be at 450 Hz and so on. The location of each of the harmonics has varying and complex effects on the air pressure levels and they produce sound waves which frequently move up and down in a fairly complex manner, rather than in straightforward regular motion. Once the airstream passes into the oral tract, it is further modified, or filtered. The effect of this filtering is that sounds at certain frequencies will be exaggerated or deleted. So, in summary, the complex waveform which characterizes speech comes about as a result of the vocal fold vibration combined with the filtering effect of the articulators and the vocal tract.

Figure 9.3 A complex speech wave

Figure 9.4 Combination of simple and complex waves in speech

Frequency and pitch

In addition to merely producing a sound by causing a body of air to vibrate, it is also possible to exert some control over the quality of the sound that is finally produced. If we were to imagine plucking an elastic band, for instance, it should be clear that certain aspects would affect the pitch of the sound. For example, if we were to tighten the string while applying the same degree of force then the pitch of the sound would rise. If we were to loosen the tension on the string, however, the sound will lower in pitch. In effect, our perception of pitch in this case relates to the number of cycles that that are completed within a given time. For example, in Figure 9.5, the portion at (b) will be higher than the portion at (a), because (b) contains more cycles. In acoustics, cycles are measured in seconds, and cycles per second are usually known as Hertz. So, a waveform of 200 Hz for instance, means that 200 cycles are completed per second.

We have mentioned that an elastic band with a relatively high tension will, when plucked, vibrate more quickly and, therefore, produce a higher pitch than a comparatively lax band. In speech, similarly, the relative pitch of a sound derives from the speed of vibration and tension of the vocal folds, combined with their inherent size and shape. Table 9.1, for example, summarizes data from Baken (1987), where average F_0 measurements are given for various groups of speakers in reading and conversational styles of speech.

Table 9.1 Average F_0 measurements

Speaker sex	Speaker age (average for group)	Style of speech task	Mean value (Hz)
Male	20.3	Spontaneous	157
Male	73.3	Spontaneous	119.3
Male	45.4	Reading	107.1
Female	24.6	Reading	224.3
Female	35.4	Reading	213.3
Female	85	Reading	199.8

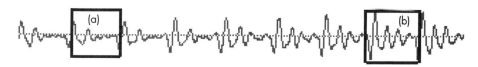

Figure 9.5 Waveform cycles

Of course there will be occasions on which pitch is absent during speech production, i.e. during voiceless sounds.

It is as well to point out at this stage that our perception of pitch does not relate in a simple way to Hertz measurements. For instance, if we were to hear two sounds one of 200 Hz and the other of 400 Hz, we would not judge the second to be twice as high as the first one. Additionally, our ears tend to be much more sensitive to pitch and to pitch changes in the lower frequencies, compared to changes in the higher frequencies. Our perception of pitch, in fact, is measured following the **mel scale** which provides a logarithmic rather than a linear scale. The mel scale, and other means for measuring perceived pitch valves, will be discussed in more details in Chapter 11.

Amplitude, intensity and loudness

We have said above that it is possible to initiate sounds with greater or lesser force, resulting in differences in perceived loudness. In order to illustrate this point, we might think of the example of producing the same syllable, once loud and once quiet. Although the syllables contain the same cycles per second, the effect of greater or lesser displacement varies, reflecting the greater or lesser disturbances of air. For the purposes of general acoustics, this displacement is known as **amplitude** but, for speech research, we usually refer to **intensity**. Intensity, therefore, is the acoustic basis of what we perceive as loudness and it is the result of the energy of the displacement of air. The relative intensity of a range of English vowel sounds is given in Table 9.2.

For a combination of speech and non-speech sounds, Fry (1979, p. 94) offers some sample decibel measurements which are summarized in Table 9.3.

Resonance

As well as each sound having its own frequency and intensity, it will also have its own quality. So, for instance, an oboe playing concert note A at 440 cycles per second will sound quite different to a French horn tuning to the same note. These differences in sounds are effected by the resonant properties of each of the instruments, i.e. its size, its shape and the material from which it is made. The resonant properties of any given speech sound are dictated by a number of factors: the size and shape of the sound source, and the size and shape of the chamber into which the sound is directed from the source. Using the example of the elastic band once more, if we just hold it between out fingers and pluck it, it will sound twangy. However, if we attach it to a simple box and pluck it, it will sound somewhat more resonant. On the other hand, if we were hold a mute inside the bell of a

French horn, the chamber into which the air is directed is made smaller, and the sound will appear thinner and less resonant.

For speech, we have seen from Tables 9.2 and 9.3 that sounds have a target frequencies and target amplitudes. However, the actual resonant quality of each of those sounds will differ, depending on the individual characteristics of the speaker. For example, males may have thicker vocal folds, which will affect the basic fundamental frequency. Other speakers

Table 9.2 The relaties intensities of a range of English vowel sounds

Sound	Intensity	Sound	Intensity
ɔ	29	m	17
ɒ	28	tʃ	16
ɑ	26	n	15
ʌ	26	d	13
ɜ	25	ʒ	13
æ	24	z	12
ʊ	24	s	12
e	23	t	11
ɪ	22	g	11
u	22	k	11
i	22	v	10
w	21	ð	10
r	20	b	8
j	20	d	8
l	20	p	7
ʃ	19	f	7
ŋ	18	θ	0

Table 9.3 Decibel (dB) values for speech and non-speech sounds

Sound	Intensity (dB)
Four-engined jet plane	130
Threshold of pain	120
Rock band	110
Symphony orchestra, fortissimo	100
Noisy underground train; loud radio music	80
Residential area, no traffic; quiet conversation	30
Quiet garden; whispered conversation	20
Watch ticking at ear	10
Threshold of audibility	0

may have larger vocal cavities where the sound is allowed to become more resonant than would be the case for speakers with smaller vocal tracts.

In phonetics research, the notion of resonance allows us to classify speech sounds using **spectra**. Spectra are defined by Fry (1979, p. 58) as 'statement[s] of what frequencies are to be found in the mixture and what their relative amplitudes are'. Later, we will examine the components of spectra in detail but, for the moment, it will suffice to state that spectral measurement allows us to measure the fundamental frequency, along with the harmonics that are present in speech.

Basic methods in acoustic analysis

As we stated at the beginning of this chapter, acoustic phonetics aims to provide a quantifiable record of speech events using instrumental techniques. These techniques are usually based around computer software packages, often interfaced with hardware which produce visual representations of and statistical measurements of speech. Although this explanation seems to represent acoustic phonetics as an exact science, we must point out that this is not the case. For instance, if we were using tape-recorded material as input, it may be the case that the quality of the recording is less than ideal (because of extraneous background noise, or inappropriate recording levels, for instance). It may also be that the chosen acoustic program fails to analyse the data in the best way, either because of its own design faults, or because we ourselves have failed to specify the correct settings for data sampling.

Because of the potential difficulties outlined above, it is important to familiarize ourselves with good practice in recording techniques, and we should also equip ourselves with a solid understanding of the characteristics and methods of whatever acoustic analysis program we happen to be using. In addition to these prerequisites to acoustic analysis, we must also acquire a firm grasp of basic procedures in acoustics, and of how acoustic representations relate to articulatory characteristics of speech. The rest of this chapter concentrates on these aspects.

Measuring frequency

We stated earlier that the overall frequency of speech is the result of a number of individual component frequencies which we referred to as the fundamental or the source and the harmonic, i.e. the filters which operate on the fundamental. The effect of the vocal tract filters is to produce peaks of amplitude at certain frequencies, and we refer to these peaks as formants. Using acoustic analysis, we can investigate each type of frequency by means of the sound spectrograph. The sound spectrograph plots frequency in Hertz (Hz) along the vertical axis and time (usually in milliseconds) along the horizontal. Spectrography typically captures frequencies of up to 5000 Hz and, although it is possible to plot frequencies in excess of 5000 Hz, these higher frequencies are not vital identifying features of speech sounds. The basic method behind sound spectrography is that the spectrograph measures all of the frequencies that are in present in speech sounds and, where acoustic energy is detected at a certain frequency, then that frequency is plotted on a so-called **spectrogram**. Frequency plotting can be performed by means of either a narrow band or a wide band spectrogram. Figure 9.6 for example, shows narrow and wide band spectrograms for Cardinal Vowel 1.

The essential difference between the two spectrograms is that the narrow band representation provides more detailed frequency information than that offered by the wide band version. Nevertheless, narrow band spectrograms take time to deal with incoming speech signals, so that there is effectively a time delay between when the signal is received and when it is analysed. In order to overcome this difficulty, and so that we can gain a real-time, dynamic understanding of speech events, we recommend the wide band spectrogram for most types of phonetic research. As well as being more efficient in representing time, wide band spectrography also allows us to see formant groupings more clearly. So, for example, we can see from Figure 9.6 that /i/ has an important band of energy in the 2500 Hz to 2800 Hz region.

It will also be clear that spectrograms are composed of varying dark and lighter portions. The relative darkness corresponds to the intensity of the speech signal, with the effect that greater intensity at certain frequencies will register as blacker on the spectrogram than less intense frequencies. Looking at Figure 9.6 again, therefore, we can see that there is greater intensity between 2500 Hz 2800 Hz than there is between 3400 Hz and 4000 Hz, for instance. More detailed aspects of the acoustic properties of vowel sounds will be explained later.

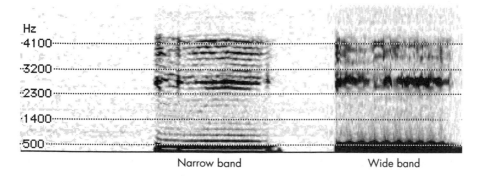

Figure 9.6 Narrow and wide band spectrograms for /i/

The formant structure in Figure 9.6 can be described as relatively regular, or periodic. Periodic sounds, as we have already seen are those whose waveform follows a regular pattern of displacement, whereas aperiodic sounds are those which disturb the air in irregular ways. In spectographic terms, the difference between periodic and aperiodic sounds is reflected by the presence or absence, respectively, of neat formant structures. Figure 9.7 shows spectrographic representations of speech sounds where irregular sounds are marked. Those sounds which are not marked are regular.

These sounds are sometimes informally referred to as 'noisy'. However, even within the category of noisy sounds, we can usually distinguish between certain varieties, such as /s/ and /ʃ/ and we will discuss this later on.

In this section, we have been referring exclusively to the frequencies which occur above the level of the fundamental, and how these are detectable on spectrograms. Although it is sometimes possible to measure the fundamental frequency using spectrography, the method involved is rather cumbersome and, for this reason, we will discuss alternative means for analysing the fundamental.

Detailed spectrographic properties of speech sounds

Understanding and interpreting acoustic patterns

At this point, we move on to investigate the acoustic structure of a range of speech sounds, i.e. vowels, diphthongs and sonorants. Of course, the precise acoustic make-up of each sound will differ for each individual speaker but there are, nonetheless, certain core features which enable us to identify these general categories in speech. It is also useful to remember two main facts which will aid our interpretation of spectrograms. First, it is the case that every speech sound has a particular spectrographic pattern associated with it. For example, a voiced plosive is represented by a break in the spectrographic pattern, along with a voicing bar. Nevertheless, it is also the case that those particular patterns may be altered by co-articulatory effects of the sort which we have mentioned in Chapter 7. For example, in Figure 9.8 /ba ba blakʃip/ ('ba ba black sheep') the first /b/ has the expected voicing bar along with the spectrographic break, whereas in the second /b/, the voicing bar is absent. This apparent anomaly can be explained by reference to the feature **voice onset time** for the plosive, i.e. the voicing onset for the second /b/ occurs simultaneously with the vowel onset, at the point where the closure phase of the plosive is released. So, it will be clear that our interpretation of spectrograms has to be allied with a detailed knowledge of articulatory phonetics.

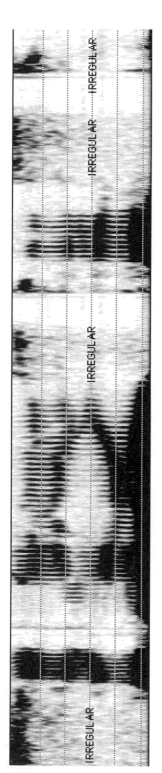

Figure 9.7 Spectrograms illustrating irregular and regular speech sounds

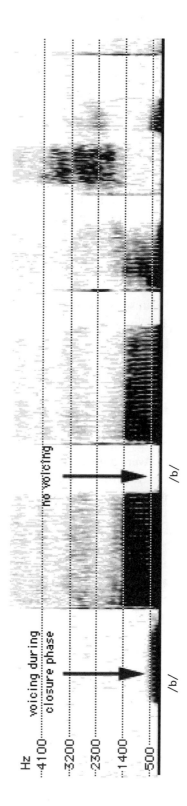

Figure 9.8 Spectrogram for /ba ba blakʃip/ ('ba ba black sheep')

Vowels

All vowels are voiced, and this means that a spectrographic representation of a vowel will contain a voicing bar, i.e. presence of energy at fundamental frequency level, usually in the region of 100–200 Hz, depending on speaker-specific characteristics. Vowels are also characterized by clear bands of energy, i.e. formants, which are quite unlike the energy distribution in other sounds. This means that vowels are usually easy to recognize on a spectrogram. Figure 9.9, for example, shows spectrograms for the eight primary Cardinal vowels. It will be clear from Figure 9.9 that, while the voicing bar and the formant arrangements are clearly indicative of the presence of a vowel, the location of and distance between each of the formants differs slightly from one another. Given that spectrograms capture the shape of resonant properties of the articulatory cavities, it will come as no surprise that different vowels differ in their spectrographic make-up, because of varying combinations of tongue height, tongue advancement and lip-rounding features. It is usually possible to differentiate formant patterns in terms of tongue height, tongue advancement and lip rounding, i.e. the three main features which are used to classify vowels. Vowel height is inversely proportional to F1 value, so that the high or close vowels have lower F1 values than low or open vowels. Tongue advancement is usually reflected in F2 values, with the effect that front vowels have higher F2s than back vowels. Finally, lip-rounding has the effect of lowering the overall energy throughout the formants.

Average formant frequencies for female speakers across a range of vowels are given in Table 9.4 (adapted from Baken, 1987, p. 358). These values will, of course, vary according to speaker and accent.

Diphthongs

As we have said above, spectrograms represent the size and shape of the articulatory cavities during the production of sounds. In the case of diphthongs, it will be clear that the tongue moves in order to produce one vowel quality followed by another, thereby modifying this size and shape of the oral cavity. The tongue movement which takes place during the production of diphthongs is represented spectrographically by a transition in the formant pattern from the first to the second vowel, or a 'bend', as shown in Figure 9.10.

As well as looking at the formants of what we might think of as straightforward diphthongs, we might also interpret slight bends to indicate that the speaker has diphthongized the target vowel sound in question, as in 'Bangor', for instance, i.e. /a/ becomes realized as [ai]. Of course, when we can uncover such narrow details of a speaker's pronunciation using

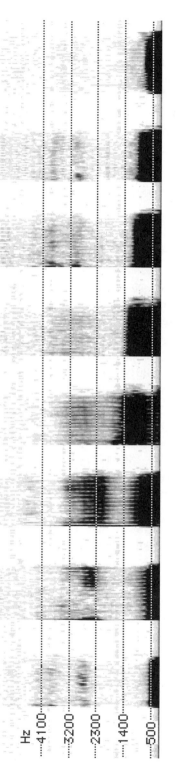

Hz
4100
3200
2300
1400
500

Figure 9.9 Cardinal vowels 1–8

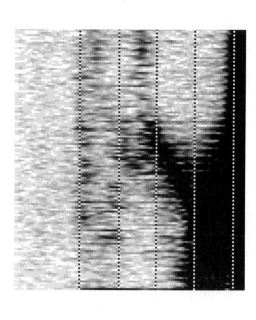

Figure 9. 10 Spectrographic representation of a diphthong

Table 9.4 Formant values for /ɪ, ɛ, æ, ɔ/

	ɪ	ɛ	æ	ɔ
F1	430	610	860	590
F2	2480	2330	2050	920
F3	3070	2990	2850	2710

spectrographic investigation, we can use the information to enhance our phonetic transcription.

Obstruents

The term 'obstruent', as we have seen in Chapter 4, covers plosives, fricatives and affricates. All of these sounds involve either a complete or almost complete obstruction to the airflow, and these degrees of stoppages have clear acoustic counterparts. In the case of plosive sounds, we will recall that there are three aspects to the articulation, i.e. the closure of the articulators, the build-up of air behind them, and the final release of the built up air. These three phases appear on the spectrogram as a break, as shown in Figure 9.11.

If the spectrogram is of good quality, it may be possible to infer the place of articulation of a plosive sound. For alveolar sounds, for instance, the second formant ought to exist at approximately 1700–1800 Hz, whereas for bilabial sounds, both the second and the third formants are comparatively low. Figure 9.12 illustrates voiced plosives at varying places of articulation, from bilabial to uvular.

For fricatives, we know that the articulation does not involve a complete stoppage of the airflow, but rather a significant obstruction to it, whereby the articulators come very close together, and the body of air is forced through a relatively narrow passage. The friction that we hear on these sounds is the result of the high frequencies which are present in this particular sound category, and high-frequency noise is easily identifiable on the spectrogram, as shown in Figure 9.13.

Although all of the sounds in Figure 9.13 are characterized by the clear fricative pattern, it is clear that they differ in terms of the amount and distribution of the frequencies within them. These differences are a direct corollary of the place of articulation of the sound. For example, in the case of /ʃ/, most of the high-frequency noise occurs between 1900 Hz and upwards to 6000 Hz, whereas /s/ is characterized by a noise pattern which only begins at approximately the 4000 Hz mark.

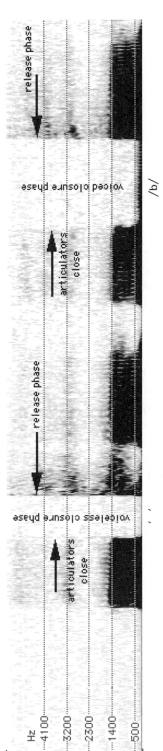

Figure 9.11 Acoustic phases of plosive consonants

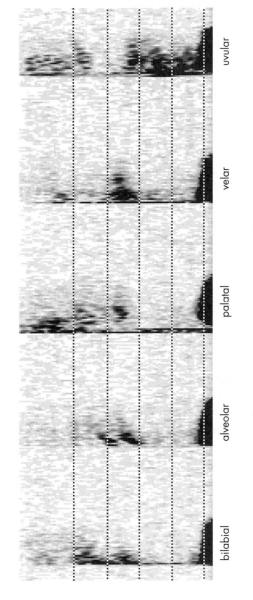

Figure 9.12 Spectrograms of consonants with varying places of articulation

Affricates

As we know from Chapter 4, the category of affricate refers to combinations of a stop and a fricative. In English, the two main affricates, i.e. /tʃ/ and /dʒ/, naturally contain the spectrographic characteristics of their individual components, i.e. a break for the stop followed by high-frequency noise for the fricative, as illustrated in Figure 9.14.

Sonorants

The sonorant category in consonant classification consists of approximants (such as /j, w, r/) the liquids (/l/) and nasals (such as /m, n/). Sonorants contrast with obstruents in so far as they involve neither a complete stoppage or nor a turbulent obstruction of the airflow. Figure 9.15 shows spectrograms of some sample sonorants in inter-vocalic position and it will be clear from the spectrograms that these sounds behave rather like vowels in so far as they exhibit a voicing bar along with formant-like structures.

Measuring pitch

We have said above that the acoustic structure of a speaker's voice consists of energy occurring at a number of frequencies. For voiceless fricatives, for instance, most of the energy occurs in the higher frequencies, starting at approximately 1200 Hz. For vowels, we have stated that their defining features are identifiable bands of frequency or formants which cluster around certain bands of frequencies. Among all of these frequencies, pitch is the most basic one that can exist in a speaker's voice and it is for this reason that it is referred to as fundamental frequency. On a spectrogram, presence or absence of pitch is indicated by the voicing bar. Figure 9.16 demonstrates, for instance, two sounds where the first exhibits a voicing bar while the second does not.

We have indicated above that spectrographic patterns correlate with the size and shape of the articulatory chambers. With regard to pitch, however, the direct correlate of the voicing bar on the spectrogram is vocal fold vibration.

Although it is relatively easy to identify whether pitch exists on a given sound, the precise measurement of pitch from a spectrogram is less than straightforward and tends to be rather cumbersome. Lehiste and Peterson (1961), for example, describe their method for measuring pitch spectrographically, using the harmonics as the guide:

> The fundamental frequency was derived by measuring the center frequency of higher harmonics on a 4 in. narrow-band

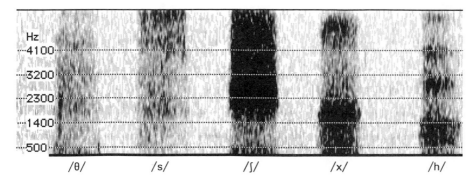

Figure 9.13 Spectrograms for fricatives at varying places of articulation

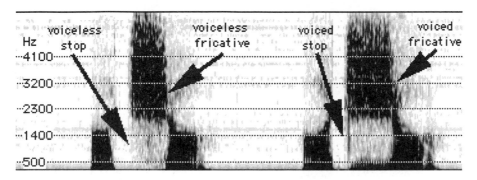

Figure 9.14 Voiceless and voiced affricates

spectrogram; the measured frequency was divided by the order number of the respective harmonic to obtain the fundamental frequency. Usually, both the 10th and 20th harmonics were measured. On these spectrograms 0.1 in represents about 88 kHz, and the individual harmonics are considerably lower. Calibration tones and repeated measurements show the accuracy to be within ± 20 Hz, and in the region of the 20th harmonic this represents an accuracy of ± 1 Hz.

Given the difficulties outlined here with respect to attempting to measure pitch from a spectrogram, we suggest the use of more efficient and easily manageable means for tracking and measuring pitch.

Pitch instrumentation

Pitch measurement is relatively easily accomplished by means of a number of commercially available acoustic analysis programs. Essentially, these

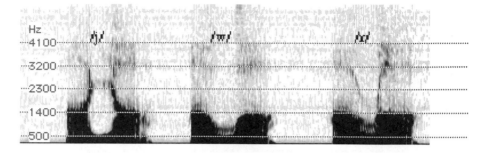

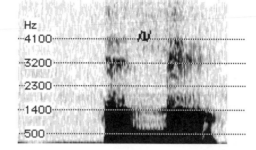

Figure 9.15 Spectrograms of sonorants

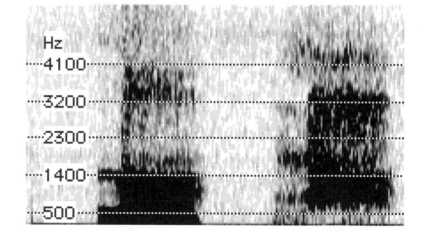

Figure 9.16 Voicing versus voicelessness

programs perform so called 'pitch-tracking routines' following a number of procedures which the user is free to choose. Depending on aspects such as the quality of the input signal, the amount of pitch detail we wish to uncover, and the particular characteristics and capabilities of the software, we can use routines such as autocorrelation, Fast-Fourier transformation and temporal structure analysis. When the user has selected one of these routines, it is possible to carry out a number of measurements of the signal. First, one may produce an F_0 contour which provides a visual representation of the pitch contour. Given this contour, it is possible to click at any point and read off the F_0 value at that particular point. The tracker

mx¬324¬mn¬162¬x¬213.138¬sd¬40.508

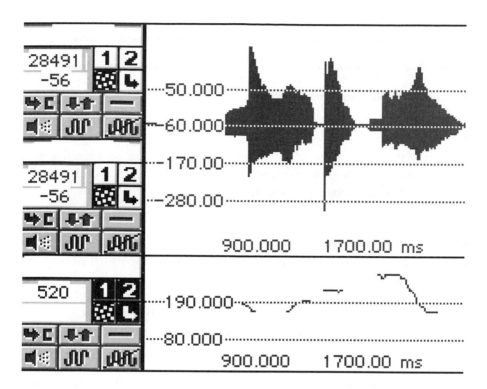

Figure 9.17 Pitch trace with statistics

will also provide a number of statistics, such as maximum, minimum, average and standard deviation. Such measurements can then be pasted into a spreadsheet program, for the purpose of performing more detailed statistical investigations. Figure 9.17 shows a sample pitch trace from Signalyze alongside its waveform, with statistics relating to the sample.

Acoustic aspects of connected speech

So far in this chapter we have been concerned with the acoustic qualities of individual speech sounds. However, we have stated that individual speech sounds are affected by surrounding sounds, so that certain features of their articulation might be altered. Although it is not the object of this chapter to discuss in detail the extent to which sounds overlap in connected speech, is useful here to schematize the situation by use of Figure 9.18, which shows that sounds to not exist as discrete entities as in the top line of the figure but, rather, frequently overlap with one another, as suggested by the lower

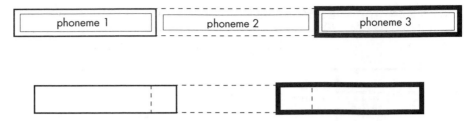

Figure 9.18 Schematic representation of co-articulation in speech

line. We describe these alterations and inter-relationships among sounds as 'co-articulation', a term which captures the dynamism of speech sound production. We now examine how aspects of connected speech are discernible use of spectrographic means.

Voice quality

In Chapter 6, we introduced the descriptive framework which is available for analysing voice quality, largely following the model established by Laver (1980), along with insights from ExtIPA. Now, however, we will examine some of the methods which are available for the acoustic investigation of voice quality, at phonation level and at the level of supraglottal voice quality types.

We have already used terms such as 'modal voice', 'harsh voice' and the like to refer to particular types of phonation modes. Acoustically, phonation modes can be investigated and quantified using **jitter** and **shimmer** as appropriate tools. Jitter refers to irregularity in the speaker's F_0, whereas shimmer refers to irregularity in the speaker's amplitude. Both jitter and shimmer offer a direct correlate to vocal harshness, insofar as the harsher the voice quality, the greater the jitter.

With regard to creaky voice, the essential characteristic is low-frequency vocal fold vibration combined with, according to Fry (1979, p. 68) 'the interspersion of larynx cycles of abnormally long duration'. We can recognize creaky voice easily from a spectrogram, where each larynx cycle corresponds to a clear vertical striation in the spectrograph, as illustrated in Figure 9.19.

Whisper, although it derives from an aperiodic sound source, is nonetheless capable of conveying intelligible speech sounds. So, while speakers may not produce sounds which derive from the periodic vibration of the vocal folds, they can still manage to produce appropriate supraglottal modifications to the speech airstream. Figure 9.20, for example, illustrates four whispered vowels along with their four modal counterparts and it can be seen that, while the voicing bar is missing from the second set of vowels and there is less overall frequency, the characteristic formant patterns of vowels are still discernible. Whispery voice, on the other hand (also known as murmur), does have voicing combined with clearer formant bars than would be the case for whisper.

Supraglottal voice quality types

In Chapter 6, we defined supraglottal voice quality types as those which involve modifications to largely the oral tract, either lengthwise or widthwise. Clearly, these settings will have an effect on the acoustic representation of the specch. For example, if we were to produce a palatalized voice, where the tongue was consistently raised towards the centre of the oral cavity then the patterns which result would contain elements which are reminiscent of a front to central vowel like pattern, much like that of Cardinal vowel 1, as in Figure 9.21 which illustrates modal followed by palatalized voice.

With velarized voice, however, the tongue is consistently raised towards the back of the oral cavity, in the position involved in the production of CV8. As illustrated in Figure 9.22 which shows modal and velarized voice, the formant patterns for the velarized portion is characterized by acoustic similarities to Cardinal Vowel 8.

Summary

In this chapter, we have summarized the main techniques which are currently in use for analysing the acoustic characteristics of speech sounds. We have indicated that while individual sounds tend to have specific acoustic patterns which can be related to features such as phonation mode, place and manner of articulation, these patterns can be modified because of the co-articulatory effects which are present in connected speech.

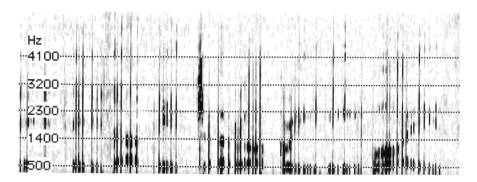

Figure 9.19 Spectrogram of creaky voice

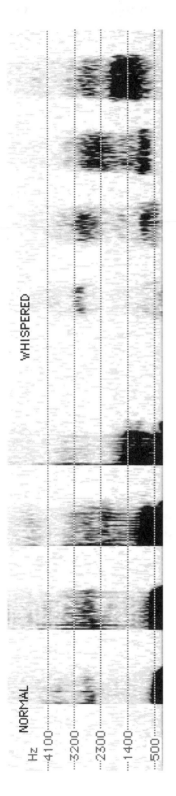

Figure 9.20 Vowels produced on modal and whisper

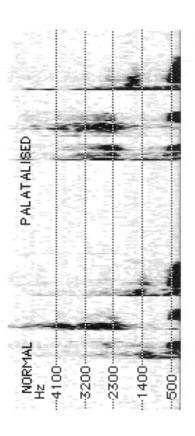

Figure 9.21 Normal and palatalized voice

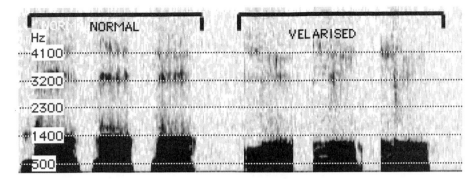

Figure 9.22 Normal and velarized voice

Further reading

For a general overview of spectrographic techniques, see Fry (1979). More recent investigative techniques and findings are presented in Johnson (1997) and Clark and Yallop (1995), whereas the central reference source for information on voice quality is Laver (1980). Baken (1987) contains useful assimilations of pitch and formant measurements from a range of studies, as well as technical detail on physical and physiological measurement procedures.

Short questions

1 What role does acoustic analysis play in the study of speech?
2 Explain how sound waveforms are produced.
3 How do wide band and narrow band spectrograms differ from one another?
4 Explain what is meant by the terms 'source' and 'filter' with regard to the production of speech.
5 How is pitch perception measured?

Essay questions

1 'There are . . . a number of features observable on spectrograms that indicate a speaker's speech habits' (Ladefoged, *1993*, p. 211). Explain how speech habits might be indicated on a spectrogram.
2 Explain how spectrographic analysis might represent articulatory distinctions in speech, as well as speaker-specific characteristics

10 The perception of speech

Introduction

When speech is produced, it is usually directed towards a listener. Listeners must then effectively perform two main tasks on the speech signal if they are to understand it correctly. First, they must perceive or hear the signal and, second, decode or deconstruct it into its meaningful components. We can only fully understand individual words and longer utterances if we are able to perceive and categorize aspects of their articulatory make-up. For instance, we know that the word 'skill' differs from 'skull' because we can perceive the difference in the vowel and relate each of the words to a particular meaning.

Clearly, the ability to hear the speech is reliant on a number of factors. First, listeners must have adequate hearing ability, so that they can perceive the full range of the frequencies contained within the sound. If fricative sounds, for instance, are to be recognized, there must be the ability to perceive high frequency. In addition to auditory acuity, there are various other factors which impinge on the accurate perception/audition of a given speech sound, such as background noise and listeners' relative familiarity with speakers' habits (a speaker may, for instance, have speech idiosyncrasies which interfere with overall intelligibility).

With regard to the decoding of the speech signal into meaningful elements, a number of neurological prerequisites and skills must be present. Listeners must, for instance, have the ability to associate sounds and combinations of sounds with particular semantic concepts. Clearly, any sort of breakdown which occurs at the hearing stage or the decoding stage has the potential to interfere significantly with the overall communicative process.

In this chapter, we explain how listeners hear speech and how they relate the aspects of speech to meaning. We also describe processes of hearing and neurological impairment and indicate the likely consequences of these impairments on speaker–listener interactions.

How listeners hear speech

As we have stated above, the perception of speech involves more than just listeners registering that some sort of sound has been produced by a speaker. In particular, we have said that the sounds must be decoded and given linguistic meaning by listeners. Our account of how listeners hear speech, however, must begin with an explanation of the mechanical aspects of the hearing system as the basis for speech perception.

Hearing, as it relates to the activity of various parts of the ear, is known as the **peripheral auditory system**. The decoding of sounds which takes place in the neural areas, however, is known as the **internal auditory system**. In the following section, we will examine the peripheral auditory system in detail; the workings of the internal auditory system will be explained later.

The peripheral auditory system

As has been explained in Chapter 9, the basis for all sound transmission, whether speech or otherwise, is a body of air in vibration. Once this vibrating body of air reaches the ear, it travels through passages known as the **outer ear**, **middle ear** and **inner ear**.

Outer ear

The outermost part of the ear, i.e. that which is visible and usually referred to commonly merely as 'the ear', is known as the **pinna** or **auricle** (*see* Figure 10.1). The pinna makes virtually no contribution to our hearing ability, except in so far as it focuses or localizes the point of entry of the sound waves into the deeper portions of the ear. From the pinna, sound travels into the ear canal, also known as the **external auditory meatus**. The ear canal is of varying size and shape, usually from approximately 2.5 cm to 5 cm long. Apart from the protective function which is performed by the ear canal (i.e. it protects the inner ear musculature), it acts as a compulsory resonator by amplifying the sound waves which pass along it. The ear canal is particularly sensitive to sounds between 3000 Hz and 4000 Hz, but it provides resonance for a greater range of frequencies, i.e. from 500 Hz up to

4000 Hz. These resonant properties mean that the ear canal allows the transmission of most of the major elements of phonological structure.

Middle ear

Canal

At the end of the ear-drum, a cavity known as the **tympanum** or **ear-drum** provides a passage for the sound waves to enter the skull. The beginning of the middle ear structure is marked by the tympanic membrane. The tympanum is an air-filled chamber which effectively provides a seal between the outer and middle ear. It consists of three connected bones, collectively referred to as the **auditory ossicles**. Individually, these bones are the **hammer** or **malleus**, the **anvil** or **incus** and the **stirrup** or **stapes** (*see* Figure 10.1). When sound reaches the tympanum, it exerts pressure which sets the bones in vibration, allowing the sound waves to be carried into the inner ear. The activity of these bones enables the tympanum simultaneously to amplify and regulate the sound level that is transmitted to the inner ear.

With regard to amplification, two features are important, i.e. the area at the so-called oval window of the stapes which is smaller than that at the entrance to the ear-drum, and the activity of the auditory ossicles which produces a greater force than that which exists at the ear-drum. The effect of these combined features is to produce a concentration of acoustic energy at the oval window which is approximately 35 times greater than that at the ear-drum.

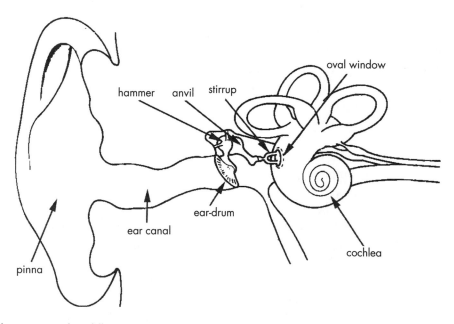

Figure 10.1 The outer and middle ear

As for the regulatory function played by the tympanum, the appropriate muscular activity of the auditory ossicles comes into operation when excessively loud sounds are presented, in order to reduce the amplitude of the signal which is carried to the inner ear. Although these muscular adjustments are efficient, they are not instantaneous so that, in the case of sudden loud noise, for instance, the transmission of damagingly or painfully high amounts of pressure to the inner ear may be unavoidable.

The pressure level within the tympanum is controlled by the **Eustachian tube** which links the middle ear to the oral cavity and whose role it is to equalize potential pressure differences between the outer and middle ear. In cases where there is an imbalance of pressure between the middle and outer ear, such as might be experienced following rapid ascent or descent, the affected individual is likely to feel dizzy or lightheaded. In such circumstances, the act of swallowing opens the Eustachian tube and allows pressure to be released from the middle ear.

Up to this point in the process of hearing, sounds exist merely as physical sensations, i.e. as vibrations in a moving body of air. However, when the air leaves the middle ear, it has to be transformed into neural signals, so that the brain can decode the sound appropriately. This transformation takes place in the inner ear.

Inner ear

The inner ear is located within the skull and it contains the **cochlea**, the organ which coverts sounds into neural impulses, (*see* Figure 10.2). The cochlea is a coiled structure, divided by two membranes the (i.e. the vestibular membrane and the basilar membrane) into sections known as the **scala vestibuli**, and the **scala tympani**.

It is the basilar membrane which begins the task of converting sound into neural impulses. When sound pressure variations meet the oval window, they are transmitted through cochlear fluid (**perilymph**) and cause movement along the basilar membrane which varies in width from one end to the other. The nature and location of the movement of the basilar membrane depends on the frequency of the sound that is presented. High-frequency sounds, for instance, produce movement near the oval window, i.e. at the basal end. Low frequencies result in movement at the apical end, known as the **helicotrema**.

The final stage in the conversion of sound impulses into neural activity takes place in the **organ of Corti** (*see* Figure 10.2), a structure consisting of hair cells resting on the basilar membrane. The displacement of the basilar membrane described above causes movement in the hair cells which is transformed into neural signals. In addition, the nerve fibres from the auditory nerve transmit the basilar movements to the auditory centre of the

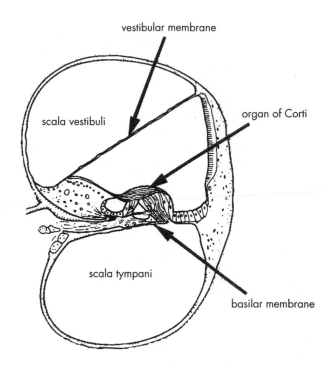

vestibular membrane

scala vestibuli

organ of Corti

scala tympani

basilar membrane

Figure 10.2 The cochlea

brain. From this point on, the brain is responsible for decoding these neural impulses into meaningful units, by means of the internal auditory system.

The internal auditory system

The internal auditory system fulfils a major role in hearing, i.e. the breaking down of speech into its component meaningful parts. We have said above that movements within the cochlea are converted into neural impulses, and this conversion takes place along the auditory nerve. The nerve might be seen as a bank of filters, where each filter is tuned to a particular frequency. So, for instance, if an external sound source occurs at a given frequency, one of the filters which is tuned to that frequency will respond and carry the sound as a neural impulse. If the sound is outside the frequency to which the filters are tuned, then the listener will simply fail to hear that sound. The ability of anybody to hear certain sounds depends on the frequency resolution capabilities of that person's inner ear fibres. There are, for example, certain sounds which are simply too high for any listener to hear. We might, in this respect, think of the ageing process, where one of the consequences may be a loss of certain filters, so that particular sounds are inaudible. The filters are properly known as **receptor neurons**, and there are approximately 28 000 of them in each ear. They are located in the **spiral ganglion** which is parallel to the organ of Corti.

As well as the pathway which exists from the ear to the brain, there are also pathways going from the brain to the ear. These bi-directional path-ways create a number of so-called **feedback mechanisms** which will be discussed later on.

Hearing impairment

As we have stated above, the process of hearing relies on a passage of air being transmitted safely from a source to a receptor, which we might refer to as the **hearing chain**. If, at any point along this hearing chain, there is an impairment in function then the strength of the acoustic signal will be diminished. As a simple illustration of impairment, we might consider the case of temporary breakdowns in understanding where, for example, lis-teners may interpret 'Do you like this dress?' as 'Do you like distress?'. For our present purposes, however, we are more interested in the effects on comprehension which result from hearing impairment.

Assessments of hearing sensitivity

The discipline of audiometry or audiology offers a number of methods, both subjective and objective, for assessing hearing ability and loss. Sub-jective methods are essentially those in which the patient is presented with a stimulus and asked to respond when the stimulus reaches certain pitch or loudness levels, for instance. These methods fall within the category of **pure tone audiometry**. With regard to objective methods of assessing hear-ing levels, two main methods exist, i.e. **acoustic admittance methods** and **electric response audiometry**. In each case, tones are relayed into the ear canal and the resulting sound pressure level in the ear is then measured. A hearing loss of 70 decibels (dB), for example, means that a sound at a given frequency must reach an intensity level of 70 dB or greater before it can be perceived by the subject. The range of normal hearing is stated in the liter-ature as being from −10 dB to +20 dB (*see* Lutman, 1983). Sounds are nor-mally presented at frequencies of 250, 500, 1000, 2000 and 4000 Hz, i.e. one octave apart. The higher the intensity level which the sound must reach before it is perceived by the subject, the more extensive is that subject's hearing loss.

Clearly, subjective methods are limited by factors such as the patient's speed of reaction but they remain the most commonly used indicators of hearing ability. As Figure 10.3 illustrates, pure tone audiometry records hearing level (HL), for each ear, in decibels against the frequency of the sound that is presented. Figure 10.3 indicates pure tone thresholds for nor-mal hearing, where the subject can perceive a sound of 500 Hz in the left ear, when that sound is presented at 10 dB increments of loudness.

Hearing levels which are lower than those indicated in Figure 10.3

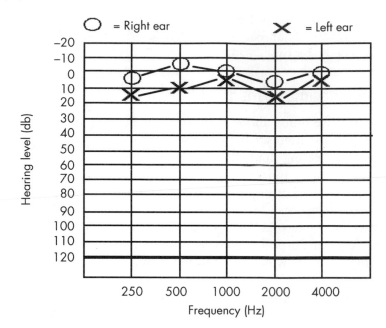

Figure 10.3 Pure tone audiogram for normal-hearing subject

suggest a below-normal hearing ability. Hearing losses are also usually described in verbal categories, i.e. from **mild** through to **profound**, based on the extent of the loss. These categories are listed in Table 10.1 below, with a brief description of the difficulties that each type of hearing loss poses for the reception of speech.

Figure 10.4, for instance, illustrates a patient whose hearing loss is profound in both ears at 1000 Hz and 2000 Hz (*see* Rahilly, 1991).

It is common to define types of hearing loss according to the age at which the hearing loss occurs relative to language development. A loss which occurs before a child has acquired the full range of linguistic resources is known as **pre-lingual**, whereas a loss which occurs after language acquisition is complete is referred to as **post-lingual**.

Table 10.1 Levels of hearing loss

Loss (dB)	Category	Description
25–40	Mild	Difficulty only with faint speech
41–55	Moderate	Frequent difficulty with normal speech
56–70	Substantial	Frequent difficulty with loud speech
71–90	Severe	Understands only shouted or amplified speech
>90	Profound	Usually cannot understand even amplified speech by hearing alone
>120	Total	No useful hearing

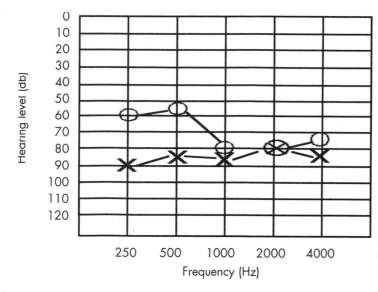

Figure 10.4 Pure tone audiogram for hearing-impaired subject

Role of the brain in speech perception

As we have stated above, the function of the auditory system is to transmit sounds. When the sound has been passed from the cochlea to the brain by means of the acoustic nerve, it gets transformed from an acoustic signal into a comprehensible message. It is at this transformation stage that the activity of the brain comes into play. The human brain is much larger in size than that of any animal, indicating that it is specialized for language in a way that animal brains are not. Although the exact function of the brain in speech perception is still poorly understood, information derived from brain scans allow investigators to monitor brain activity while a subject performs a variety of listening and speaking tasks.

The brain consists of billions of **neurons**, or nerve cells, along with a number of other sections, all of which contribute to the complex structure and functioning of the brain. It is common practice to categorize the parts of the brain into **hemispheres** and **lobes**, and it has been shown that damage to the left and the right hemispheres have specific effects on language reception and production. For example, patients who suffer damage to the right side of their brain frequently lose the ability to understand certain formulaic linguistic expressions, which they will tend to interpret literally. A subject who is presented with the phrase 'I was walking on eggshells', for instance is likely not to grasp the metaphorical intention of the speaker. On the other hand, a subject whose left hemisphere is damaged is likely to encounter difficulty understanding simple words, such as 'pen', or will be unable to select a named object in a picture.

It is possible to think of the brain as providing a set of operations on the speech sound which effectively discriminate, ever more narrowly, aspects of the incoming signal. The first stage of the decoding process takes place in the **primary auditory cortex** whereby listeners perceive presence or absence of voice. In the **secondary auditory cortex** then, changes in the pitch make-up of the signal are perceived. The final stage of message perception and decoding occurs in the **temporal cortex**.

Models of speech perception

When the process of decoding each of the incoming speech sounds is complete, the listener must then establish the linguistic meaning of the utterance. We can state that both parts of the brain are involved and demand a decoding of grammatical, syntactic and semantic information. Although we can track the perception of speech via the auditory system to the brain, we do not know exactly how the incoming neurological signals are actually converted into linguistic concepts (the last stage of the speech chain we introduced in Chapter 1). Neurolinguists and psycholinguists have speculated on this problem, though unfortunately not all branches of linguistics and phonetics have co-operated closely enough to integrate their various insights. (Much of the following discussion is based on Ball, 1993.)

Passive listener model

Crystal (1987) has suggested that models of speech perception can be divided into those that require solely a passive role for the listener, and those that demand an active role. We could envisage a passive model as one where the incoming signals are matched to a set of templates stored in the language areas of the brain. If a match is found then the signal is recognized and interpreted, if no match is found (as for example when we listen to a foreign language we do not know) then no interpretation is possible.

This approach naturally opens up a large number of questions. First, we need to consider what kind of templates might be involved. Certainly, we would expect some of them to be phonological units (such as phonemes), because we can recognize individual sounds. But psychoacoustic experimentation (*see* Chapter 11) suggests we interpret incoming speech in larger units as well, such as syllables or complete words (though in this last case it is likely that only common words would be stored as wholes). It is even possible that common phrases (especially semantically empty ones such as greetings) would be stored as unanalysed wholes.

We also must ask how robust such templates would have to be. For example, we might have to use a template-matching procedure under unfavourable acoustic conditions (such as loud background noise); we have to match incoming signals from a large number of different speakers using different fundamental frequencies, and different voice qualities, and so on; we also have to deal with input from speakers using different regional or social varieties of the language. We all know of instances when such circumstances have, in fact, resulted in an inability to comprehend a message, so clearly there are limits to the flexibility of templates. Moreover, the point about regional and social varieties raises the question whether we store two templates for common words with differing phonological realizations (such as northern English [bʊs] versus southern English [bʌs] for 'bus'), but only one for words that differ only in phonetic realization (e.g. Hiberno–English [miθ̪] versus southern English [mit] for 'meet').

Naturally, if the passive listener approach is not supported by evidence, then many of these questions become irrelevant. There is, however, support for a template type model from some psycholinguistic investigations. It is known that speakers are very apt to ignore some slips of the tongue (whether accidental or deliberate), and to 'hear' what the speaker is assumed to have meant. By 'hear' we don't mean that listeners pretend to hear the correct message, but that they claim not to have noticed the mistake. Examples might be where listeners hear a phrase such as 'the man are here', and claim to have heard 'the men are here'; or where they hear [aɪ ˈhɒt aɪ ˈθ3d ˈdʒɒn] and claim to have heard [aɪ ˈθɔt aɪ ˈh3d ˈdʒɒn] ('I thought I heard John').

Active listener model

An alternative account of speech perception has been proposed by numerous researchers: one where the listener has to take an active role in the interpretation process. Numerous versions of this view exist (such as 'motor theory' and 'analysis by synthesis', *see* Ryalls, 1996), but here we will outline the general approach, only touching on these alternatives. In active listener models it is assumed that the speech production and perception processes somehow work in tandem. By this we mean that the decoding of a heard message operates through listeners referring across to how they would produce particular sounds themselves: listeners' knowledge of speech articulation acts as a link between the incoming acoustic signal and the identification of phonetic and then phonological and higher linguistic units.

In order to illustrate this approach we can look at a couple of specific suggestions as to how it might work. The 'motor theory' of speech perception (*see* Lieberman and Blumstein, 1988) basically takes the view that listeners model the articulations of the speaker internally. Lieberman and Blumstein (1988) give the example of the acoustic difference between the

/d/ found before a high front vowel (e.g. [diː] as in 'deep'), and that before a high back vowel (e.g. [duː] as in 'do'). These differences are to do with formant transitions, yet listeners are still able to identify the segments as both being [d]. Lieberman and Blumstein (1988, p. 147) argue that this is because the listeners sense the articulatory movements that went into producing the types of [d], and so decode the acoustic pattern using their prior knowledge of the articulatory gestures and the anatomical apparatus involved in the production of speech.

An alternative theory under this general heading is that known as 'analysis by synthesis'. Here it is assumed that the perception and production pathways are mediated by sets of features that speakers use to analyse speech. Listeners use a set of acoustic rules to analyse the incoming signal into these features; these rules are also used to generate a copy of the incoming signal as if for production (though normally this 'echo' will not actually be spoken). The listeners' perceptual system then allows a comparison of the features identified for the incoming signal with those of the 'outgoing' signal and so matches them.

A joint approach

As Crystal (1987, p. 148) points out, it is likely that both the above main approaches have something to contribute to our understanding of how we interpret spoken messages. Active theories might well explain, for example, our ability to adjust for accent and individual differences discussed above more plausibly than do template accounts. On the other hand, passive approaches allow for the fact that certain types of people may be unable to produce speech for pathological reasons but can still comprehend it (e.g. certain types of aphasia patients), and for the fact we can understand speech from speakers which we would not be likely to 'silently model' (e.g. speakers with dysfluent speech or strong foreign accents).

In theoretical terms, the active model can be criticized for adding to the complexity of any account through the addition of the intermediate, articulatory modelling stage in speech perception; on the other hand, the passive model can be criticized for *not* linking speech production and perception in any meaningful way.

A compromise, therefore, might be posited whereby templates are used as a short-cut to speech interpretation for speech signals that fit within the norm expected for a particular spoken variety, but where articulatory modelling is available to back this up for unusual or unclear input signals. Such a model of speech production and perception is shown in simple form in Figure 10.5.

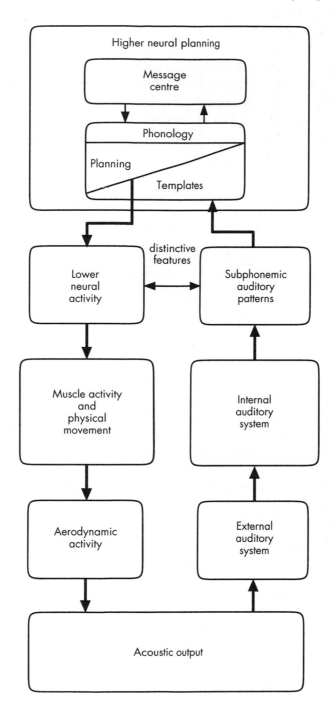

Figure 10.5 A model of speech perception

Summary

In this chapter, we have shown that the process of speech perception involves the successful completion of a number of neural and cerebral activities. We have also indicated that a break-down of any of these activities is likely to have a significant effect on communication. We have also considered different views of how the interpretation process actually operates. In the next chapter, we move on to examine which particular aspects of the acoustic signal are important for listeners' decoding of sounds.

Further reading

Most phonetics textbooks provide straightforward accounts of basic audition. For more detailed explanations of the anatomy and physiology of hearing, however, *see* Perkins and Kent (1986) and Denes and Pinson (1973). Ryalls (1996) provides a good introduction into speech perception.

Short questions

1 List the stages involved in a listener's reception of a speech sound.
2 How is hearing ability measured?
3 What function is played by the Eustachian tube?
4 Suggest one reason for deterioration in hearing, as a result of either ageing or injury.
5 What effects is brain injury likely to have on the decoding of speech?

Essay questions

1 Explain in detail how a listener manages to perceive an incoming speech signal.
2 What role does the brain play in the decoding of speech?
3 In cases of communication breakdown, suggest likely points of impairment along the 'communication chain'.

11　Perceptual phonetics

Introduction

In Chapter 10 we examined the working of the peripheral auditory system and explained how sound is transformed from acoustic waves to neural impulses. We also introduced briefly the role of the brain in decoding those neural impulses, so that listeners manage to make sense of the message that they receive. In this chapter, we move on to look in more detail at what types of sounds and what aspects of sounds can be perceived by listeners, and how those aspects can be measured. The whole area of testing what listeners can hear is known as **psychoacoustics**. Clearly, while the discipline of psychoacoustics can offer interesting insights into aspects of speech perception, it falls short of being an exact science, because of the inherent subjectivity of listeners' responses. Therefore, this chapter discusses perceptually derived, rather than quantifiable physical data.

Methods of psychoacoustic investigation

Within the area of psychoacoustics, various types of investigation are common. Audiometry, for example, has produced a great deal of information on hearing abilities among various populations. We know, for instance, that young people tend to have sharper hearing abilities than older people, and that the maximum human sensitivity for sound perception is 3000 Hz. Nevertheless, not all of these frequencies are used for the purposes of speech perception. In fact, speakers will rarely use frequencies of less than 125 Hz or more than 8000 Hz, even if the speech output is filtered. In telephone systems, for instance, speech tends to be subjected to filtering from 200 Hz to 4000 Hz without intelligibility being significantly affected. Only sounds which rely on higher frequencies for differentiation, such as the fricatives, might be problematic in this context. Figure 11.1 presents the average limits in hearing for normal listeners, demonstrating that the threshold of hearing differs according to the intensity level of the sound which is presented.

In Chapter 10, we stated that there are frequency aspects of the speech signal, which allow us to differentiate general sound categories from one another. We saw, for instance, that vowels were distinguished from consonants because vowels possess a clear set of formants. To state what is perhaps obvious, if there are certain acoustic features that are responsible for differentiating sounds then the implication is that listeners are capable of perceiving these differences. In order to investigate precisely what listeners perceive, psychoacoustics provides a number of subjective measurement scales. The **mel scale**, as illustrated in Figure 11.2, investigates how listeners perceive pitch and allows us to assess whether a given sound is heard as being, for instance, twice as high or half as high as another sound. So, a sound with a mel value of 500 would be perceived as twice as high as a sound whose value is 250.

Unlike pitch, which is measured linearly in Hertz, mels proceed along a logarithmic scale. Table 11.1 shows a range of pitch measurements matched up with their equivalent mel values. The table also demonstrates that the ear is more sensitive to pitch changes in the lower frequencies than in the higher frequencies. At the lowest level, a frequency difference of

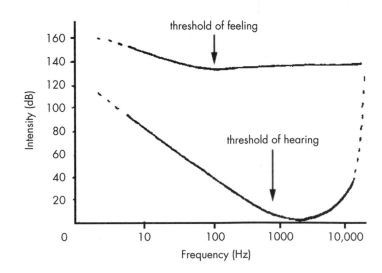

Figure 11.1 Average limits in hearing for normal listeners

Table 11.1 Pitch measurements matched with their equivalent in mels

Pitch (mels)	Frequency (Hz)
0	20
250	160
500	394
750	670
1000	1000
1250	1420
1500	1900
1750	2450
2000	3120
2250	4000

140 Hz is sufficient to produce a difference of 250 mels, whereas at the highest level, a frequency change of 880 Hz is required in order for the listener to register a difference of 250 mels.

Increasingly, in phonetics research, use is being made of the **Bark** scale which, along similar lines to the mel scale, also demonstrates the relationship between measurable acoustic frequency and perceived frequency. This relationship is shown in Figure 11.3. As was the case for the mel scale, the Bark scale shows that listeners' auditory systems are more sensitive to pitch changes in the lower frequencies than the higher ones.

While the mel and Bark scales are used to assess perceived pitch, perceived loudness is measured on the **phon** scale. The phon scale aims to quantify the perceived loudness of any sound irrespective of the physical intensity of that sound. It also takes account of the fact that listeners may hear sounds which have different frequencies but the same intensities as *not* having the same level of loudness. On the other hand, listeners may perceive sounds with the same frequencies but different intensities as being identically loud. Still in the area of loudness studies, the **sone** scale also

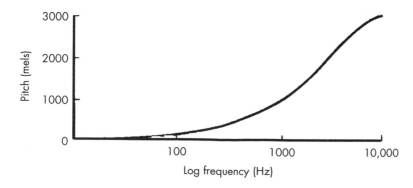

Figure 11.2 The mel scale

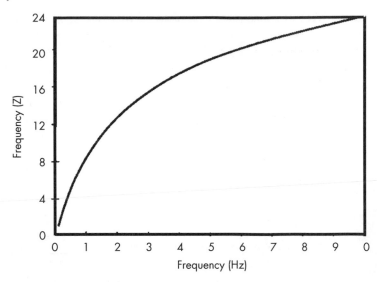

Figure 11.3 The Bark
scale

offers a numerical index for perceived loudness. Figure 11.4 shows how the
factors of frequency and intensity interact to produce varying levels of
loudness. For example, a listener judges a sound of two sones as being
twice as loud as a sound of one sone.

A further perceptual area which is investigated is the so-called **threshold
of hearing**. As we have explained in Chapter 10, an individual's overall
hearing ability is assessed by means of audiometric testing which identifies
the loudness level which has to be achieved before any sound can be perceived. Threshold of hearing tests, however, examine the thresholds or differences which distinguish one sound from another in the perception of the
listener. These differences are known as **difference limens** or **just noticeable
differences** and are measured in terms of frequency and intensity. For
example, it has been stated that a pitch change of 88 Hz is necessary before
listeners will recognize a rising tone (*see* Ainsworth and Lindsay, 1986).
With regard to just noticeable differences in intensity, a sound of 100 Hz
with a loudness level of 5 db would have to be doubled to 10 db before a
change would be perceived. However, the same tone presented at 100 db
need only be changed by six per cent in order for the change to be noticeable.

Experimental procedures in psychoacoustics

Given that psychoacoustics relies on essentially subjective and perceptual
responses from listeners, and that we wish our comments to be as representative as possible of how listeners respond to acoustic cues, it is important to devote some attention to the business of how listeners are
chosen for experimentation. In psychoacoustic pursuits, we are not usually
interested in the judgements of trained listeners such as phoneticians or

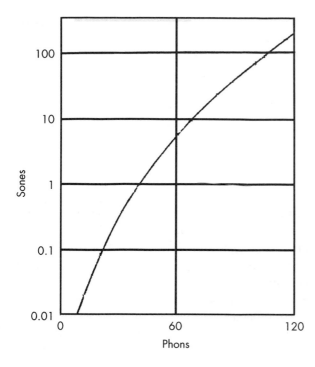

Figure 11.4 Levels of loudness measured in phons and sones

language instructors. This is largely because such people are likely to have acquired detailed listening skills which are not representative of those which exist in the rest of the population. Instead, so-called 'naïve listeners' are chosen, i.e. those who have no special training in linguistics or phonetics skills. The subjects will, of course, be chosen according to strict sampling criteria since particular listener characteristics (age, for example) are likely to have significant effects on the results.

As well as choosing listeners wisely, it is also crucial that suitable data is presented to the listener for experimentation purposes. Clearly, the kind of data chosen will depend on the object of the investigation, e.g. whether pitch or loudness or individual speech sounds. In some cases, natural speech constitutes suitable material for investigation but, when we intend to examine the precise acoustic cues which enable listeners to differentiate between one sound and another, synthetic speech is often required. The value of synthetic speech lies in the fact that it can be controlled and manipulated by the investigator (who can, for instance, alter voice onset time (VOT) and examine the effect of the manipulation on listeners) and it is not vulnerable to aspects of speaker variation. Different types of control on the part of the investigator are exercised according to whether the experiments are of the **limits** or **constant stimuli** type. In limits experimentation, the investigator changes the value of the stimulus in a series of fixed steps, whereas in constant stimuli tests, a variety of random stimuli are presented to the subject, who must identify one according to set criteria. In addition to such investigator controlled experimentation, it is also possible to place the manipulation of the stimuli within the control of the subject, in so-called **adjustment** studies, where the subject makes adjustments to the stimuli.

While it is always desirable to have studio quality recordings of whatever speech sample is being used, some recordings may involve masking of the speech signal (i.e. where noise at various frequencies is added to the signal), in order to simulate the kind of background noise which frequently accompanies naturalistic conversation.

Psychoacoustic experiments are interested in four principle aspects of listeners' responses to experimental material, i.e. **detection**, **discrimination**, **identification** and **scaling**. Detection consists of subjects stating the point at which the sound stimulus is detectable, as in loudness studies, for example, where subjects locate the decibel level which enables them to hear the sound in question. Discrimination is the process which allows listeners to spot difference limens between sounds in terms of pitch, loudness, or segmental articulatory aspects. Listeners might, for example, be asked to discriminate the point at which the movement of the tongue movement from [i] to a position close to the palate begins to produce friction. Identification is the activity whereby listeners are asked to label sounds in terms of a set of categories which have been provided by the experimenter. For example, subjects may have to choose whether a given sound is accompanied by labialization or not. Finally, scaling procedures ask listeners to respond to sounds using either numerical or perceptual scales. A subject may be asked, for example, to state whether a given sound is twice as high as another (see the use of the mel scale in this respect), or whether a greater pitch difference is involved. In the next section, we move on to examine the acoustic cues which allow listeners to discriminate between various categories of speech sounds.

Acoustic cues in speech perception

On the basis of the types of experimentation outlined above, phoneticians have managed to identify the central acoustic cues which enable listeners to differentiate speech sounds from one another. Using such experimentation, it has been possible to demonstrate that listeners possess **categorical perception**, i.e. the ability to identify categorically the point at which one sound begins to sound like another. We might envisage, for example a situation in which we produce Cardinal Vowel 1 and, while maintaining the voiced phonation, round the lips. According to the notion of categorical perception, it would be possible to identify the point at which the /i/ quality disappears and /y/ begins to emerge. We will now examine the acoustic cues for identifying presence or absence of phonation, place of articulation, manner of articulation and vowel distinctions.

Phonation differences

We have stated earlier that the voiced–voiceless contrast is crucial for conveying linguistic distinctions. Because of this, it is obviously important to examine how listeners identify phonatory differences in speech. We have already seen in Chapter 9 that voiced sounds are distinguished acoustically from voiceless sounds because of the presence of fundamental frequency and the periodicity which exists in voiced sounds. So, the acoustic cues of low-frequency energy and periodicity combine to indicate the presence of voicing to a listener.

Of course, we know from an articulatory standpoint that voicing distinctions are not conveyed merely by the presence or absence of voiced phonation for the duration of that sound. In the sequence /paba/, for instance, it is clear that there is a voicing distinction between the /p/ and the /b/, but the distinction may not merely be one of voice or voicelessness during the closure phase of each of the plosives, but rather a result of activity at or immediately following the release phase. At the release phase of the /p/, some time elapses before the vowel begins, whereas the /b/ is released simultaneously with the start of the vowel. For the voiceless and the voiced plosives respectively, we say that a long VOT versus a short VOT exists, and it is during the long VOT for voiceless plosives that we hear the aspiration, or noise, which characterizes such plosives.

Two further acoustic features which enable listeners to identify voicing concern duration and intensity cues. First, the relative duration of the vowel and consonant segments is relevant, where the consonant occurs in word-final position. The effect is that a voiced consonant will be perceived where there is a long vowel followed by a short consonant. So, for example, in a realization such as [biː] followed by an alveolar consonant, the final consonant will be heard as [d] rather than [t]. In the opposite case, i.e. where a short vowel is followed by a long consonant, the consonant will be heard as voiceless. With regard to intensity, those sounds which are perceived as having greater intensity (i.e. fortis sounds) are usually perceived as being voiceless, which those with comparatively less intensity (lenis sounds) are likely to be heard as voiced.

So, listeners perceive voice as a result of either simple presence of voiced phonation, or because of specific VOT and segment length cues. With regard to the perception of articulatory aspects of consonants, we now move on to consider the aspects which allow listeners to hear place and manner of articulation.

Place of articulation

Consonant place of articulation is conveyed acoustically by means of formant transitions, i.e. either from a vowel to a following consonant, or to a vowel from the preceding consonant. In these cases, we are particularly interested in the F2 transition of the vowel which can have either a minus or a plus value. If the F2 has a minus value, then the frequency of the vowel is moving towards or away from a frequency which is lower than normal for that vowel, and the place of articulation of the consonant can be identified as bilabial. If, on the other hand, the F2 has a plus value then the movement is either towards or away from a frequency that is higher than usual, and a velar place of articulation is indicated. Less significant transitions, either in the plus or minus direction, suggest an alveolar place of articulation.

It is also possible to infer place of articulation for fricative sounds due to the extent and distribution of acoustic noise that exists. For example, /ʃ/ tends to have a concentration of noise between approximately 1900 Hz and 6000 Hz, corresponding to the post-alveolar central stricture, whereas the noise for the alveolar /s/ occurs between 4000 Hz and 8000 Hz.

Manner of articulation

As we have stated in Chapter 9, there are some easily identifiable cues which enable us to read manner of articulation from a spectrograph. Plosives, for instance are recognizable by means of a break in the spectrographic pattern, whereas fricatives are characterized by high-frequency noise. In psychoacoustic terms, plosives are heard where there is an interruption of the speech signal lasting from approximately 40 to 120 milliseconds. For fricatives, the high-frequency or noise aspect lasts approximately 70–140 milliseconds. Affricates, i.e. combinations of stop and fricative, are identifiable on the basis of these combined acoustic cues, i.e. interruption followed by high-frequency noise.

With regard to other manners of articulation, there are also psychoacoustically relevant cues. It is important to point out first that approximants, nasals and laterals are all characterized by the presence of voice. In addition to the voicing cue, nasals are identified where there is low-frequency resonance just above the level of F_o, combined with zero energy until about the 2000 Hz level. Approximants and laterals, while both marked by vowel-type formants, are distinguishable on the basis of the duration of the formant transitions and, usually, the transitions for laterals are more rapid than those for approximants.

Acoustic cues for vowels

We know by now that part of the essential definition of a vowel is that it is voiced. Therefore, for listeners to identify a vowel, low-frequency energy (i.e. Fo) must be present. In addition to this feature, the location of and relationship between the vowel formants provides cues for recognition of particular varieties of vowels. Of course, while is possible to identify general targets for formants according to a given vowel sound, the precise location of these formants will differ for individuals and for groups of speakers. However, the overall pattern of formant arrangements, in spite of frequency variation at F1 and F2, will usually be easily discernible and these patterns are discussed in Chapter 9. Lip-rounding, for example, has an effect on vowel formants, so that lip-rounded vowels exhibit an overall weaker distribution of energy through the formants.

To a lesser extent, vowel duration and intensity aspects may also be responsible for listeners' discrimination of vowels. For instance, it is the case that vowel length is distinctive in some languages (in Danish, [vilə] means 'wild' whereas [viː lə] means 'rest'), so that listeners identify words on the basis of vowel length before the final consonant is uttered. With regard to intensity, it is sometimes suggested that low vowels display greater intensity than high vowels, but this effect is not significant.

Conclusion

Throughout this chapter, we have discussed the acoustic cues which enable listeners to identify individual speech sounds. Together, these constitute the major aspects of speech recognition and discrimination. Of course, psychoacoustic investigations encompass a greater range of features than those explained in this chapter. For instance, they are also interested in the particular aspects of laryngeal activity which allow listeners to identify pitch transitions in speech. Clearly, if an impairment to the auditory system such as deafness occurs, then the listener loses the ability to discriminate crucial speech cues, and the communicative process breaks down.

Further reading

For an in-depth account of the acoustic cues to vowels and consonants, Fry (1979) is recommended (*see also* the 'Further reading' section of Chapter 9). With regard to psychoacoustic methods in particular, useful background material is to be found in Richards (1976) and Johnson (1997).

Short questions

1 What is meant by the term 'psychoacoustics'?
2 Explain how the mel and the Bark scales are used in psychoacoustic experimentation.
3 How is perceived intensity measured?
4 Explain the term 'just noticeable difference' as it relates to frequency and intensity.
5 What acoustic cues do listeners use to decide whether a consonant is voiced or voiceless?

Essay questions

1 Explain how listeners use a variety of acoustic cues to identify features of vowels and consonants.
2 Design a psychoacoustic experiment in which you will investigate a listener's perception of pitch.
3 Imagine you are a telecommunications software engineer and that you need to produce a communications system capable of conveying detailed speech information. How would you establish the type of information that must be captured by your system?

12 Instrumental phonetics

Introduction

In previous chapters we have introduced the notion of acoustic analysis, and the sound spectrograph and its modern computer-based versions. We have also briefly reviewed some of the experimental approaches phoneticians have taken to the study of speech perception. However, these are not the only forms of instrumental phonetics. Over the last century phoneticians have developed a range of instruments to analyse speech production, transmission and perception. In this chapter we will review a range of approaches to the instrumental investigation of speech production, and illustrate them with examples of the sorts of data that are acquired from them.

A short cautionary note is needed, however, before we proceed. Students of phonetics may well develop an idea that speech description using impressionistic transcription is wholly subjective and imprecise, whereas instrumental approaches are always objective and precise. On the one hand, transcription if learned properly can be an objective and testable approach to describing speech sounds; on the other, the results from instrumental analyses may themselves be difficult to interpret, as it may be unclear which part of a printout refers to which section of the speech. All instruments have in-built limitations (perhaps to do with speed of data acquisition, or ability to cover all relevant parameters), so no approach to phonetic description can give all the answers, but using transcription and instrumentation together can get us quite a way along the road.

Muscle control for speech

The production of speech requires initiation of an airstream, phonatory activity within the larynx and articulatory activity within the pharynx and nasal and oral cavities. At all these stages, relevant muscle activity is needed, and so at a very basic level the study of muscle activity will help the phonetician understand how the speech process operates. Interest in muscle activity goes back over 100 years, but it is only in the last 50 or so years that the technology has been available to study this area fully. This technique is known as **electromyography** (EMG), and will be described in this section.

EMG is based on the fact that when muscles are activated minute electrical charges can be detected. These charges can be measured through the use of electrodes, and the resulting patterns of electrical discharges can be compared to the speech signal (assuming this is recorded separately) when electromyography is used by the speech scientist. This results in our ability to note which muscles are activated at which point in time during the speech event.

To be able to record the very small levels of electrical discharge involved in muscle contraction (these are measured in microvolts), electrodes have to be placed either into the muscle concerned, or very close to it. These electrodes are of two main types: intra-muscular (needle or hooked wire) electrodes which are placed into the relevant muscle, and surface electrodes which are placed on the surface of the skin immediately above the relevant muscle. The former type would need to be used by the speech scientist to investigate activity in speech muscles such as in the larynx which are away from the surface of the skin, whereas the latter have been used for facial muscles, such as the orbicularis oris which controls lip posture in speech. However, even surface muscles may be investigated through intra-muscular electrodes. This is because interest may lie in a small muscle surrounded by larger ones which would affect the signal if a surface electrode were used, or (as in the case of orbicularis oris) a muscle might consist of several subdivisions which can only be satisfactorily distinguished through the use of an intra-muscular electrode.

This technique has been used to investigate many of the muscles involved in speech production, and has informed phoneticians' models of speech production. However, in recent times there has been probably as much work done with EMG in the investigation of speech disorders. These range from voice disorders due to laryngeal muscle problems to acquired neurological disorders such as dysarthria and apraxia of speech. Research has also been directed towards stuttering in an attempt to find out what patterns of muscular contraction occur during a dysfluent episode.

Figure 12.1 shows a EMG traces of some of the muscles involved in lip movement for the phrase [epapapə], spoken by a French sufferer of Friedreich's ataxia (though this trace shows an almost normal pattern at conversational speaking rate). The muscles concerned are mentalis (MENT), orbicularis oris superior (OOS), orbicularis oris inferior (OOI), depressor labii inferior (DLI) and anterior belly of the digastric (ABD); a voicing trace is also included. We can clearly see the peaks of muscles activity co-occurring with the production of the [p] segments (*see* Gentil, 1990).

Airflow in speech

As we noted in Chapter 2, a moving body of air is essential for speech, and by far the most commonly used airstream is the pulmonic egressive one. The muscular activity used to set this airflow in motion can, of course, be investigated through the use of EMG; however, this does not tell us anything about the volumes of air flow involved, their speed and their direction. If we wish to find out this kind of information we must employ a technique known as **aerometry.**

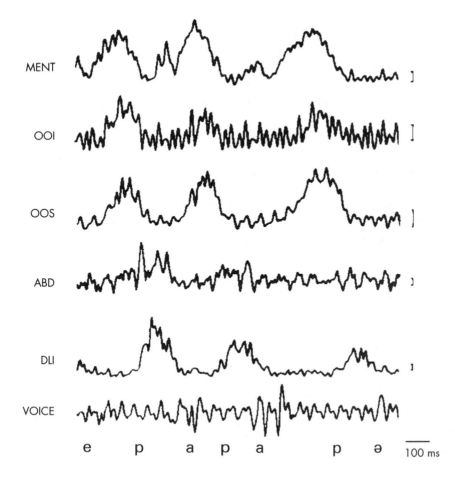

Figure 12.1
Averaged intergrated EMG for the phrase [epapapə]. Brackets indicate 100 μV (Courtesy Michèle Gentil)

Most aerometry systems are designed to investigate several aspects of speech aerodynamics of interest to phoneticians. These include – as noted above – the volume velocity and direction of airflow, but also intra-oral and nasal air pressures (and in some instances other air pressure readings), all linked to a speech signal taken from a microphone. Often, aerometry is used in addition to other equipment (for example, electrolaryngography), and so traces can be produced showing the interaction of aerodynamics and vocal fold activity etc.

Aerometry systems are normally based around an airtight mask that fits over the nose and mouth. The measurement of air pressures and flows requires suitable transducers to be fitted within the mask. These convert pressures into electrical signals that can be fed to a personal computer for storage and display. The speech signal itself has to be recorded via a mask microphone (i.e. one fitted within the mask: an external microphone would only pick up a very muffled signal). The mask microphone, however, does not produce the clearest of signals, as the speaker's voice is bound to be affected by the wearing of the mask. This is one of the main drawbacks of aerometry systems, together with the fact that face masks can never be absolutely airtight and some leakage is bound to occur.

To illustrate typical aerometry results, we can see in Figure 12.2 oral and nasal air pressures and nasal airflow for repetitions of the syllable /si/ in a dysarthric and hypernasal speaker. Figure 12.3 illustrates oral and nasal flow together with an EGG signal (i.e. electroglottography: what we term electrolaryngography in the following section) for the word 'hamper' ([hæmpɚ] in American English pronunciation). These figures show how aerometry allows us to compare a variety of aerodynamic activities during speech, and then link these to other types of measurement.

Phonation

To examine phonatory activity the phonetician must obtain information about the position and movement of the vocal folds within the larynx. This can be done either directly or indirectly. Direct observation normally is undertaken through the use of an endoscope: a long narrow tube that can be attached, for example, to a video recorder. A rigid endoscope can be inserted into the oral cavity, and views of the larynx and vocal folds obtained with the subject uttering a low back vowel. Few other sounds are possible, because the presence of the endoscope does not allow normal tongue movement. Alternatively, a flexible nasendoscope can be used, passed through the nasal cavity into the nasopharynx. This does allow a wider range of speech sounds to be uttered, but is of course still very invasive. Because of the speed of vocal fold vibration, the movements of the folds are difficult to see and so analyse. High-speed photography can get

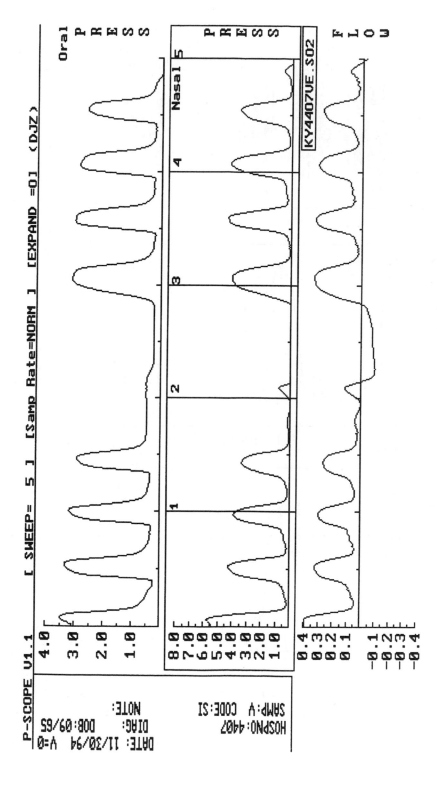

Figure 12.2 Oral and nasal air pressures and nasal airflow for repetitions of /si/ in a dysarthric and hypernasal speaker
(Courtesy David Zajac)

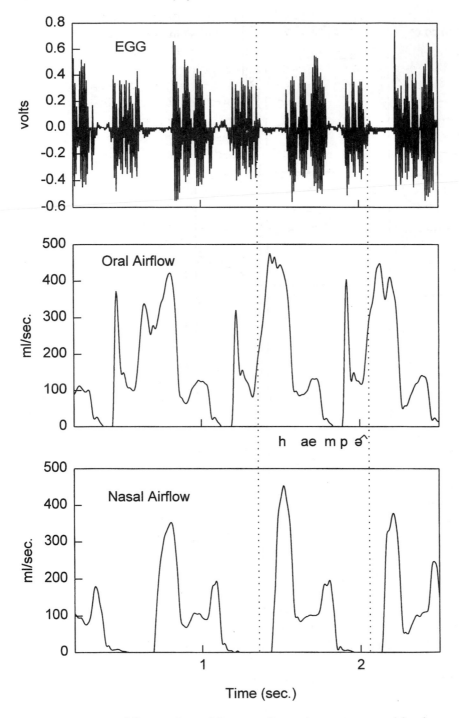

Figure 12.3 Oral flow and nasal flow together with an EGG signal for 'hamper'

round this problem, but is very expensive. Normally, stroboscopic light, carried down the endoscope, is utilized. Stroboscopic light consists of very rapid flashes of light, in this case triggered by the speaker's own voice (when analysed acoustically or through electrolaryngography). If the light flashes are synchronized with the speed of vocal fold vibration, we see what appears to be a static view of the folds, if a slight delay is built in we see the movement of the folds from vibratory cycle to vibratory cycle: caught, as it seems, in slow motion. An example of this technique (**stroboscopic endoscopy**) is given in Figure 12.4, where normal vocal fold vibrations are pictured together with electrolaryngographic readouts.

Indirect examination of phonation is achieved through the use of the **electrolaryngograph** (ELG), also termed 'electroglottograph' (EGG). With this technique, two electrodes are placed externally on the subject's throat either side of the larynx. A weak current is passed from one electrode to the other through the larynx, and the equipment measures the varying impedance offered to this current by the vocal folds. This clearly differs from moment to moment during normal voicing, and particular patterns are also characteristic of creak, whisper and other phonation types. This basic information is displayed on the computer screen in what is termed the Lx waveform. However, a variety of other measures are also possible in current models of the electrolaryngograph. First, the pitch of the voice can be computed from looking at cycle to cycle variations in vocal fold vibration frequency; this is displayed on the Fx waveform. The system is also able to compute closed quotient and open quotient measures during voicing, and this can be especially useful in examining disordered voice quality.

Recent versions of the electrolaryngograph have included full acoustic analysis as well as vocal fold measures. This allows plotting of measures of intensity against vocal fold frequency, and the viewing of the speech waveform together with Lx or Fx waves, and so on. Figure 12.5 and Figure 12.6 show modal and creaky voice types; in both cases the speech signal is shown in the top of the figure with vocal fold trace (Lx trace) below (vocal fold closure upward).

In Figure 12.5 the acoustic waveform has a regularly repeating pattern (or periodicity), whereas the laryngograph waveform shows a clear pattern of regular vocal fold closures. However, Figure 12.6 shows creaky voice, and the two waveforms illustrate that creaky voice is associated with cycles of alternating large and small duration and amplitude, while the vocal folds show rapid closure but slow opening.

We illustrate in Figure 12.7 some of the other measurements available to ELG users:

- DFx1 – Larynx frequency distribution. This analysis shows the probability of larynx vibrations over the range of frequencies normally found

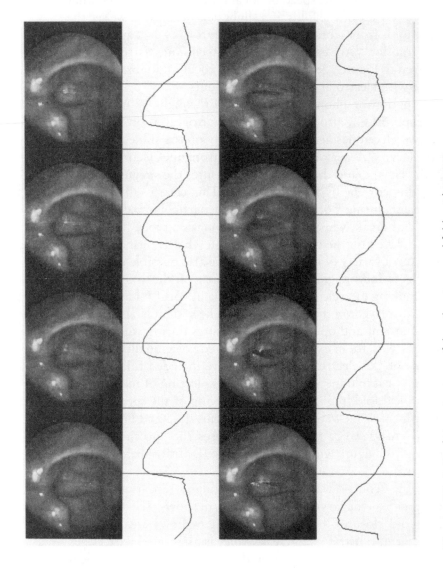

Figure 12.4 Stroboscopic views of the vibrating vocal folds with ELG Lx trace (Courtesy Adrian Fourcin, Evelyn Abberton and Laryngograph Ltd)

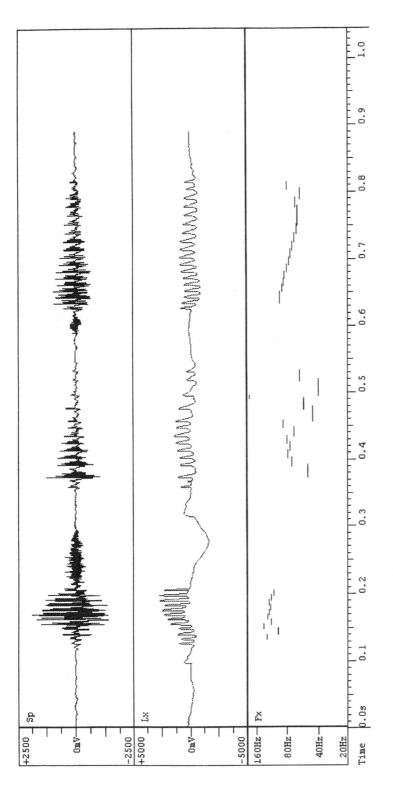

Figure 12.5 Speech (upper) and Lx (middle) and Fx (lower) ELG waveforms for modal voice quality uttering the phrase 'This won't do' (Courtesy Adrian Fourcin. Evelyn Abberton and Laryngograph Ltd)

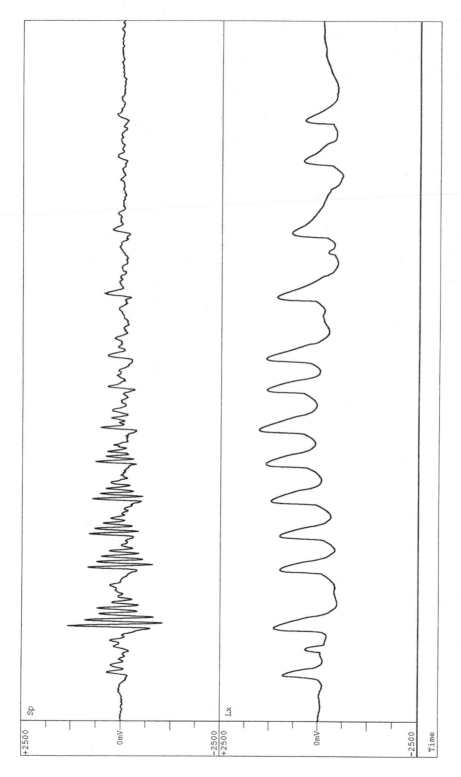

Figure 12.6 Speech (upper) and Lx (lower) ELG waveforms for creaky voice quality uttering 'aren'ʲ' (Courtesy Adrian Fourcin, Evelyn Abberton and Laryngograph Ltd)

in voice production. The speaker in Figure 12.7(a) shows a well-defined range, and a clear modal (most prominent) frequency.

- CFx – Larynx frequency cross-plot. This analysis shows the degree of regularity in the speaker's vocal fold vibration sequences. Irregularities show up as points plotted away from the main diagonal on the graph. In Figure 12.7(b) we can see that the speaker shows very few points of irregularity.
- VRP – The phonetogram. This graph shows the range of acoustic intensities in the voice plotted against their corresponding vocal fold frequencies. Phonetograms of normal voice have patterns similar to that shown in Figure 12.7(c) so this measure provides a useful initial analysis of disordered voice types.
- QxFx – Closed phase ratio. This measure provides the ratio of closed phase duration (i.e. the time when the vocal folds are held together) to the duration of the total larynx period. The longer the closed phase, the 'better' is the voice quality perceived. The example in Figure 12.7(d) shows the closed phase ratio for a normal speaker.

Velic action

In this section we will describe how speech scientists have investigated nasality in speech. Nasal and nasalized segments have characteristic acoustic features (described in Chapter 9), and so can be examined solely through spectrographic analysis. However, there have been approaches to this area that have relied on the articulatory aspects of nasality. Nasal and nasalized sounds are produced with a lowered velum, with air escaping only through the nasal cavity (in the case of nasal sounds), or through both the nasal and the oral cavities (in the case of nasalized ones). This gives us two possible ways to examine nasality: either through looking at velum position (raised or lowered), or though measuring egressive air flow from the nasal cavity.

The method employed in instrumental phonetics to measure velum position is the velotrace. The **velotrace** is a mechanical device, part of which actually rests directly on the upper surface of the velum. A narrow flexible part of the velotrace is placed through the nostril and the nasal cavity onto the upper surface of the velum, and is able to move up and down as the velum itself moves up and down. This portion acts as a lever, and is joined outside the nasal cavity by a series of joints and other levers leading ultimately to a computer that records the movements of the levers and plots them against the speech signal (recorded via a microphone). In this way the physical movement of the velum can be examined at different points of the speech signal.

However, the velotrace is invasive, and requires complex and expensive equipment. The alternate approach is to look at airflow at the nares. This

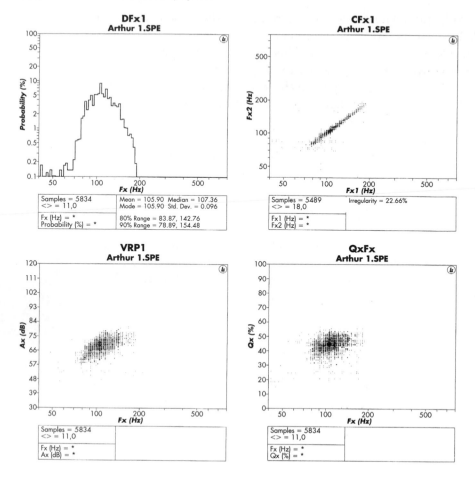

Figure 12.7 A series of ELG measurements of the same subject: **(a)** DFx1; **(b)** CFx; **(c)** VRP1; and **(d)** QxFx (Courtesy Adrian Fourcin, Evelyn Abberton and Laryngograph Ltd)

was touched on when we discussed aerometry above, but very often phoneticians (especially those helping speech pathologists looking at abnormal nasalance in speakers) will require something less expensive and complex than full aerometry equipment. **Nasometers** are designed to look at nasal airflow through the use of small microphones rather than the pressure and flow meters described earlier. Further, airtight masks are usually avoided, thus making the equipment easier to use for the subject (though not so accurate for the phonetician).

A typical nasometer is that produced by Kay Elemetrics, which uses two microphones, one above the other, separated by a metal plate. The whole is mounted on a series of straps that can be fitted to the head of the subject, so that the upper microphone records nasal output, and the lower oral output. The software that comes with the equipment allows the ratio of oral to nasal airflow to be calculated and displayed in a variety of ways on the screen. Figure 12.8 shows the utterance 'a hamper' (in southern British pronunciation: [ə 'hæmpə]), and one can clearly see the increase in nasalization from the oral, through the nasalized, to the nasal segment.

Nasometers are clearly more user-friendly than the velotrace in measuring nasality. However, it must be remembered that this equipment is less accurate than the aerometer described earlier.

Articulation

As we have seen, phoneticians have been successful in developing instrumentation that directly or indirectly measures many aspects of speech other than the articulation of individual sounds. The measurement of the movement of the articulators within the oral cavity has, however, proved to be especially difficult. Certain places of articulation (e.g. bilabial, labiodental, interdental) can be seen by an observer, and so recorded photographically or on video-tape. Other places, and subtle distinctions of manner (e.g. between stop, affricate and fricative), cannot be easily observed. An early attempt to surmount these difficulties came with the development of direct **palatography**.

Palatography is the measurement of tongue-palate contact patterns through taking an image of the palate (i.e. palate patterns are measured but not tongue patterns). In direct palatography this is done by coating the roof of the mouth with a charcoal-based powder, and then requiring the subject to utter a single segment that involves tongue–palate contact (that is to say any consonant between the dental and velar places of articulation). The contact will disturb the charcoal coating, and this will be wiped off from

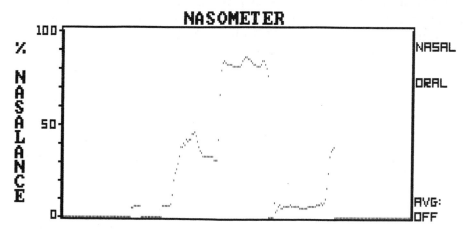

Figure 12.8 Nasometer trace for 'a hamper'

the area where the tongue has contacted the palate. By using a mirror inserted slightly into the subject's mouth, a photographic record can be made of the pattern of disturbance (and so the area of contact) for any particular sound.

This technique has clearly several drawbacks. First, speakers can only utter a single sound at a time: this is not a normal way of speaking and so may affect the results. Second, there is always a danger that subjects may raise their tongue only slightly after making the utterance and thereby wipe off a different section of the powder. Finally, the resultant photograph shows the entire area of the palate contacted during the sound in question: we cannot ascertain which parts were contacted at the beginning of the articulation, and which other parts were added in or taken away as the articulation proceeded. A slight variant of direct palatography was indirect palatography. This used an artificial palate designed to fit the subject's mouth closely. This had the powder sprayed onto it, and was removed following the making of a sound to be measured externally.

Electropalatography (EPG) was developed from the 1970s onwards to overcome these disadvantages. EPG is dynamic, and so we can see which parts of the palate are contacted at which point during articulation. It does not involve the use of charcoal powder, but instead a very thin artificial palate fitted with a large number of electrodes which fire when contacted by the tongue. This means we no longer have the problem of only uttering one sound at a time, or accidentally interfering with the powder coating.

There are currently three different EPG systems in regular use: the Rion system from Japan, the Reading-EPG3 system from Great Britain, and the Kay Elemetrics Electropalatometer system from the USA, all running through personal computers and displaying results on the PC screen (and of course these can be printed from the computer). They all differ slightly in terms of the shape of the artificial palate (e.g. the Reading system covers just the palate, whereas the Kay system covers the upper dentition as well), the number of electrodes (Reading: 62, Rion: 63, Kay: 96), and the

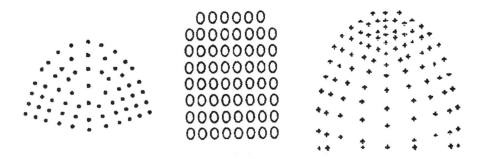

Figure 12.9 EPG electrode patterns for the Rion (left), Reading (centre), and Kay (right) systems

patterns of the electrodes (*see* Figure 12.9). As we have noted, these systems are dynamic: that is to say they can show the patterns of contact at various points during an utterance. To do this there must be rapid continuous sampling of the electrodes, for example 100 or 200 times a second. (EPG3 samples 100 frames of data a second; the Kay system also samples at 100 frames a second, with the system taking 1.7 milliseconds to complete a sweep of all the electrodes.) As we can see from Figure 12.10 a series of frames can be displayed on the computer screen and printed, and from this series the phonetician can identify the frames where maximum contact for a consonant takes place, where contact just begins and where it ends, and so on.

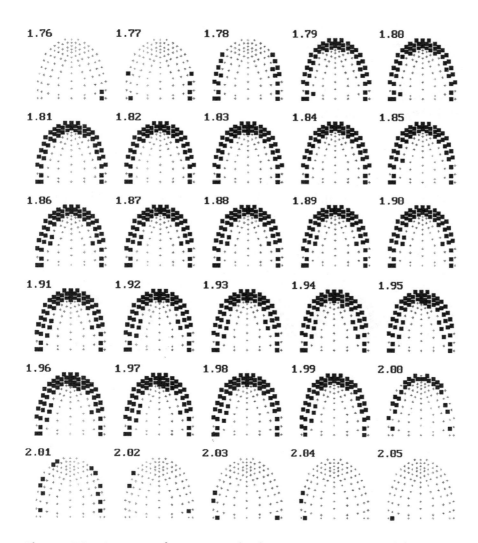

Figure 12.10 An EPG frames series for the utterance [udu], sampling every 10 milliseconds

Once data has been collected, data reduction techniques are available that allow the researcher to compare speakers or speech events in a principled manner. The Reading EPG3 system, for example, has software aiding in the calculation of centre of gravity (i.e. where the main concentration of activated electrodes is situated); anteriority index (an index that gives preference to clear anterior or posterior contact patterns); assymmetry index (compares left and right side patterns), and others (described in Hardcastle and Gibbon, 1997).

The use of EPG in the study of speech can be seen in Figure 12.11 and Figure 12.12 below. Here we compare the production of final alveolars following a vowel, and following the same vowel and /ɹ/ in a rhotic accent of English (Northern Irish English). It can be clearly seen that the presence of the /ɹ/ moves the plosive contact from alveolar to post-alveolar.

Tracking

We have seen how the EPG can tell us much about the contact patterns between the tongue and the roof of the mouth. However, there are many sound types (such as vowels and labials) which cannot be examined via EPG, and we must remember it tells us little about tongue position or shape. The dream of the phonetician has always been to somehow see the movements of all the articulators during speech, and articulator tracking is one step towards this goal. Tracking involves placing one or more small pellets (made of gold, for example) on the articulator(s) under investigation, and then tracking the movements of the pellet(s). These movements can then be displayed on a computer screen and printed out and, as long as the

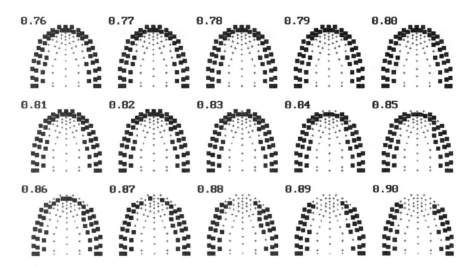

Figure 12.11 EPG patterns of alveolar stops in the word 'caught' in a rhotic accent of English

phonetician also has recorded certain anatomical landmarks (such as the chin, or the palate), it is possible to see how the articulator moves in time in relation to the landmarks.

Two main tracking systems have been used in speech research: **X-ray microbeam** and **electromagnetic articulography** (EMA). The X-ray microbeam technique involves the use of computer-controlled small doses of X-rays that are sufficient to record the movement of the pellets attached to the articulators. The dosage is small enough to allow reasonably long recording sessions with minimal danger to subjects. This technique has been used to study both normal and disordered speech (*see* review in Ball and Gröne, 1997), but due to the expense involved in setting up and acquiring the equipment, only a very few research centres have ever used it.

EMA (also known as EMMA for electromagnetic mid-sagittal articulography) is considerably less expensive and requires much less laboratory space than X-ray microbeam. Electromagnetic articulography is a non-invasive, and biologically safe instrumentation system that records and displays articulatory movements. At present there are three different commercially available systems that differ in technical details: the Carstens Electromagnetic Articulograph AG 100 (Schönle et al., 1987; Tuller et al., 1990), the Electromagnetic Midsagittal Articulometer EMMA (Perkell et al., 1992), and the Movetrack from Sweden (Branderud, 1985).

EMA works as follows (*see* full details in Ball and Gröne, 1997): a transmitter coil generates an alternating magnetic field; the strength of the field decreases with the distance from the transmitter. A receiving coil positioned with its axis in parallel to the transmitter induces an alternating low voltage, that changes with the distance of the receiver from the transmitter.

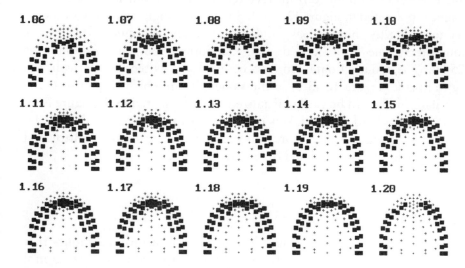

Figure 12.12 EPG patterns of alveolar stops in the word 'court' in a rhotic accent of English

By using two transmitter coils with different frequencies the distance between the receiver and the transmitter can be calculated from the strength of the voltages induced in the receiver. But when the detector is tilted, distances appear to be too large, and the position of the detector cannot be determined. Therefore a third signal from a third transmitter has been added, which allows an iterative correction of the tilt angle. The three signals from the transmitters can be interpreted as radii of three circles around the transmitters. If the receiver coil is tilted these three circles do not intersect at one point, since all three radii are too great. In a step-by-step algorithm the radii are then reduced by the same factor till intersection occurs at a single point. This point represents the actual coil position.

The transmitter coils are aligned in parallel and perpendicular to the midsagittal plane on a light-weight helmet, worn around a speaker's head. The positions of the coils are in front of the forehead, the mandible and the neck. In this manner the speaker's head is just inside the alternating electromagnetic field. Up to five detector coils can be fixed on the articulators for simultaneous recording (about 800 Hz): e.g. the upper and lower lips, the mandible, the tongue tip and the tongue dorsum. The speech signal is also recorded as an acoustical reference (about 16 kHz). Detector coils, which are 4 mm to 2 mm in size, are fixed with surgical glue (Hystoacryl). From these coils a very small wire, about 0.4 mm in diameter leads out of the corner of the mouth (for coils that are fixed on the tongue surface) to the pre-amplifier of the recording unit of the device.

Electromagnetic articulography provides a two-dimensional midsagittal display of articulatory movements. As a constant reference structure the shape of the palate can be recorded. An example of the two-dimensional time history data obtained from receivers placed on four locations on the tongue is presented in Figure 12.13(a). Shown is a single repetition of a subject repeating the phrase 'Say ladder again'. The movement trajectories from the tongue have been digitally smoothed following sampling at 625 Hz. The acquired data can also be displayed as receiver paths in the sagittal plane. Figure 12.13(b) is the same data in which the form of the articulator paths can be easily visualized. Also presented in the figure is an outline of the hard palate taken during the experimental session. EMA studies are producing ever more information on articulator control and movements in both normal and disordered speech.

Imaging

The tracking systems we have just looked at both involve techniques that provide some kind of image of the vocal tract (especially the supraglottal vocal tract). There are other imaging techniques that do not normally

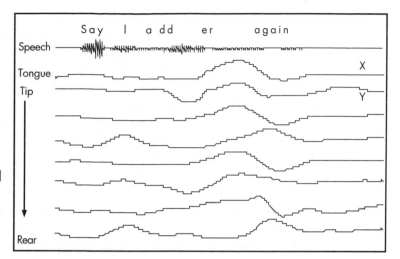

Figure 12.13a
Vertical (y) and horizontal (x) movement trajectories from four receivers on the tongue. (Courtesy Vince Gracco)

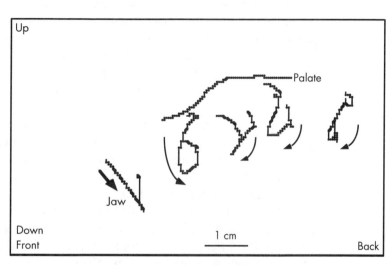

Figure 12.13b
Tongue and jaw paths in occlusal space associated with the word 'ladder'. Arrows indicate the direction of the motion. (Courtesy Vince Gracco)

involve the tracking of affixed pellets, but instead provide an image of all or parts of the structures within the relevant part of the vocal tract. The oldest of these techniques is **X-radiography** (which, of course, we have just looked at in its microbeam form), but more recently researchers have applied both the **ultrasound** and **magnetic resonance imaging** (MRI) techniques to the study of speech production.

X-radiography was developed at the end of the nineteenth century when it was discovered that these rays (part of the general spectrum of rays, including radio waves, and rays of light and heat, but at the very low frequency end of this spectrum) penetrate materials that would normally reflect light. Another important aspect of X-rays is differential absorption: that is to say, material of different densities will absorb X-rays to different degrees. This means that if we record X-rays on photographic plates (or similar, such as cine or video), materials of different densities will be distinguishable.

X-rays have been used in medical research since their discovery, and phonetics research has also made use of them for most of this time: researching both normal and disordered aspects of speech production. A wide range of X-ray techniques have been developed, involving greater or lesser degress of clarity; still, cine and video pictures; and varying degrees of dosage of radioactivity. Because of concerns about safety, phoneticians have been moving away from X-radiography recently (with the exception of the microbeam studies referred to above, but this equipment is almost prohibitively expensive), and have instead turned to other imaging techniques described in this section.

Ultrasonic investigations of speech have utilized the fact that pulses of ultrasound (sounds with frequencies of 2–20 MHz) reflect off physical structures (such as the tongue or larynx). Computer-based analysis allows us to measures distances derived from the time it takes the pulses of ultrasound to travel from the transmitter to the structure and back to the receiver. As different densities of physical structure (such as soft tissues or bone) have different acoustic resistance, it is also possible to distinguish these. The ultrasound transducer is held beneath the chin and sound waves pass into the tongue from the bottom. When the waves reach the airspace in the oral cavity, they reflect back to the transducer (meaning the waves cannot pass over airspace). A computer within the machine reconstructs the images from the reflected echoes, in real-time, creating 30 or more scans per second of the tongue surface.

A lot of ultrasound work in phonetics has dealt with tongue movement and shape. X-ray studies have always been much better at sagittal (i.e. side) views of the tongue, rather than frontal views (as the mass of the jaw bone interferes with clear reading of the X-rays). Ultrasound investigations have enabled us to look at the surface of the tongue from the front: which, of course, is essential in studying the grooved and slit fricatives discussed in Chapter 5. Figure 12.14 shows tongue shapes for a variety of front and central vowels that have been constructed from ultrasound data.

The final instrumental technique we will look at is magnetic resonance imaging (MRI). Magnetic resonance imaging (or nuclear magnetic resonance imaging) is a non-invasive imaging technique giving three-dimensional views of biological tissue with good resolution compared to many other approaches (particularly of the soft tissue of the vocal tract). Its main drawback currently is temporal, in that, due to the time required to obtain a magnetic resonance image, static images only are possible (though recent developments towards a more dynamic system can produce images very frequently: up to four times a second).

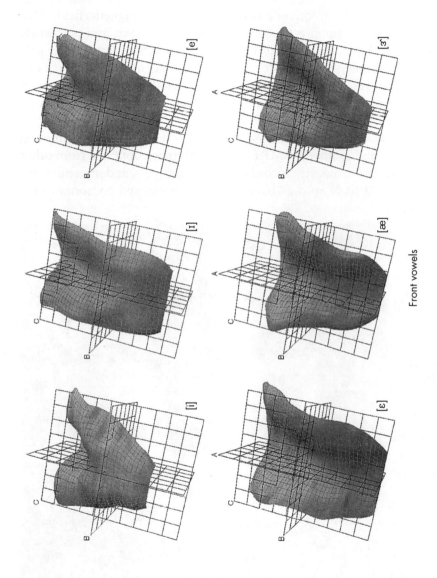

Front vowels

Figure 12.14 Ultrasound of the tongue with front vowels (Courtesy Maureen Stone)

MRI works by taking advantage of the magnetic properties of hydrogen nuclei protons, which occur abundantly in biological tissue (Moore, 1992). If a large and constant magnetic field is applied to the biological tissue (for example, the vocal tract), then the protons in the area concerned will align parallel to that field. The next step in the imaging procedure requires the application of a radio frequency orthogonal to the magnetic field. This results in the dipoles tipping away from their primary axis and precessing in a cone-shaped spinning path. During the free induction decay of the precession of the dipole, a small electromotive force is emitted. This force can be detected by a receiver which is tuned to the radio frequency used, and in the final stage of imaging, the electromotive force is converted via a processor unit to an image (*see* Morris, 1986).

The majority of MRI studies on speech have concentrated on examining the vocal tract, and comparing MRI results with those obtained from other methods (such as the acoustic record or X-radiography), and investigations of errors in MRI data. Studies have looked at vowel and consonant pro-

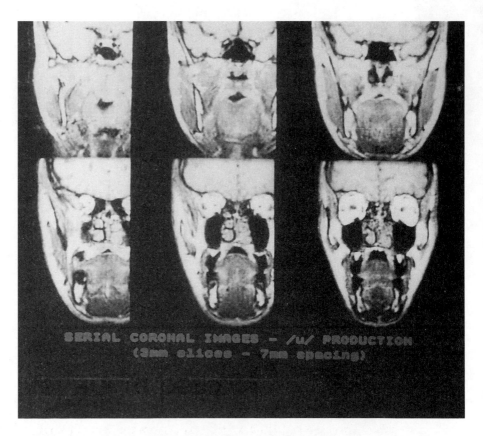

Figure 12.15 MRI images: serial coronal images of the production of /u/ (3 mm slices, 7 mm spacing) (Courtesy Christopher Moore)

duction, and both normal and pathological speech. Figure 12.15 illustrates some of the images obtained during one such study, and demonstrates a series of MRI 'slices' through the oral cavity (working from the back to the front) to give us front views of the production of the vowel /u/.

Conclusion

As we have demonstrated in this chapter, there exists a wide range of instrumentation for the investigation of the speech production process (not all of which have been included here, of course). The trend in the future appears to be to integrate different measurement techniques to provide a multi-parameter analysis package. For example, acoustic information via sound spectroscopy can be included together with ELG/EGG traces, EPG frames, and EMA tracks from different articulator points. Such multi-parameter data will allow us better to understand the complex interaction of articulators in speech production.

Further reading

Instrumental phonetic studies are mostly reported in the main phonetics journals, such as *Journal of Phonetics, Journal of the Acoustical Society of America, Journal of Speech Language and Hearing Research, Language and Speech, Phonetica*, and *Speech and Language Imaging*. Serious students of phonetics are recommended to consult these journals to follow developments in the discipline.

However, collections that survey instrumental phonetics are available, and among the more recent are Ball and Code (1997), Kent *et al.* (1991) and Lass (1996).

Short questions

1 How is muscle control for speech production investigated?
2 What do aerometry systems measure and how do they do this?
3 What are the strengths and weaknesses of the nasometer and the velotrace?
4 What are the strengths and weaknesses of endoscopy and electrolaryngography/electroglottography?
5 How does EPG work?
6 Describe the operation of electromagnetic articulography.
7 How does ultrasonic imaging work, and why is it preferable to X-radiography?
8 Describe the operating principle underlying magnetic resonance imaging.

Essay Questions

1   Describe with reference to previous studies, the development of speech imaging techniques (including speech tracking) over the last 30 years.
2   Undertake, with the guidance of your tutor, a practical investigation of any aspects of speech production, using any one or combination of the techniques described in this chapter.

Appendix 1: Phonetics charts

AIRSTREAM TYPES

Œ	oesophageal speech	И	electrolarynx speech
Ю	trachaeo-oesophageal speech	↓	pulmonic ingressive speech

PHONATION TYPES

V	modal voice	F	falsetto
W	whisper	C	creak
V̤̣	whispery voice (murmur)	V̰	creaky voice
V̤	breathy voice	C̣	whispery creak
V!	harsh voice	V!!	ventricular phonation
V̬!!	diplophonia	Ṿ!!	whispery ventricular phon.

SUPRALARYNGEAL SETTINGS

L̝	raised larynx	L̞	lowered larynx
Vᶶ	labialized voice (open round)	Vʷ	labialized voice (close round)
V͍	spread-lip voice	Vᶹ	labio-dentalized voice
V̺	linguo-apicalized voice	V̻	linguo-laminarized voice
V˞	retroflex voice	V̪	dentalized voice
V̳	alveolarized voice	V̳ʲ	palatoalveolarized voice
Vʲ	palatalized voice	Vˠ	velarized voice
Vʶ	uvularized voice	Vˤ	pharyngealized voice
V̝ˤ	laryngo-pharyngealized voice	Vᴴ	faucalized voice
Ṽ	nasalized voice	V͊	denasalized voice
J̞	open jaw voice	J̝	close jaw voice
J˂	right offset jaw voice	J˃	left offset jaw voice
J̟	protruded jaw voice	Θ	protruded tongue voice

USE OF LABELED BRACES & NUMERALS TO MARK STETCHES OF SPEECH AND DEGREES OF QUALITY

[ˈðɪs ɪz ˈnɔ˞məl ˈvɔɪs {V!3 ˈðɪs ɪz ˈveri ˈhɑ˞ʃ ˈvɔɪs V!3} ˈðɪs ɪz ˈnɔ˞məl ˈvɔɪs wʌns ˈmɔ˞ {V!1 ˈðɪs ɪz ˈles ˈhɑ˞ʃ ˈvɔɪs V!1}]

THE INTERNATIONAL PHONETIC ALPHABET (revised to 1993, updated 1996)

CONSONANTS (PULMONIC)

	Bilabial	Labiodental	Dental	Alveolar	Postalveolar	Retroflex	Palatal	Velar	Uvular	Pharyngeal	Glottal
Plosive	p b			t d		ʈ ɖ	c ɟ	k ɡ	q ɢ		ʔ
Nasal	m	ɱ		n		ɳ	ɲ	ŋ	N		
Trill	ʙ			r					R		
Tap or Flap				ɾ		ɽ					
Fricative	ɸ β	f v	θ ð	s z	ʃ ʒ	ʂ ʐ	ç ʝ	x ɣ	χ ʁ	ħ ʕ	h ɦ
Lateral fricative				ɬ ɮ							
Approximant		ʋ		ɹ		ɻ	j	ɰ			
Lateral approximant				l		ɭ	ʎ	L			

Where symbols appear in pairs, the one to the right represents a voiced consonant. Shaded areas denote articulations judged impossible.

CONSONANTS (NON-PULMONIC)

Clicks	Voiced implosives	Ejectives
ʘ Bilabial	ɓ Bilabial	' Examples:
ǀ Dental	ɗ Dental/alveolar	p' Bilabial
ǃ (Post)alveolar	ʄ Palatal	t' Dental/alveolar
ǂ Palatoalveolar	ɠ Velar	k' Velar
ǁ Alveolar lateral	ʛ Uvular	s' Alveolar fricative

OTHER SYMBOLS

ʍ   Voiceless labial-velar fricative

w   Voiced labial-velar approximant

ɥ   Voiced labial-palatal approximant

ʜ   Voiceless epiglottal fricative

ʢ   Voiced epiglottal fricative

ʡ   Epiglottal plosive

ɕ ʑ   Alveolo-palatal fricatives

ɺ   Alveolar lateral flap

ɧ   Simultaneous ʃ and x

Affricates and double articulations can be represented by two symbols joined by a tie bar if necessary.

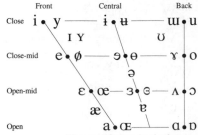

VOWELS

	Front	Central	Back
Close	i • y	ɨ • ʉ	ɯ • u
	ɪ Y	ʊ	
Close-mid	e • ø	ɘ • ɵ	ɤ • o
		ə	
Open-mid	ɛ • œ	ɜ • ɞ	ʌ • ɔ
	æ	ɐ	
Open	a • ɶ		ɑ • ɒ

Where symbols appear in pairs, the one to the right represents a rounded vowel.

SUPRASEGMENTALS

ˈ   Primary stress

ˌ   Secondary stress   ˌfoʊnəˈtɪʃən

ː   Long   eː

ˑ   Half-long   eˑ

˘   Extra-short   ĕ

| Minor (foot) group

‖   Major (intonation) group

.   Syllable break   ɹi.ækt

‿   Linking (absence of a break)

TONES AND WORD ACCENTS

LEVEL		CONTOUR	
̋e or ˥	Extra high	ě or ˇ	Rising
é ˦	High	ê ˆ	Falling
ē ˧	Mid	᷄e ˀ	High rising
è ˨	Low	᷅e ˬ	Low rising
̏e ˩	Extra low	᷈e ˷	Rising-falling
↓	Downstep	↗	Global rise
↑	Upstep	↘	Global fall

DIACRITICS   Diacritics may be placed above a symbol with a descender, e.g. ŋ̊

̥	Voiceless	n̥ d̥	̤	Breathy voiced	b̤ a̤	̪	Dental	t̪ d̪
̬	Voiced	s̬ t̬	̰	Creaky voiced	b̰ a̰	̺	Apical	t̺ d̺
ʰ	Aspirated	tʰ dʰ	̼	Linguolabial	t̼ d̼	̻	Laminal	t̻ d̻
̹	More rounded	ɔ̹	ʷ	Labialized	tʷ dʷ	̃	Nasalized	ẽ
̜	Less rounded	ɔ̜	ʲ	Palatalized	tʲ dʲ	ⁿ	Nasal release	dⁿ
̟	Advanced	u̟	ˠ	Velarized	tˠ dˠ	ˡ	Lateral release	dˡ
̠	Retracted	e̠	ˤ	Pharyngealized	tˤ dˤ	̚	No audible release	d̚
̈	Centralized	ë	̴	Velarized or pharyngealized	ɫ			
̽	Mid-centralized	ě	̝	Raised	e̝	(ɹ̝ = voiced alveolar fricative)		
̩	Syllabic	n̩	̞	Lowered	e̞	(β̞ = voiced bilabial approximant)		
̯	Non-syllabic	e̯	̘	Advanced Tongue Root	e̘			
˞	Rhoticity	ɚ a˞	̙	Retracted Tongue Root	e̙			

Appendix 2: Languages cited in the text

Language	Language Group	Geographical Area
|Gui	Central Khoisan	Botswana
!Xóõ	Southerm Khoisan	Botswana
Abkhaz	North Caucasian	Abkhazia (Georgia)
Acehnese	Austronesian	Indonesia
Agul	North Caucasian	Russia
American English	Indo-European (Germanic)	USA
Amharic	Semitic	Ethiopia
Amuzgo	Otomanguean-Amuzgoan	Mexico
Arabic	Semitic	Middle East, North Africa
Archi	North Caucasian	Russia
Arrernte	Australian	Australia
Bengali	Indo-European (Indo-Iranian)	Bangladesh, India
Brazilian Portugese	Indo-European (Romance)	Brazil
British English	Indo-European (Germanic)	Great Britain
Bura	Afro-Asiatic	Nigeria
Burmese	Sino-Tibetan	Burma
Cantonese	Sino-Tibetan	Kwangtung, southern China
Catalan	Indo-European (Romance)	Catalonia (Spain)
Chengtu Chinese	Sino-Tibetan	Szechuan (China)
Chinese (Mandarin)	Sino-Tibetan	northern China
Chipewyan	Athabaskan	north and central Canada
Comanche	Uto-Aztecan	Oklahoma (USA)
Czech	Indo-European (Slavonic)	Czech Republic

Language	Language Group	Geographical Area
Dutch	Indo-European (Germanic)	Netherlands, Belgium
Dyirbal	Pama-Nyungan	N. Queensland (Australia)
Edo	Niger-Congo	Nigeria
Efik	Niger-Congo	Nigeria, Cameroon
English	Indo-European (Germanic)	UK, USA, Canada, Australia, New Zealand, South Africa, Caribbean, etc.
Etsako	Niger-Congo	Nigeria
Ewe	Niger-Congo	Ghana, Togo
Farsi	Indo-European (Indo-Iranian)	Iran
Finnish	Uralic	Finland
French	Indo-European (Romance)	France, Belgium, Canada, Luxembourg, Monaco, Switzerland, French Guiana, Haiti, Caribbean, Polynesia etc.
Fula	Niger-Congo	northern West Africa
Galician	Indo-European (Romance)	Galicia (Spain)
Gbaya	Niger-Congo	N. Central Africa
German	Indo-European (Germanic)	Germany, Austria, Belgium, Switzerland
Gimi	Papuan	Papua-New Guinea
Greek	Indo-European (Hellenic)	Greece, Cyprus
Guaraní	Tupi	Paraguay
Gujerati	Indo-European (Indo-Iranian)	Gujerat State, India
Hanunóo	Austronesian	Mindoro (Philippines)
Hausa	Afro-Asiatic	Nigeria, Niger, Chad, Togo, Ghana, Burkina Faso, Cameroon

Hawaiian	Austronesian	Hawaii (USA)
Hebrew	Semitic	Israel, world-wide
Hiberno-English	Indo-European (Germanic)	Ireland
Hindi	Indo-European (Indo-Iranian)	India, Fiji, Guyana, Mauritius, Trinidad, Surinam, East Africa, South Africa
Hungarian	Uralic	Hungary, Romania, Slovakia
Icelandic	Indo-European (Germanic)	Iceland
Igbo	Niger-Congo	Nigeria
Ingush	North Caucasian	Ingushetia (Russia)
Inuit	Eskimo-Aleut	Greenland, north Canada, Alaska, Siberia
Irish	Indo-European (Celtic)	Ireland
Isoko	Niger-Congo	Nigeria
Italian	Indo-European (Romance)	Italy, Switzerland, San Marino
Jalapa Mazatec	Oto-Manguean	Mexico
Japanese	possibly Altaic	Japan
Javanese	Austronesian	Java (Indonesia)
Kabardian	North Caucasian	Russia, Turkey
Kalispel	Salishan	Washington State, Montana (USA)
Kele	Austronesian	Papua-New Guinea
KiChaka	Niger-Congo	Tanzania
Kikuyu	Niger-Congo	Kenya
Korean	Altaic	North and South Korea
Kurdish	Indo-European (Indo-Iranian)	Turkey, Iraq, Syria, Iran, Armenia
Kwakw'ala	Wakashan	Vancouver Island, British Columbia (Canada)
Lappish	Uralic	Norway, Sweden, Finland, Russia
Lendu	Nilo-Saharan	Democratic Republic of Congo
Malagasy	Austronesian	Madagascar, Comoros

Language	Language Group	Geographical Area
Malayalam	Dravidian	Kerala, Laccadive Is. (India), Fiji
Marathi	Indo-European (Indo-Iranian)	Maharashtra (India)
Margany	Pama-Nyungan	Queensland (Australia)
Margi	Afro-Asiatic	Nigeria
Marshallese	Austronesian	Marshall Is., Nauru
Melpa	Papuan	Papua-New Guinea
Mid-Waghi	Papuan	Papua-New Guinea
Montana Salish	Salishan	Montana (USA)
Mpi	Sino-Tibetan	Thailand
Navajo	Athabaskan	Arizona, Utah, New Mexico (USA)
Ngwe	Bantoid	Cameroon
Nitinaht	Wakashan	British Columbia
Nupe	Niger-Congo	Nigeria
Oaxaca Chontal	Tequistlatecan Hokan	Mexico
Palantla Chinantec	Oto-Manguean	Mexico
Pedi	Niger-Congo	South Africa
Polish	Indo-European (Slavonic)	Poland
Portugese	Indo-European (Romance)	Portugal, Brazil, Angola, Mozambique, Guinea-Bissau, Timor, Goa (India)
Quechua	Quechuan	Peru, Ecuador, Bolivia, Colombia, Argentina, Chile
Russian	Indo-European (Slavonic)	Russia, former soviet states
Salish	Salishan	N.W. USA
Scots Gaelic	Indo-European (Celtic)	Scotland, Nova Scotia (Canada)
Scottish English	Indo-European (Germanic)	Scotland
Sherpa	Sino-Tibetan	Nepal, China, India
Shona	Niger-Congo	Zimbabwe, Zambia, Mozambique
Sindhi	Indo-European (Indo-Iranian)	Sindh (Pakistan), India

Sinhalese	Indo-European (Indo-Iranian)	Sri Lanka
Skagit	Salishan	Washington State (USA)
Slovene	Indo-European (Slavonic)	Slovenia, Austria, Italy
Spanish	Indo-European (Romance)	Spain, Mexico, USA, Central America, South America, Caribbean, etc
St Lawrence Island Yupik	Eskimo-Aleut	Alaska (USA)
Sundanese	Malayo-Polynesian	Java
Swahili	Niger-Congo	East Africa
Swedish	Indo-European (Germanic)	Sweden, Finland
Swiss German	Indo-European (Germanic)	Switzerland
Taba	Austronesian	Malaku (Indonesia)
Tabassaran	North Caucasian	Dagestan (Russia)
Tamazight Berber	Afro-Asiatic	Morocco, Algeria
Tamil	Dravidian	Tamil Nadu (India), Sri Lanka, South Africa, Malaysia, Singapore, Fiji
Tereno	Arawakan	Brazil
Thai	Tai	Thailand
Tibetan	SIno-Tibetan	Tibet, India, Nepal, Bhutan
Tigre	Semitic	Ethiopia, Eritrea, Sudan
Tikar	Niger-Congo	Cameroon
Tiv	Niger-Congo	Nigeria, Cameroon
Tlingit	Na-Dené Tlingit	Alaska (USA), British Columbia (Canada)
Toda	Dravidian	India
Tsou	Austronesian	Taiwan
Turkish	Altaic	Turkey, Cyprus
Twi	Niger-Congo	Ghana
Ubykh	North Caucasian	Turkey
Uduk	Nilo-Saharan	Sudan
Urdu	Indo-European (Indo-Iranian)	Pakistan, India

Language	Language Group	Geographical Area
Urhobo	Niger-Congo	Nigeria
Uzere Isoko	Niger-Congo	Nigeria
Vietnamese	Austro-Asiatic	Vietnam, Laos, Cambodia
Walmatjari	Pama-Nyungan	Western Australia
Warja	Afro-Asiatic	Nigeria
Warlpiri	Pama-Nyungan	Northern Territory (Australia)
Watjarri	Pama-Nyungan	Western Australia
Welsh	Indo-European (Celtic)	Wales, Patagonia
Xhosa	Niger-Congo	South Africa
Yeletnye	Papuan	Papua-New Guinea
Yoruba	Niger-Congo	Nigeria, Benin, Togo, Sierra Leone
Zhongshan Chinese	Sino-Tibetan	China
Zulu	Niger-Congo	South Africa

References

Abberton, E., Fourcin, A. 1997: Electrolaryngography. In Ball, M.J., Code, C. (eds), *Instrumental Clinical Phonetics*. London: Whurr, 119–148.

Abercrombie, D. 1967: *Elements of General Phonetics*. Edinburgh: Edinburgh University Press.

Ainsworth, W.A., Lindsay, D. 1986: Perception of pitch movement on tonic syllables in British English. *Journal of the Acoustical Society of America 79*, 472–480.

Baken, R.J. 1987: *Clinical Measurement of Speech and Voice*. London: Taylor & Francis.

Ball, M.J. 1993: *Phonetics for speech pathology* (2nd edition). London: Whurr.

Ball, M.J., Code, C. (eds) 1997: *Instrumental Clinical Phonetics*. London: Whurr.

Ball, M.J., Gröne, B. 1997: Imaging techniques. In Ball, M.J., Code, C. (eds), *Instrumental Clinical Phonetics*. London: Whurr, 194–227.

Barton Payne, P. 1990: *MacPHONETIC™* (User's Manual). Edmonds, WA: Linguist's Software, Inc.

Bolinger, D. 1961: Contrastive accent and contrastive stress. *Language 37*, 83–96. The Hague: Mouton

Branderud, P. 1985: Movetrack – a movement tracking system. *Proceedings of the French – Swedish Symposium on Speech, 22–24 April 1985*. Grenoble: GALF, 113–122.

Brosnahan, L., Malmberg, B. 1970: *Introduction to Phonetics*. Cambridge: Cambridge University Press.

Brown, G. 1990: *Listening to Spoken English* (second edition). London: Longman.

Catford, I. 1977: *Fundamental Problems in Phonetics*. Edinburgh: Edinburgh University Press.

Catford, I. 1988: *A Practical Introduction to Phonetics*. Oxford: Oxford University Press.

Chao, Y. R., Yang, L.S. 1947: *Concise Dictionary of Spoken Chinese*. Cambridge, MA: Harvard University Press.

Chomsky, N., Halle, M. 1968: *The Sound Pattern of English*. New York: Harper & Row.

Clark, J., Yallop, C. 1995: *An Introduction to Phonetics and Phonology* (2nd edition). Oxford: Blackwell.

Couper-Kuhlen, E. 1986: *An Introduction to English Prosody*. London: Edward Arnold.

Cruttenden, A. 1997: *Intonation* (second edition). Cambridge: Cambridge University Press.

Crystal, D. 1969: *Prosodic Systems and Intonation in English*. Cambridge: Cambridge University Press.

Crystal, D. 1987: *The Cambridge Encyclopedia of Language*. Cambridge: Cambridge University Press.

Crystal, D., Davy, D. 1969: *Investigating English Style*. London: Longman.

Culbertson, W., Tanner, D. 1997: *Introductory Speech and Hearing Anatomy and Physiology Workbook*. Boston, MA: Allyn & Bacon.

Duckworth, M., Allen, G. Hardcastle, W.J., Ball, M.J. 1990: Extensions to the International Phonetic Alphabet for the transcription of atypical speech. *Clinical Linguistics and Phonetics* **4**, 273–280.

Denes, P., Pinson, E. 1973: *The Speech Chain*. New York: Anchor Books.

Edwards, M.L. 1986: *Introduction to Applied Phonetics: Laboratory Workbook*. San Diego, CA: College-Hill Press.

Farnetani, E. 1997: Coarticulation and connected speech processes. In Hardcastle, W., Laver, J. (eds), *The Handbook of Phonetic Sciences*. Oxford: Blackwell, 371– 404.

Fry, D.B. 1979: *The Physics of Speech*. Cambridge: Cambridge University Press.

Gentil, M. 1990: EMG analysis of speech production patterns with Friedreich disease. *Clinical Linguistics and Phonetics* **4**, 107–120.

Gimson, A.C. 1989: *An Introduction to the Pronunciation of English* (fourth edition). London: Edward Arnold.

Grunwell, P. 1987: *Clinical Phonology* (second edition). London: Croom Helm.

Halliday, M.A.K. 1967: *Intonation and Grammar in British English*. The Hague: Mouton.

Halliday, M.A.K. 1970: *A Course in Spoken English: Intonation*. Oxford: Oxford University Press.

Hardcastle, W., Gibbon, F. 1997: Electropalatography and its clinical applications. In Ball, M.J., Code, C. (eds), *Instrumental Clinical Phonetics*. London: Whurr, 149–193.

Hirose, H. 1997: Investigating the physiology of laryngeal structures. In Hardcastle, W., Laver, J. (eds), *The Handbook of Phonetic Sciences*. Oxford: Blackwell, 116–136.

Hixon, T.J. 1973: Respiratory function in speech. In Minifie, F.D., Hixon, T.J., Williams (eds) *Normal Aspects of Speech, Hearing and Language*. Englewood Cliffs, NJ: Prentice Hall, 75–125.

Hodson, B.W. 1980: *The Assessment of Phonological Processes*. Danville, IL: Interstate Inc.

Ingram, D. 1981: *Procedures for the Phonological Analysis of Children's Language*. Baltimore, MD: University Park Press.

IPA 1989: Report on the 1989 Kiel Convention. *Journal of the International Phonetic Association* **19**, 67–80.

IPA 1993: Council actions on the revisions of the IPA. *Journal of the International Phonetic Association* **23**, 32–34.

IPA 1995: Correction to the IPA chart. *Journal of the International Phonetic Association* **25**, 48.

IPA 1999: *The Handbook of the International Phonetic Association*. Cambridge: Cambridge University Press.

Johnson, K. 1997: *Acoustic and Auditory Phonetics*. Oxford: Blackwell.

Kahane, J., Folkins, J. 1984: *Atlas of Speech and Hearing Anatomy*. Columbus, OH: Bell & Howell.

Kent, R.D. 1997a: Gestural phonology. In Ball, M.J., Kent, R.D. (eds), *The New Phonologies*. San Diego, CA: Singular Publishing Group, 247–268.

Kent, R.D. 1997b: *The Speech Sciences*. San Diego, CA: Singular Publishing Group.

Kent, R.D., Atal, B., Miller, J. (eds) 1991: *Papers in Speech Communication: Speech Production*. Woodbury, NY: Acoustical Society of America.

Ladd, D.R. 1986: Intonational phrasing – the case for recursive prosodic structure. *Phonology Yearbook* **3**, 311–340.

Ladefoged, P. 1982: *A Course in Phonetics* (second edition). New York: Harcourt, Brace Jovanovich.

Ladefoged, P. 1993 *A Course in Phonetics* (third edition). Fort Worth, TX: Harcourt Brace College Publishers.

Ladefoged, P, Maddieson, I. 1996: *The Sounds of the World's Languages*. Oxford: Blackwell.

Lass, N. (ed.) 1996: *Principles of Experimental Phonetics*. St Louis, MI: Mosby.

Laufer, A. 1991: Does the 'voiced epiglottal plosive' exist? *Journal of the International Phonetic Association* 21, 44–45.

Laver, J. 1980: *The Phonetic Description of Voice Quality*. Cambridge: Cambridge University Press.

Laver, J. 1994: *Principles of Phonetics*. Cambridge: Cambridge University Press.

Lehiste, I., Peterson, G.E. 1961: Some basic considerations in the anaysis of intonation. *Journal of the Acoustical Society of America* 33, 419–425.

Lieberman, P. 1967: *Intonation, Perception and Language*. Research Monograph 38. Cambridge, MA: MIT Press.

Lieberman, P., Blumstein, D. 1988: *Speech Physiology, Speech Perception and Acoustic Phonetics*. Cambridge: Cambridge University Press.

Lutman, M.E. 1983: The scientific basis for the assessment of hearing. In Lutman, M.E., Haggard, M.P. (eds), *Hearing Science and Hearing Disorders*. London: Academic Press.

McCawley, J.D. 1978: What is a tone language? In Fromkin, V.A. (ed.), *Tone: A Linguistic Survey*. New York: Academic Press, 113–131.

Moore, C. 1992: The correspondence of vocal tract resonance with volumes obtained from magnetic resonance images. *Journal of Speech and Hearing Research* 35, 1009–1023.

Morris, P. 1986: *Nuclear Magnetic Resonance Imaging in Medicine and Biology*. Oxford: Oxford University Press.

Nakagawa, H. 1996: A first report on the click accompaniments of ǀGui. *Journal of the International Phonetic Association* 26, 41–54.

Ní Chasaide, A., Gobl, C. 1997: Voice source variation. In Hardcastle, W., Laver, J. (eds), *The Handbook of Phonetic Sciences*. Oxford: Blackwell, 427–461.

O'Connor, J.B. 1980: *Better English Pronunciation* (second edition). Cambridge: Cambridge University Press.

O'Connor, J.D., Arnold, G.E. 1973: *Intonation of Colloquial English* (second edition). London: Longman.

Pandeli, H., Eska, J., Ball, M. J. and Rahilly, J. 1997: Problems of phonetic transcription: the case of the Hiberno-English flat alveolar fricative. *Journal of the International Phonetic Association*, 27, 65–75.

Perkell, J., Cohen, M., Svirsky, M., Matthies, M., Garabieta, I., Jackson, M. 1992: Electromagnetic midsaggital articulometer system for transducing speech articulatory movements. *Journal of the Acoustical Society of America* 92, 3078–3096.

Perkell, J. 1997: Articulatory processes. In Hardcastle, W., Laver, J. (eds), *The Handbook of Phonetic Sciences*. Oxford: Blackwell, 333–370.

Perkins, W., Kent, R.D. 1986: *Textbook of Functional Anatomy of Speech, Language and Hearing*. London: Taylor & Francis.

Pierrehumbert, J. 1980: The phonology and phonetics of English intonation. Unpublished PhD dissertation, MIT.

Pike, K.L. 1943: *Phonetics*. Ann Arbor, MI: University of Michigan Press.

Pike, K.L. 1948: *Tone Languages*. Ann Arbor, MI: University of Michigan Press.

Pike, K.L. 1962: Practical phonetics of rhythm waves. *Phonetica* 8, 9–30.

Pullum, G.K., Ladusan, W. 1996: *Phonetic Symbol Guide*. Chicago: University of Chicago Press.

Quirk, R., Duckworth, A. P. , Svartvik, J., Rusiecki, J. P. L., and Colin, A. J. T. 1964: Studies in the correspondence of prosodic to grammatical features in English. In *Proceedings of the 9th International Congress of Linguists*. The Hague: Mouton, 679–691.

Rahilly, J. 1991: *Intonation Patterns in Normal-hearing and Postlingually-deafened Adults in Belfast*. Unpublished doctoral dissertation, Queen's University, Belfast.

Richards, A. 1976: *Basic Experimentation in Psychoacoustics*. Baltimore: University Park Press.

Rosenthal, J.B. 1989: A computer-assisted phonetic transcription skill development program. *Folia Phoniatrica* **41**, 243.

Ryalls, J. 1996: *An Introduction to Speech Perception.* San Diego, CA: Singular Publishing Group.

Schönle, P. , Wenig, P. , Schrader, J., Höhne, J., Bröckmann, E. and Conrad, B. 1987: Electromagnetic articulography – use of alternating magnetic fields for tracking movements of multiple points inside and outside the vocal tract. *Brain and Language* **31**, 26–35.

Seikel, J.A., King, D., Drumright, D. 1997: *Anatomy and Physiology for Speech and Language.* San Diego, CA: Singular Publishing Group.

Shadle, C. 1997: The aerodynamics of speech. In Hardcastle, W., Laver, J. (eds), *The Handbook of Phonetic Sciences.* Oxford: Blackwell, 33–64.

Shriberg, L., Hincke, R., Trost-Steffen, C. 1987: A procedure to select and train persons for narrow phonetic transcription by consensus. *Clinical Linguistics and Phonetics* **1**, 171–189.

Shriberg, L., Kwiatowski, J. 1980: *Natural Process Analysis (NPA): A procedure for phonological analysis of continuous speech samples.* New York: Macmillan.

Strevens, P. 1978: A rationale for teaching pronunciation. *English Language Teaching Journal* **28**, 182–189.

Tench, P. 1978: On introducing parametric phonetics. *Journal of the International Phonetic Association* **8**, 34–46.

Tench, P. 1996: *The Intonation Systems of English.* London: Cassell.

Trager, G.L., Smith, H.L., Jr. 1951: *An Outline of English Structure.* (Studies in Linguistics: Occasional Papers 3). Norman, OK: Battenburg Press.

Tuller, B., Shao, S., Kelso, J. 1990: An evaluation of an alternate magnetic field device for monitoring tongue movements. *Journal of the Acoustical Society of America* **88**, 674–679.

Wells, J. 1990: *Accents of English* (three volumes). Cambridge: Cambridge University Press.

Westermann, D., Ward, I.C. 1933: *Practical Phonetics for Students of African Languages.* (Republished 1990, edited by J. Kelly. London: Kegan Paul International.)

Weiner, F.F. 1979: *Phonological Process Analysis (PPA).* Baltimore, MD: University Park Press.

Zajac, D., Yates, C. 1997: Speech aerodynamics. In Ball, M.J., Code, C. (eds), *Instrumental Clinical Phonetics.* London: Whurr, 87–118.

Index